Hiking
Oregon's
Eagle Cap Wilderness

by
Fred Barstad

FALCON™

HELENA, MONTANA

A FALCON GUIDE

Falcon Press is continually expanding its list of recreational guidebooks. All books include detailed descriptions, accurate maps, and all the information necessary for enjoyable trips. You can order extra copies of this book and get information and prices for other Falcon guidebooks by writing Falcon Press, P.O. Box 1718, Helena, MT 59624 or calling toll free 1-800-582-2665. Also, please ask for a free copy of our current catalog. Our e-mail address is: falconbk@ix.netcom.com

©1996 by Falcon Press Publishing Co., Inc.,
Helena and Billings, Montana.
Reprinted 1997
10 9 8 7 6 5 4 3 2

Printed in the United States of America.

All black-and-white photos by author unless noted otherwise.
Cover photo by David Jensen.

Library of Congress Cataloging-in-Publication Data

Barstad, Fred.
    Hiking Oregon's Eagle Cap Wilderness/ by Fred Barstad.
        p.   cm.
    ISBN   1-56044-399-5 (pbk.)
    1. Hiking—Oregon—Eagle Cap Wilderness—Guidebooks.
    2. Eagle Cap—Wilderness (Or.)—Guidebooks.   I. Title.
    GV199.42.O72E343   1996
    796.5'1'097957—dc20   96-988
                                                                          CIP

 Text pages printed on recycled paper.

CAUTION

Outdoor recreational activities are by their very nature potentially hazardous. All participants in such activities must assume the responsibility for their own actions and safety. The information contained in this guidebook cannot replace sound judgment and good decision-making skills, which help reduce the risk exposure, nor does the scope of this book allow for disclosure of all the potential hazards and risks involved in such activities.

Learn as much as possible about the outdoor recreational activities you participate in, prepare for the unexpected, and be cautious. The reward will be a safer and more enjoyable experience.

CONTENTS

CONTENTS

CONTENTS

ACKNOWLEDGMENTS

I would like to thank Gary Fletcher for hiking with me, contributing pictures, and editing the text. I also want to thank Kerry Searles, Lowell Euhus, Ettore Negri and Jerry Lavender for hiking with me on these trails and contributing pictures. Thanks also to Casey Barstad, Brian Barstad, Doug Cracraft, Oliver Boeve and Dave Kaufman for hiking and camping with me and keeping me company over many miles. Also of great help were Bill George for hiking with me and sharing his knowledge of the area and Vic Coggins, of the Oregon Department of Fish and Wildlife, for information on the bighorn sheep and mountain goats.

Thanks also to the employees of the U.S. Forest Service at Wallowa Mountain Visitors Center for much information on trail status and maintenance. Most of all I thank my wife Suzi Barstad for hiking and camping with me and for her endless hours of typing and editing to get this book ready for publication.

OVERVIEW MAP

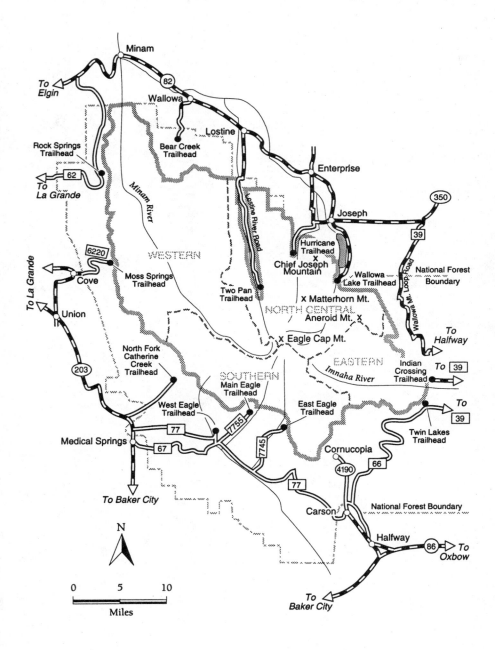

LEGEND

State or Other Principal Road	(000)	Campground	⛺
Forest Road	0000	Bridge	
Paved Road		Cabins/Buildings	■
Gravel Road		Peak/Elevation	9,782 ft.
Unimproved Road		Falls	
Trailhead/Parking	◯ Ⓟ	Pass/Saddle	) (
Main Trail(s)		Snowfield	
Climbing Route		Gate	
Alternate/ Secondary Trails/ Cross Country Trails		Cliffs	
River/Creek		Map Orientation	N
Lake			
Ditch		Scale	0 0.5 1 Miles

USGS TOPOGRAPHIC MAPS

Index to USGS 7.5 Minute Quadrangles

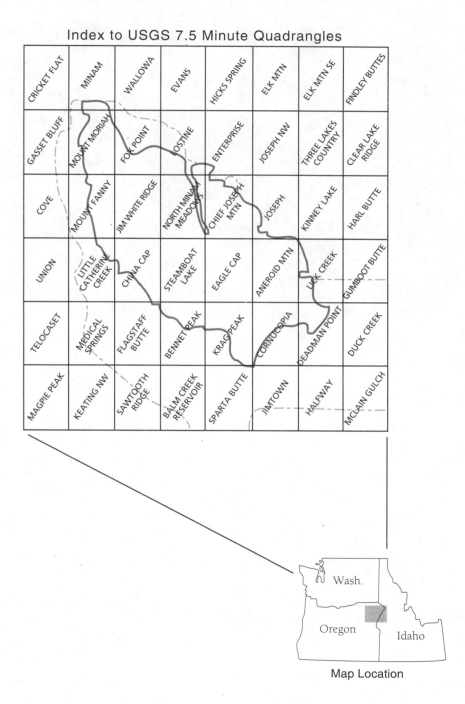

Map Location

Twin Peaks from Falls Creek Trail. *Photo by Gary Fletcher.*

INTRODUCTION

Eagle Cap Wilderness is the premier backpacking country of Oregon. It covers 580 square miles of the Wallowa Mountains, in the northeast corner of Oregon. Anywhere you look in the Wallowas you will find absolutely breathtaking mountain scenery. There are fifty-two named high lakes, of which nearly all have an abundance of trout just waiting to take your bait. Many miles of rivers drain from the high alpine mountains through densely forested canyons. These rivers also have many trout, and several have received National Wild River status for their "outstandingly remarkable" characteristics. The abundance and diversity of animal life in the Wallowa Mountains is sensational.

The trails in this book, with a couple of exceptions, are within or lead into Eagle Cap Wilderness. The Wilderness encompasses nearly all of the high country of the Wallowa Mountains. It also includes much of the foothill and canyon country surrounding the Wallowa Mountains.

At this time, permits are required to enter Eagle Cap Wilderness. These self-issue permits are available at major trailheads or at Forest Service offices. Much of the Wilderness is used very little. Part of the purpose of this book is to encourage backpacker use of these areas, and thereby to disperse the traffic so that overused areas can recover somewhat. If you are interested in solitude, check out the trails with a "light" traffic rating.

The Wallowa Mountains are steepest on the north side. On the north-central side there are almost no foothills between the Wallowa Valley and the alpine peaks. To the east, timbered ridges cut by deep canyons connect the Wallowa Mountains with Summit Ridge. Summit Ridge overlooks the Snake River in Hells Canyon National Recreation Area.

On the south side, timbered foothills lead up to the high peaks. The western and northwestern part of the Wallowa Mountains are made up of ridges of moderate elevation. These ridges are separated by deep canyons. The average elevation of the ridges in the western part of the range is a little more than 7,000 feet. This is about 2,000 feet lower than the average ridge top elevation in the central and north-central part of the range.

The major drainages of the Wallowas radiate in all directions from the center of the range. From the summit of Eagle Cap Mountain most of the major drainages can be seen heading out in all directions.

The high country of the Wallowas shows much evidence of glacial carving. The larger valleys are the typical U shape of glacial valleys. There are also many cirques and hanging valleys. Most of the ice is now gone with only a few stagnant patches left. The large moraine that holds Wallowa Lake is evidence of large glaciers once here.

Life Zones

There are four distinct life zones in the Wallowa Mountains. The transitional zone reaches up to about 6,000 feet in most places. Ponderosa pine is the typical tree of this zone, with Douglas-fir and true fir in wetter locations.

From approximately 6,000 to 7,500 feet elevation is the Canadian zone. Here the typical tree is lodgepole pine. There are also fir and spruce in the Canadian zone. Mountain hemlock also thrive in this zone on wetter slopes.

Above the Canadian zone up to the timberline at about 8,500 feet, is the Hudsonian zone, with its subalpine fir and white bark pine. In a few scattered locations in this zone there are stands of limber pine. The Wallowas are the only range in Oregon that have limber pine.

The highest peaks and ridges reach into the Arctic alpine zone. There are almost no trees here, only scattered elfenwood, very small weather-beaten trees. At 9,700 feet on the south side of Aneroid Peak a three-foot-tall whitebark pine survives the harsh climate. This may be Oregon's highest altitude tree.

Large Animals

The Wallowa Mountains are blessed with abundant animal life. There are more deer, elk, and even bear in this county than there are humans. Mule deer are the most common large animal. They range throughout the mountains, up to and including the alpine zone in the summer and fall. These deer generally drop to lower elevations in winter. However, it sometimes takes a lot of snow to move them down. Big bucks usually stay high as long as they can. In years of light snow I have seen deer higher than 8,000 feet in late January.

Bighorn Rams. *Photo by Gary Fletcher.*

There is also a fairly large population of white-tailed deer in some canyon bottoms and around the edges of the mountains. Whitetails are common in the Wallowa Valley. Elk inhabit the entire area. They are most common in the eastern, southern, and western parts of the Wallowas. There are some scattered herds in the higher central parts too. Elk seem to like more moderate terrain than mule deer. Elk are usually not seen on the rugged cliffs and ridges of the central part of the range.

Black bears live in all parts of the Wallowas. They are probably more common in the middle and upper Minam River Canyon, but they can show up anywhere. They are generally not a problem, but it always pays to keep a clean camp and hang your food anyway. They do raid the dumpsters at Wallowa Lake almost every year. Be very careful around mothers with cubs. The cubs are cute, but mamas can be dangerous. In spring watch for bears grazing in open moist areas. They eat the wild onions that grow there.

Cougars are fairly common in the Wallowas. They are not often seen by hikers, but don't be too surprised if you turn back on a trail and find large cat tracks on top of your tracks. Cougars are curious and may follow a hiker for some distance. This has happened to me at least four times. Since 1994 the use of dogs for hunting cougar has been banned, and cougars have become more common. As yet, they have not been a major problem for people in this area. However, the idea of a one-hundred-pound cat watching you makes some people very nervous.

Bighorn sheep were once native to the Wallowa Mountains, but vanished about 1945, possibly from disease contracted from domestic sheep. Bighorns were reintroduced from Alberta, Canada, in 1964 but many in the Wallowa Mountains died in the late 1980s. Now they seem to be doing fine. The largest ram ever found in the United States came from the Wallowa Mountains. Bighorns normally roam the north-central part of the range, at 9,000 feet or higher during summer.

Mountain goats are not native to the Wallowas. They were introduced in 1950 from northern Washington, and more were released in the 1980s from Olympic National Park, Washington, and Misty Fiords National Monument, Alaska. They can be seen on or near the tops of Hurwal and Hurricane divides or near the top of Chief Joseph Mountain. Please watch the goats and sheep from a distance. They are sensitive to human intrusion.

Smaller Animals

Coyotes are found everywhere in the Wallowas. It is common to hear them at night. Pikas can be seen or heard in most rock slides. Red diggers, a type of ground squirrel, are common in meadows at lower altitudes. Golden eagles can be seen soaring along the ridges, and grouse are quite common as well. Some of the ridge tops crawl with lady bugs in early summer.

There are many other small animals in these mountains; watch and you will see them. Rattlesnakes are not found in the higher parts of the Wallowas. However, there are some in the canyon bottoms in the western part of the range. Rattlesnakes usually live below 4,000 feet here.

USING THIS BOOK

Trail Ratings

The trails in this book are rated as easy, moderate, or strenuous, with length or time involved not considered. Only steepness of the grade, roughness of the trail, extent of erosion or rockiness, and elevation changes are considered.

Trails that are rated "easy" will generally have gentle grades and be mostly smooth; however, there may be short sections of rocky or eroded areas. Nearly anyone in reasonable condition can hike easy trails, given enough time.

Trails rated as "moderate" will climb or descend more steeply than easy trails. They may climb 500 or 600 feet per mile and have fairly long stretches of rough or eroded sections. A backpacker in good physical condition can hike these trails with no problem. However, people in poor condition and small children may find them grueling.

Trails rated as "strenuous" are best done by expert backpackers and mountaineers. These trails may climb 1,000 feet or more per mile and may be very rough in spots.

All hikes are measured in one way diatances unless otherwise specified.

Climbing and Scrambling Ratings

The ratings in the climbing section of this book are not the same as the trail ratings. What is rated as an easy climb is at least as difficult as a strenuous trail, and the climbs get more difficult from there. While most of the climbing routes described are not technical (requiring ropes and protective hardware), they do require more stamina than many hikers have.

Use discretion and common sense when visiting a new area. There is an old saying that there are bold climbers and there are old climbers, but there are no old, bold climbers. With that advice, warm up on a few routes that may be well below your limit; get used to the area before pushing the limits of your ability. Mountain travel is typically classified as follows:

Class 1 — Trail hiking.

Class 2 — Hiking over rough ground such as scree and talus; may include the use of hands for stability.

Class 3 — Scrambling that requires the use of hands and careful foot placement.

Class 4 — Scrambling over steep and exposed terrain; a rope may be used for safety on exposed areas.

Class 5 — Technical "free" climbing where terrain is steep and exposed, requiring the use of ropes, protection hardware, and related techniques.

Some "strenuous" climbs may have considerable exposure on its scrambles. Most climbs in this book are considered Class 3 with the exception of Twin Peaks and Bonneville Mountain, which may be Class 4 and require a rope, and the Dihedrals, which are Class 5.

Parklike area along East Fork Eagle Creek.

Maintenance Ratings

Trails that have yearly maintenance will usually be cleared of obstructions by midsummer each year. If the rating is infrequent, that means that the trail is scheduled to be maintained every 2 to 3 years, but in reality it may be only every 5 to 6 years. If the rating is rare or seldom, it may be a very long time between maintenance, and you should expect to have to climb over a few logs. Trails with no maintenance are not kept up by the Forest Service, but many horsemen cut logs so they can get their pack strings through. On these trails there may be long stretches with blowdowns and badly eroded sections.

Traffic Ratings

If the traffic rating is heavy, you should expect to meet people every few minutes to few hours, and many of the better campsites may be taken. You will probably meet one to five parties per day on trails with a moderate rating. On trails with a light traffic rating, it is unlikely you will meet more than one or two parties a day, and it may be days or even weeks before you see anyone else. These are average figures for summer and fall months; no one can say for sure how many people you will encounter on any trail on a given day.

Following a Faint Trail

Most of the trails in this book are easy to follow. Some, however, have short stretches that have become faint or nonexistent because of natural causes, such as blown down timber or wash outs, or they have become overgrown with vegetation. Animals can also make trails difficult to follow by making their own trails that cross or fork off from the main trail. In areas where cattle graze, particularly in portions of southern Eagle Cap Wilderness, this can be a major problem. You must be able to follow a faint trail when hiking the less used trails in the Wallowa Mountains.

The first thing to do before trying to follow one of these less-traveled trails is to carefully read its entire description in this book. The description will tell you if route finding skills are required to follow the trail safely. Next, get a good topo map of the area. These maps are listed at the beginning of each trail description. All the United States Geological Survey (USGS) maps listed are 7.5 minute quadrangles. The Imus Geographics Wallowa Mountains Eagle Cap Wilderness map, listed on most of the trail descriptions, covers the entire area. This map is a smaller scale than the USGS maps, but it is very accurate on both the trails and the roads leading to the trailheads. The Imus Geographics map is available at most outdoor stores in the area and at major outlets in larger cities.

Be sure you have a compass and know how to use it. Remember that a compass does not necessarily point to true north. It points to magnetic north, which is approximately 18 degrees east of true north in this area. Nearly all maps show an area's declination. Another helpful navigational instrument is an altimeter. Altimeters work very well if you use them correctly. However, they run on air pressure, which is always changing, so they need to be set at each known altitude point. This means several times a day, if possible.

While you are hiking, watch ahead for blazes cut into the bark of trees, and rock cairns on the ground. Logs that have been sawed off may also be an indicator of the trail's route. Trees missing some branches on one side may show that the trail passes on that side of the tree. Through thick woods, look for narrow strips where the trees are much smaller or nonexistent; this could be the route that was once cleared for the trail. All of these things are not positive signs that you are going the right way, but when taken together, with good compass and map skills they make it much easier to follow a faint trail.

Passing Stock on the Trail

If you meet parties with pack or saddle stock on the trail, try to get as far off the trail as possible. Horsemen prefer that you stand on the downhill side of the trail, but there is some question whether this is the safest place for a hiker. If possible, I like to get well off the trail on the uphill side. It is often a good idea to talk quietly to the horses and their riders as this seems to calm many horses. If you have the family dog with you, be sure to keep it restrained and quiet, as many horse wrecks are caused by dogs.

Environmental Concerns

Making campfires and cutting switchbacks have probably the most negative impact on the environment where hikers are concerned. As traditional and nice as campfires are, their use should be limited. Small fires in certain areas at low elevations may be okay if regulations permit, but building fires in alpine meadows, or any alpine area, is definitely not good practice. It takes many years for the fragile alpine environment to recover from just one small campfire. Take along a backpack stove; it is easier to use anyway. If you must build a fire, make sure to extinguish it completely.

Cutting switchbacks is extremely hard on trails and hillsides. This practice causes much erosion and destroys plant life. Although horses can damage trails that are not designed or maintained for them, hikers do much damage also. It is always best to stay on the main trail and not take shortcuts.

Do not dismantle rock cairns, as they may be the only thing marking the route in some areas. Please leave cabins and mine sites as you found them; these are a historical part of the wilderness.

Campsite selection is also important in trying to maintain the environment. Make camp in the timber if possible and try to avoid camping in meadows. Be careful not to trample vegetation. Camp well away from lakes and at least some distance back from streams. Check Forest Service regulations about campsite selection. When leaving, pack out your trash and any other trash you find. If we all do our part, we can keep our wild areas beautiful and clean forever. Further information for trail descriptions are listed at the beginning of each chapter. A list of addresses and phone numbers for these sources can be found in the Appendix.

Personal Safety

There are a few simple things you can do that will improve your chances of staying healthy while you are in the wilderness. One of the most important is to be careful of your drinking water supply. All water should be boiled, chemically treated, or filtered before drinking, washing utensils, or brushing your teeth. The water may look clean and pure, and it may be, but you can never be sure.

Check the weather report before you head into the mountains and canyons of Eagle Cap Wilderness. Cold stormy weather, with rain, snow, and high winds are possible at all times of the year. Thunderstorms with accompanying heavy rain, hail, and wind are common during summer. Do not stay on ridges or other exposed places during a lightning storm. Very few people are struck by lightning, but you do not want to be one of them. Nighttime temperatures in the high valleys and on the ridges can drop to freezing in July and August and far below that in September. These extreme low temperatures usually occur on clear nights after the passing of a cold front.

There is at least some avalanche danger on the winter skiing routes mentioned in this book. It is a good idea to take a class in avalanche safety before venturing into the back country in winter. Avalanche transceivers should be carried by each member of the party, and everyone should know how to use them properly. Be sure that all your transceivers are the same frequency. For futher information about no trace techniques and wilderness safety refer to *Wild Country Companion*, another Falcon book.

Many of the glacier-carved lakes in Eagle Cap have shorelines that drop off abruptly, and children should be watched at all times when near the water. The water in most lakes is very cold, so swimming time should be limited. Mosquitoes can be a major annoyance in many places, so take along repellent and make sure the netting on your tent is in good shape. Ticks can also be a nuisance in early summer. If you venture to any of the lakes in winter, be careful of thin ice covering the lakes.

Finally, be sure to let someone know where you are going and when you plan to return. Of all the safety tips, the most important is to take your brain with you when you go into the wilderness. Without it, no tips will help, and with it, almost any obstacle can be overcome. Think about what you are doing, be safe, and have a great time in the outdoors.

NORTH CENTRAL REGION

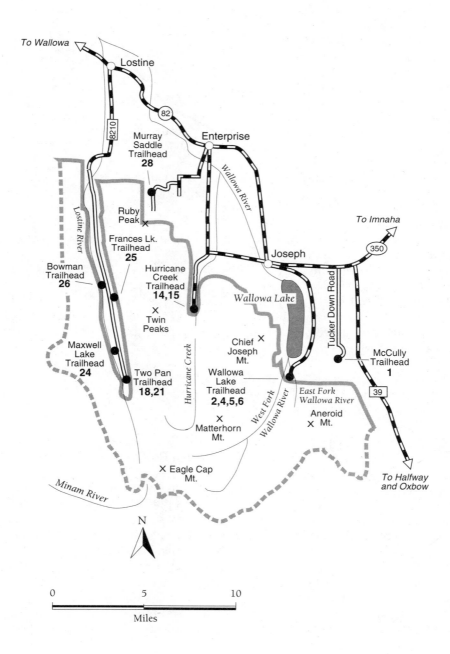

To Wallowa

Lostine

8210

82

Murray
Saddle
Trailhead
28

Enterprise

Wallowa River

Ruby
Peak ×

To Imnaha

350

Frances Lk.
Trailhead
25

Lostine River

Joseph

Bowman
Trailhead
26

Hurricane
Creek
Trailhead
14,15

Wallowa Lake

Tucker Down Road

× Twin
Peaks

McCully
Trailhead
1

Maxwell
Lake
Trailhead
24

Chief ×
Joseph
Mt.

39

Two Pan
Trailhead
18,21

Wallowa
Lake
Trailhead
2,4,5,6

Hurricane Creek

West Fork Wallowa River

East Fork
Wallowa River

Aneroid
× Mt.

× Matterhorn
Mt.

× Eagle Cap
Mt.

Minam River

To Halfway
and Oxbow

N

0   5   10
Miles

1   MCCULLY BASIN

Trail 1812

General description: A backpack of 10.5 miles from McCully Trailhead to Tenderfoot Trail 1819.

Difficulty: Moderate.

Trail maintenance: Yearly.

Best season: Mid-June through mid-October for hiking, and December through March for skiing. There is some avalanche danger in winter.

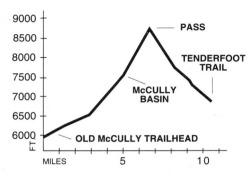

Traffic: Light except during October and November hunting season, light to moderate horse traffic, light ski traffic in winter.

Elevation gain: 3,180 feet. Loss: 1,930 feet.

Maximum elevation: 8,700 feet.

Maps: Imus Geographics Wallowa Mountains Eagle Cap Wilderness, or Joseph and Aneroid Mountain USGS quads.

For more information: U.S. Forest Service at Wallowa Mountain Visitors Center, Enterprise, Oregon.

Finding the trail: Go east from Joseph 5.5 miles on the Imnaha Highway, and turn right on Tucker Down Road. Go 5 miles to McCully Trailhead parking area, which is on the right side of the road 1 mile past the Ferguson Ridge Ski area access road.

0.0	Trail begins at New McCully Trailhead.
0.9	Old McCully Trailhead.
2.0	Trail enters Eagle Cap Wilderness.
5.5	Trail crosses McCully Creek.
7.0	Trail crosses pass into Big Sheep Creek drainage.
10.5	Trail junction with Tenderfoot Wagon Road Trail 1819.

The trail: The area around McCully Trailhead was burned in 1988 in the Canal Forest Fire. A new trailhead (El 5,520 ft.) was put in after the fire, so this trailhead has changed from where it was in 1988.

From the hitching rail on the south side of the parking area the trail heads west and crosses McCully Creek. If you are not on horseback, there is a foot bridge 40 yards upstream from the crossing. After crossing the foot bridge, the trail heads south for 30 yards and then makes a switchback to the right. Seventy-five yards past the switchback, the trail joins the roadbed, which is McCully Basin Trail. Turn left on the road and follow it 0.8 mile to Old McCully Trailhead, where the trail leaves the burn area. Be careful not to take the Mount Howard Trail, an unused jeep road, which switches back to the right 0.5 mile, after leaving the New McCully Trailhead.

From the old trailhead (El 6,080 ft.), follow the trail south, passing the Eagle Cap Wilderness boundary (El 6,500 ft.) 2 miles from the trailhead. At 5.5 miles (El 7,600 ft.) the trail crosses McCully Creek and enters McCully Basin. At McCully Basin the character of the forest changes from the dense transitional and Canadian zone forests below to the more open subalpine type. This opener country affords inspiring views of the peaks that surround this lovely alpine

1   *McCully Basin*

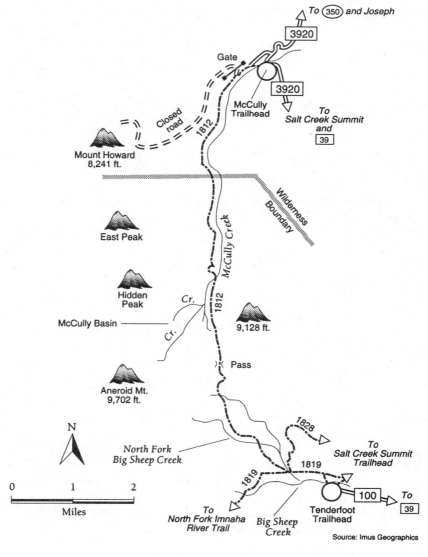

Source: Imus Geographics

basin. To the southwest is 9,702-foot high Aneroid Peak. The highest living tree in Oregon, a scruffy little whitebark pine, grows near the summit of this peak. East and Hidden Peaks are to the west of the basin and Ferguson Ridge is to the east. McCully Basin is used as a base camp for telemark skiers in the winter.

From McCully Basin, the trail continues south, climbing to the pass (El 8,700 ft.) dividing McCully Creek drainage and North Fork Big Sheep Creek drainage. South of the pass the trail switchbacks down into the basin at the head of the North Fork of Big Sheep Creek. Here the trail becomes harder to see. Continue south, following the cairns. Cross a small rise and go along the left side of a meadow. At the south end of the meadow, the trail turns left (El 7,770 ft.), 8.75 miles from McCully Trailhead. Three quarters of a mile farther along, the trail crosses a creek (El 7,240 ft.). A short distance after crossing the creek, the trail becomes difficult to see again. Go down the left side of a small open slope, and find the trail again at the bottom of the opening (El 7,110 ft.). Descend another 0.75 mile to the southeast, to the junction with Tenderfoot Wagon Road Trail 1819. This junction (El 6,770 ft.) is 10.5 miles from McCully Trailhead. See Hike 97 Tenderfoot Wagon Road. The last 3.5 miles of this trail requires some route finding skills to follow. If you want to leave the wilderness by a different route, and have a car parked at Tenderfoot Trailhead, then turn left at the junction with Tenderfoot Wagon Road Trail and follow the old wagon road, 1 mile, to Tenderfoot Trailhead. See Hike 97 Tenderfoot Wagon Road for directions to Tenderfoot Trailhead.

2   EAST FORK WALLOWA RIVER

Trail 1804

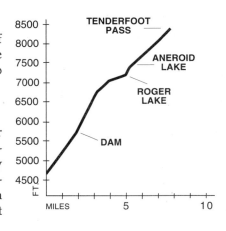

General description: A backpack of 8.5 miles to Tenderfoot Pass, or a 6 mile backpack or long 12 mile day hike to Aneroid Lake and back.
Difficulty: Moderate.
Trail maintenance: Yearly.
Best season: July through Sep-tember to Aneroid Lake, mid-July through September above Aneroid Lake and January through April for skiing. There is considerable avalanche danger on this trail in winter when snow conditions are right for it.
Traffic: Heavy to Aneroid Lake, then moderate past the lake, with heavy horse traffic to Aneroid Lake.
Elevation gain: 2,850 feet to Aneroid Lake, 3,850 feet to Tenderfoot Pass.
Maximum elevation: 8,500 feet.

Maps: Imus Geographics Wallowa Mountains Eagle Cap Wilderness, or Joseph and Aneroid Mountain USGS quads.

For more information: U.S. Forest Service at Wallowa Mountain Visitors Center, Enterprise, Oregon, and Wallowa Lake General Store, in the resort area at the south end of Wallowa Lake, and Wing Ridge Ski Tours in Joseph, Oregon for winter use. The trail crosses Pacific Power and Light Company land at first, but soon enters Wallowa Whitman National Forest. No special permission is necessary to cross this PP and L land.

Finding the trail: From Joseph take Oregon Highway 82, 7 miles south, passing Wallowa Lake, to Wallowa Lake Trailhead (El 4,650 ft.).

2   East Fork Wallowa River

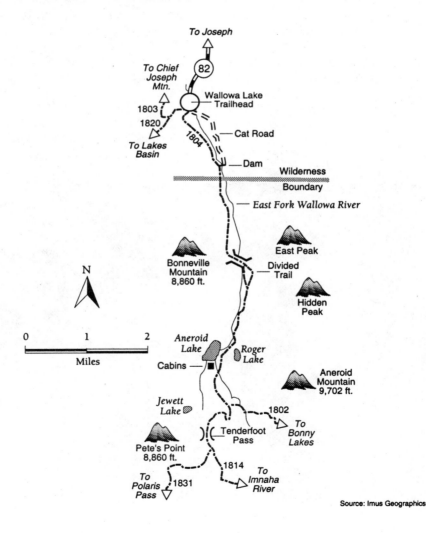

Source: Imus Geographics

0.0	Trail begins at Wallowa Lake Trailhead.
2.0	Dam on river next to trail.
2.2	Trail enters Eagle Cap Wilderness.
3.8	Trail crosses East Fork Wallowa River on bridge.
5.5	Trail passes Roger Lake.
6.0	Trail passes Aneroid Lake.
7.0	Trail junction with Bonny Lake Trail.
8.5	Trail comes to Tenderfoot Pass and trail becomes North Fork Imnaha River Trail 1814.

The trail: The trail leaves the trailhead parking area on the east side. It forks a few yards after leaving the parking lot. Take the left fork. A short distance up the trail a "cat road" turns off to the left. This road was built to facilitate the rebuilding of the dam, which is the intake for the power house at the south end of the parking area. This road may be used as an alternate trail. If you use the cat road, be sure to turn right and cross a second bridge just below the metal gate a little more than 1 mile up the road. This will put you back on the main trail. Generally, it is best to take the trail, as the road is much steeper.

The trail climbs for 2 miles to a dam (El 5,800 ft.). The pipe you may have noticed across the river, when you were coming up the trail, is the penstock which connects the dam and the powerhouse.

The Eagle Cap Wilderness boundary is 0.25 mile past the dam. The elevation at the wilderness boundary is 5,920 feet. Just before reaching the wilder-

Heading for Aneroid Lake in winter. *Photo by Gary Fletcher.*

ness boundary sign, the unmarked route to Bonneville Mountain turns off to the right. See Climb 5 Bonneville Mountain East Side.

At 3.8 miles, the trail crosses the East Fork on a bridge (El 6,900 ft.). A short distance above the bridge the trail divides. Going up, the trail to the right is usually used. The trail comes back together again, in a short distance, at 7,120 feet elevation. The unmarked climbing route to Aneroid Mountain turns off, to the left, 0.25 mile beyond the point where the trails come back together. See Climb 1 Aneroid Mountain.

The trail climbs gently above this point, going through the timber on the east side of the lush meadows along the river. There are several beaver dams in the river as it flows through the meadows. The ponds behind these beaver dams have lots of small brook trout that can be easily caught on a worm or fly. The trail passes Roger Lake (El 7,420 ft.) at 5.5 miles. Aneroid Lake (El 7,500 ft.), is 0.5 mile past Roger Lake. There is a camping area at the north end of Aneroid Lake. A marked side trail leads to the campsites. Some cabins, which are not open to the public, are at the south end of the lake.

The trail passes Aneroid Lake on the left (east) side. It then climbs for 1 mile, into an open meadow, and to the junction with Bonny Lakes Trail 1802. See Hike 98 Bonny Lakes. The elevation at this junction is 7,820 feet.

After passing the Bonny Lakes junction, the trail winds its way up through mostly open slopes, dotted with whitebark pines, to Tenderfoot Pass. The pass (El 8,500 ft.) is 1.5 miles past the Bonny Lakes Trail junction. Jewett Lake (El 8,300 ft.) is to the right about 0.5 mile off the trail a short distance below the pass.

At Tenderfoot Pass, East Fork Wallowa River Trail becomes North Fork Imnaha River Trail 1814. See Hike 93 North Fork Imnaha River. Return by the same trail, or check Hikes 93, 3, and 4 for a loop trip over Polaris Pass and back to Wallowa Lake Trailhead.

3 POLARIS PASS

Trail 1831

General description: A high altitude 7.5-mile trail connecting the North Fork Imnaha River Trail with the West Fork Wallowa River Trail.
Difficulty: Strenuous.
Trail maintenance: Yearly.
Best season: August and September.
Traffic: Light to moderate.
Elevation gain: Heading west 680 feet. Loss: 2,300 feet.
Maximum elevation: 8,890 feet.
Map: Aneroid Mountain USGS quad.

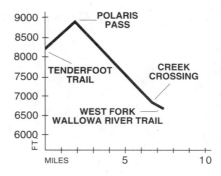

For more information: U.S. Forest Service at Wallowa Mountain Visitors Center, Enterprise, Oregon.

Finding the trail: Trail leaves the North Fork Imnaha River Trail 1814, 0.3 mile south of Tenderfoot Pass. See Hike 2 East Fork Wallowa River and Hike 93 North Fork Imnaha River 1814. The elevation at this junction is 8,210 feet.

0.0	Trail begins at junction with North Fork Imnaha River Trail.
2.0	Trail crosses Polaris Pass.
6.5	Trail crosses creek.
7.5	Trail junction with West Fork Wallowa River Trail.

The trail: Polaris Pass Trail leaves North Fork Imnaha River Trail 1814 and heads southwest through open alpine terrain. It drops slightly at first, then climbs in an ascending traverse for nearly 2 miles. The trail switchbacks four times as it climbs the last 300 feet to Polaris Pass (El 8,890 ft.).

3   *Polaris Pass*

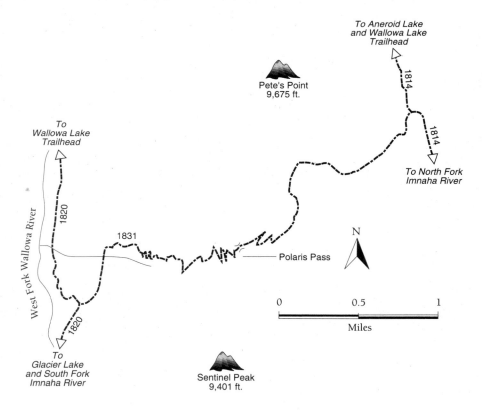

The view in all directions is spectacular from Polaris Pass. Looking to the east down the North Fork of the Imnaha River the country is typical of the Eastern Wallowas. The rock is dark brown and gray, not the the lighter colored granite and limestone you see looking west into the central part of the range. The country to the east is also far less rugged. A wide range of alpine flowers bloom in August above timberline near Polaris Pass. Some mountain goats can also be found in this area.

After crossing Polaris Pass, the trail switchbacks continuously; first through open scree slopes, and then through thickening timber. The trail drops steadily, losing over 2,000 vertical feet in the 4.5 miles to the first creek crossing (El 6,810 ft.). Beyond the creek crossing the trail makes a descending traverse for 1 more mile to the junction with the West Fork Wallowa River Trail 1820. See Hike 4 West Fork Wallowa River . This junction (El 6,590 ft.) is 7.5 miles from the North Fork Imnaha River Trail 1814.

The upper part of Polaris Pass Trail is very dry in late summer. Water should be carried along as it is hard to come by. Use caution on this trail in questionable weather; it can be very stormy near the top.

4   WEST FORK WALLOWA RIVER

Trail 1820 and 1806

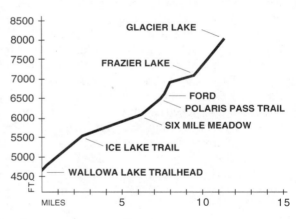

General description: An 11.6 mile backpack from Wallowa Lake Trailhead to Glacier Lake. The first part of this trail may be used to reach Hike 6 Ice Lake, Hike 7 Lakes Basin, and Hike 3 Polaris Pass.
Difficulty: Easy to Six Mile Meadow, and moderate from there to Glacier Lake.
Trail maintenance: Yearly.
Best season: June through October to Six Mile Meadow, July through September to Glacier Lake.
Traffic: Very heavy to Six Mile Meadow, heavy from there to Glacier Lake. Heavy horse traffic to Six Mile Meadow.
Elevation gain: 3,516 feet.
Maximum elevation: 8,166 feet.
Maps: Imus Geographics Wallowa Mountains Eagle Cap, or Joseph, Aneroid Mountain and Eagle Cap Mountain USGS quads.

For more information: U.S. Forest Service at Wallowa Mountain Visitors Center, Enterprise, Oregon and Wallowa Lake General Store, in the resort area at Wallowa Lake.

Finding the trail: The trail begins at Wallowa Lake Trailhead. See Hike 2 East Fork Wallowa River for directions to the trailhead. Like Hike 2, this trail goes through PP and L land at first. It also goes a short distance through Wallowa Lake State Park before reaching the national forest. No special permission is needed to cross these lands on the trail.

0.0	Trail begins at Wallowa Lake Trailhead.
0.3	Trail junction with Chief Joseph Mountain Trail.
2.6	Trail junction with Ice Lake Trail.
6.0	Trail reaches Six Mile Meadow and junction with Lakes Basin Trail.
7.5	Trail junction with Polaris Pass Trail.
8.0	Trail fords West Fork Wallowa River.
8.7	Trail passes Frazier Lake.
9.0	Trail junction with Hawkins Pass Trail.
11.6	Trail reaches Glacier Lake.

The trail: Go around the cable gate on the left side of the parking area. Fifty yards up the trail is a signboard with a trail map of the area (El 4,650 ft.). Take the trail to the right.

One third mile from the trailhead is Chief Joseph Mountain Trail 1803 junction (El 4,790 ft.). See Hike 5 Chief Joseph Mountain. Bear left at this junction and follow West Fork Trail south, passing Wallowa Whitman National Forest and Eagle Cap Wilderness Boundary signs. At 1.25 miles the trail goes through an area that was hit by an avalanche a few years ago. This area of broken and knocked down trees shows the power of even a fairly small avalanche. The trail continues to climb gently, crossing a bridge at 2 miles (El 5,260 ft.). At 2.3 miles (El 5,380 ft.) there is a switchback which allows the trail to climb to a better crossing of a side creek. One quarter mile farther, the trail is elevated slightly in a couple of places to make crossing a wet area easier. At 2.6 miles, Ice Lake Trail 1808, turns off to the right (El 5,530 ft.). See Hike 6 Ice Lake.

Beyond the Ice Lake junction, the trail gradually climbs for 3.3 miles to Six Mile Meadow (El 6,080 ft.). At Six Mile Meadow there is a trail junction with Trail 1810, which turns right and goes to the Lakes Basin. See Hike 7 Lakes Basin. Six Mile Meadow used to be heavily used as a camping area, now the meadow is closed to camping to allow it to repair itself from the damage caused by years of heavy use. Most of the West Fork Wallowa River is quite fast flowing, and hard to fish, however here at Six Mile Meadows there are some slower areas in the river, and some good catches of brook trout can be had.

From Six Mile Meadows, the West Fork Trail heads on up the West Fork Wallowa River. Soon it climbs some distance away from the river, up the east side of the canyon through thinning timber to the junction with Polaris Pass Trail 1831 (El 6,590 ft.) Polaris Pass Trail junction is 7.5 miles from Wallowa Lake Trailhead. See Hike 3 Polaris Pass.

A few feet past Polaris Pass Trail junction the trail crosses a creek. A quarter mile farther, the West Fork of the Wallowa River flows through a short steep canyon to the right of the trail. In the canyon is a waterfall. Another quarter mile and the trail fords the West Fork Wallowa River (El 6,900 ft.). This crossing can be hazardous during periods of high water. It is always a wet crossing.

The next 0.75 mile from the ford to Frazier Lake is one of the most spectacular parts of the West Fork Trail. There are huge limestone cliffs across the river to the east and south. These cliffs are overlaid with brown sedimentary

4   *West Fork Wallowa River*

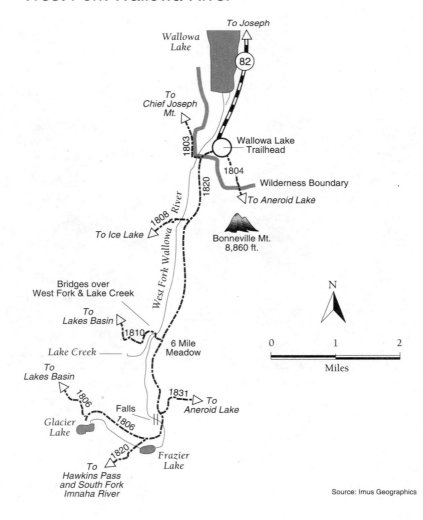

Source: Imus Geographics

rock. The trail and river canyon in this area make a curve to the right (west). When you get near Frazier Lake, there is a waterfall dropping over the limestone cliffs.

At Frazier Lake (El 7,127 ft.) there are several good campsites, and brook trout are here for the catching. Frazier Lake is also notorious for its mosquitoes. The trail goes around the right (north) side of the lake and climbs very slightly for 0.2 mile to the junction with South Fork Imnaha River Trail 1820 (El 7,140 ft.). See Hike 92 South Fork Imnaha River. The Imnaha River Trail turns to the left (southwest). After passing the junction, the West Fork Wallowa River Trail changes trail number to 1806. It climbs a couple of switchbacks then heads northwest, staying well above the creek bed. It continues to climb in an ascending traverse through thinning timber to Glacier Lake (El 8,166 ft.). Glacier Lake is 11.6 miles from Wallowa Lake Trailhead.

Glacier Lake is in a very picturesque alpine setting. It is one of the most photographed lakes in the Wallowas. The lake may be frozen over, at least partly, well into July. There are plenty of good campsites around the lake. Fishing for small brook trout is generally good in Glacier Lake. To continue on past Glacier Lake, see Hike 13 Glacier Pass.

East and West Fork Wallowa River Canyons over Wallowa Lake.

Trail 1803

General description: A long day hike of 14 miles round trip, or a moderate backpack, from Wallowa Lake Trailhead to the meadows at the base of the face of Chief Joseph Mountain. This trail is used to access several climbing routes on Chief Joseph Mountain.
Difficulty: Moderate.
Trail maintenance: Yearly.
Best season: The first 4 miles are usually snow free, or nearly so, from mid-April to mid-November. The upper 3 miles are best done Mid-June through mid-October.

Traffic: Heavy foot and horse traffic June through August. Light to moderate traffic the rest of the time.
Elevation gain: 2,830 feet.
Maximum elevation: 7,620 feet.
Map: Chief Joseph Mountain USGS quad
For more information: Wallowa Lake General Store at Wallowa Lake, and U.S. Forest Service at Wallowa Mountain Visitors Center, Enterprise, Oregon.
Finding the trail: Take the West Fork Wallowa River Trail 1820, for 0.3 mile from Wallowa Lake Trailhead (El 4,790 ft.). See Hike 4 West Fork Wallowa River. See Hike 2 East Fork Wallowa River for directions to the Wallowa Lake Trailhead.

0.0   Trail junction with West Fork Wallowa River Trail.
0.2   Bridge over West Fork Wallowa River.
1.2   Bridge over B C Creek.
3.4   Trail switches back to the south.
4.4   Trail switches back in open area.
7.0   End of trail at the base of cliffs on Chief Joseph Mountain.

The trail: Turn right off West Fork Trail at the Chief Joseph Trail junction, then bear left. The trail to the extreme right goes a short distance to a viewpoint of the falls in the Wallowa River, and returns to the parking area through the Pacific Power and Light campground.

Two tenths of a mile after leaving the West Fork Wallowa River Trail the Chief Joseph Mountain Trail crosses a bridge over the West Fork Wallowa River (El 4,770 ft.). Past the bridge the trail climbs some switchbacks then heads north. Six hundred yards after crossing the bridge the unmarked route

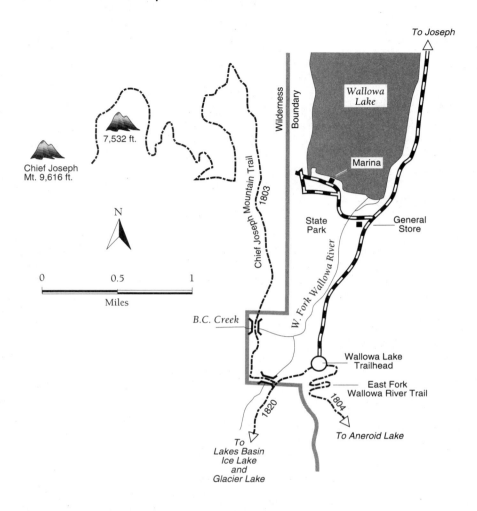

to the Dihedrals Rock Climbing Area, turns to the left (south). See Climb 17 Dihedrals. Seven-tenths of a mile from the West Fork Trail there is a viewpoint on the right with a good view of Wallowa Lake. Three-tenths of a mile farther is a bridge over B C Creek (El 5,030 ft.). B C Creek bridge is a good turn around point for the less serious hikers. This small creek forms an almost continuous waterfall as it plunges off the side of Chief Joseph Mountain. A short distance past B C Creek two climbing routes to the summit of Chief Joseph Mountain turn off to the left. There are no visible signs where these routes leave the trail. See Climb 8 B C Ridge and Climb 9 Marina Ridge.

   Three and four tenths miles from the West Fork Trail, the trail switches back to the south. After a mile or so of heading south, in and out of side draws, it enters a semi-open slope of sagebrush and scattered trees. The trail crosses the open slope to another switchback at 4.4 miles (El 6,350 ft.). Another climbing route to the summit of Chief Joseph Mountain leaves the trail at this point. See Climb 7 First Chute. These open slopes become a flower garden in late June. The principle flowers are arrowleaf balsamroot and lupine, but there are also many other types.

Make the switchback and climb gently, crossing the open slope again, and re-enter the timber at the ridge top (El 6,450 ft.). At 5.7 miles (El 6,950 ft.), the trail enters another open hillside. It continues to climb gently, re-entering the timber at 7,220 feet elevation. The trail then climbs through thinning alpine timber to a point at the base of Chief Joseph Mountain. Here it ends at 7,620 feet elevation, 7 miles from the West Fork Wallowa River Trail. The return trip to Wallowa Lake Trailhead is made by retracing the same route, as no loop trips are possible without bushwhacking.

This is a beautiful place to camp and admire the view, or to make a base camp, for climbing Chief Joseph Mountain. Lack of water is a problem. If the snow is all melted there may be no water close by.

A short climb (150 yards) to the right (west) from the end of the trail brings you to the top of point. This point is marked with a rock pile and a wooden cross. From this point (El 7,650 ft.), there is an excellent view of the face of Chief Joseph Mountain, the surrounding alpine country, and the Wallowa Valley. Look for mountain goats high on the cliffs above. There are also mule deer (some very large bucks) and a few elk in this area. There is occasional rock fall off the face of Chief Joseph Mountain, so it is best not to camp to close too the face. The view is better a little farther back anyway.

A break on Chief Joseph Mountain Trail. *Photo by Ettore Negri.*

6   ICE LAKE

Trail 1808

General description: A backpack or long day hike of 5.1 miles from West Fork Wallowa River Trail to Ice Lake (7.7 miles one way if coming all the way from Wallowa Lake Trailhead). Ice Lake is the normal base camp for parties climbing The Matterhorn. Ice Lake is often seen in photographs, as it is one of the most beautiful lakes in the Wallowa Mountains.

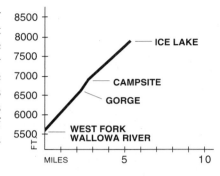

Difficulty: Moderate.

Trail maintenance: Yearly.

Best season: July through September.

Traffic: Heavy, with heavy horse traffic.

Elevation gain: 2,360 feet from West Fork Wallowa River Trail junction; 3,240 feet from Wallowa Lake Trailhead.

Maximum elevation: 7,850 feet.

Maps: Imus Geographics Wallowa Mountains Eagle Cap Wilderness, or Aneroid Mountain and Eagle Cap Mountain USGS quads.

For more information: Wallowa Lake General Store at Wallowa Lake and U.S. Forest Service at Wallowa Mountain Visitors Center, Enterprise, Oregon.

Finding the trail: Take the West Fork Wallowa River Trail 1820 from Wallowa Lake Trailhead. Go 2.6 miles south to the junction with Ice Lake Trail (El 5,530 ft.). See Hike 4 West Fork Wallowa River.

0.0	Trail junction with West Fork Wallowa River Trail.
0.1	Bridge over West Fork Wallowa River.
1.3	Trail approaches Adam Creek.
2.3	Trail overlooks gorge.
2.5	Trail crosses stream.
2.7	Campsite on the right of the trail.
5.1	Trail junction with the around the lake trail, at Ice Lake.

The trail: Ice Lake Trail turns right (west) off the West Fork Wallowa River Trail, and soon crosses a bridge over the West Fork of the Wallowa River. It then begins climbing in gentle but steady switchbacks through fairly open slopes studded with Indian paintbrush. At 1.3 miles (El 6,150 ft.) the trail approaches Adam Creek, which is more like a waterfall than a creek at this point. Two and a quarter miles from the West Fork Trail junction (El 6,550 ft.) the trail overlooks a gorge with Adam Creek rushing through it. There are falls at the upper end of the gorge. From here the upper falls of Adam Creek can be seen in the distance. One quarter mile farther (El 6,730 ft.) there is a side stream crossing the trail. The steep gray and brown slopes of Hurwal Divide are above and to the right. Another 0.25 mile and the trail comes into a semi-open basin with a good campsite on the right side of the trail (El 6,800 ft.).

A few yards past the campsite the trail crosses a small stream and begins another series of switchbacks. The trail climbs in switchbacks to the junction with the trail which circles Ice Lake (El 7,844 ft.). This junction is 5.1 miles from the West Fork Trail. There is a bridge across Adam Creek a few yards to the left on the trail around the lake.

Good campsites are available at Ice Lake, but before camping here Forest Service regulations should be checked. There may be areas which are closed to camping. Firewood is somewhat scarce and fires may be prohibited. This alpine area is not the place to have campfires anyway. This is a high use area, so please take care not to damage it further.

The view from anywhere around the lake is spectacular. Flowers start to bloom as soon as the snow leaves (late June). Mule deer are common around the lake. Mountain goats and bighorn sheep may sometimes be seen from Ice Lake. These animals are usually on the ridges to the north. Ice Lake is the normal base camp for climbing Matterhorn Mountain, Sacajawea Peak, Hurwal Divide, and Craig Mountain. See Climb 10 Matterhorn Mountain from Ice Lake. Fishing for brook trout is very good in Ice Lake.

6   *Ice Lake*

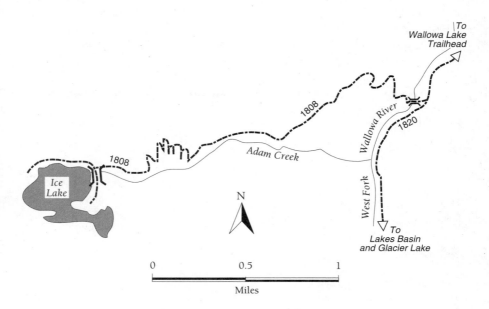

Ice Lake. *Photo by Gary Fletcher.*

From Ice Lake a route is possible over the high pass (El 8,900 ft.) to the south via Razz Lake, to the Lakes Basin. This route involves some skill in route finding and some rough scrambling. It should be led only by experienced hikers or mountain climbers. By using this rough cross-country route to Razz Lake, a loop trip can be made through the Lakes Basin, and back down to the West Fork Wallowa Trail to Six Mile Meadow, then on down the West Fork Wallowa River Trail to Wallowa Lake Trailhead.

7   LAKES BASIN

Trail 1810

General description: A 5.9 mile backpack from West Fork Wallowa River Trail 1820 to Hurricane Creek Trail 1807. This trail is one of the main access routes to the popular Lakes Basin area.

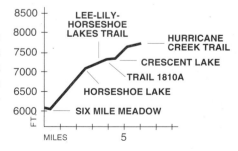

Difficulty: Moderate.
Trail maintenance: Yearly.
Best season: Late June through September.
Traffic: Very heavy, with heavy horse traffic.

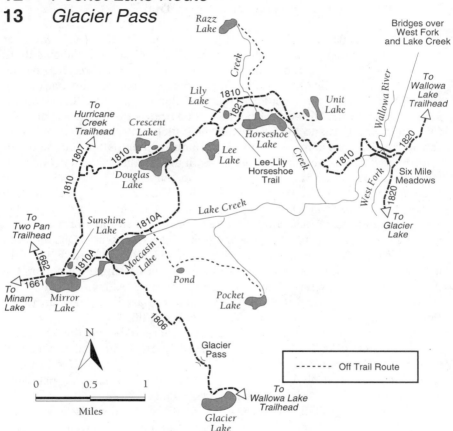

Elevation gain: 1,610 feet from West Fork Wallowa River Trail; 3,040 feet from Wallowa Lake Trailhead.
Maximum elevation: 7,690 feet.
Maps: Imus Geographics Wallowa Mountains Eagle Cap Wilderness, or Aneroid Mountain and Eagle Cap Mountain USGS quads.
For more information: U.S. Forest Service at Wallowa Mountain Visitors Center, Enterprise, Oregon.
Finding the trail: From Wallowa Lake Trailhead go 6 miles south on the West Fork Wallowa River Trail to Six Mile Meadow and the junction with Lakes Basin Trail. See Hike 4 West Fork Wallowa River, and Hike 2 East Fork Wallowa River for directions.

0.0	Trail junction with West Fork Wallowa River Trail.
0.2	Bridge over West Fork Wallowa River.
3.0	Horseshoe Lake and trail junction with Lee, Lily, Horseshoe Lakes Trail.
3.5	Trail creek crossing and Razz Lake Route junction.
4.0	Trail junction with Lee, Lily, Horseshoe Lakes Trail.
4.5	Trail junction with Lakes Basin Alternate and Douglas Lake.
5.0	Trail passes Crescent Lake.
5.9	Trail junction with Hurricane Creek Trail.

The trail: Lakes Basin Trail turns right (west) off the West Fork Wallowa River Trail. A quarter mile from the junction it crosses the West Fork Wallowa River on a bridge. There is a good campsite on the right just before crossing the bridge. Camping in Six Mile Meadow is prohibited, so please camp back in the trees. After crossing the West Fork, the trail soon crosses Lake Creek on another wooden bridge. After crossing the second bridge, the trail heads up Lake Creek for a short distance. It then begins the switchbacks heading up to Horseshoe Lake. The trail climbs steadily for 2.75 miles, then flattens out on top of some huge flat rock outcroppings. One-fourth mile farther is the junction with Lee, Lily, Horseshoe Trail 1821 and Horseshoe Lake (El 7,133 ft.). Horseshoe Lake is 3 miles from the West Fork Trail. See Hike 10 Lee, Lily, Horseshoe Lakes. Fishing for small brook trout is generally excellent in Horseshoe Lake. Small flies and rooster tails attract the fish, as do regular old worms.

At the junction the main trail bears to the right (northwest). One hundred fifty yards past the junction the unmarked route to Unit Lake heads to the right up a small gully. See Hike 8 Unit Lake Route. After passing the junction, the trail climbs gradually for 0.5 mile to a creek crossing. A few feet before the crossing is the unmarked spot where the route to Razz Lake takes off to the right. See Hike 9 Razz Lake Route. The elevation at this turn off is 7,240 feet. The trail continues to climb gradually 0.5 mile more to the junction with Lee, Lily, Horseshoe Lake Trail. See Hike 10 Lee, Lily, Horseshoe Lakes. One-half mile farther is the junction with Trail 1810A. (El 7,300 ft.). See Hike 11 Lakes Basin Alternate. Trail 1810A goes to Moccasin and Mirror Lakes. A path goes straight ahead a few yards to the east end of Douglas Lake.

At this junction Trail 1810 turns to the right (west) and heads for Crescent Lake and Hurricane Creek Trail. Turn right, and climb slightly for 0.5 mile more to a creek crossing at the outlet of Crescent Lake (El 7,350 ft.). There are good campsites on the west side of Crescent Lake. Past Crescent Lake the trail continues to climb with some switchbacks for 0.9 mile to the junction with Hurricane Creek Trail 1807 (El 7,690 ft.). See Hike 14 Hurricane Creek. The junction with Hurricane Creek Trail is 5.9 miles from the West Fork Wallowa River Trail.

Hurwal Divide ends in spectacular cliffs just to the north of Crescent Lake. Just before reaching Hurricane Creek Trail junction, the bright white limestone peak of Matterhorn Mountain can be seen by looking to the north. All the lakes in the Lakes Basin have good fishing, and there are campsites scattered throughout the area. Mule deer are common, and a few bears inhabit the Lakes Basin. Usually bears are not a problem, but it doesn't hurt to hang your food and keep a clean camp. This is an extremely popular area you may not be alone at any of the lakes in July or August.

8   UNIT LAKE ROUTE

General description: A short 0.5 mile off-trail route, from Horseshoe Lake to Unit Lake.
Difficulty: Easy, but requires route finding skills.
Trail maintenance: None.
Best season: Mid-June through mid-September.
Traffic: Light.
Elevation gain: 197 feet. Loss: 323 feet.
Maximum elevation: 7,330 feet.
Map: Eagle Cap Mountain USGS quad.
For more information: U.S. Forest Service at Wallowa Mountain Visitors Center, Enterprise, Oregon.
Finding the trail: The route to Unit Lake leaves Lakes Basin Trail 1810, 150 yards past (west northwest of) Lee, Lily, Horseshoe Lake Trail junction, near Horseshoe Lake. See Hike 7 Lakes Basin Trail 1810, map on p. 27.

0.0   Trail junction with Lakes Basin Trail near Horseshoe Lake.
0.5   Unit Lake.

Unit Lake. *Photo by Lowell Euhus.*

The trail: The route, which is a path up a small gully at this point, heads to the right (northeast) and climbs for 200 yards. Here the path flattens out (El 7,330 ft.) and begins to drop down to the east. Do not drop down; turn left (north) off the path, in the flat area. Climb over a small rocky rise and drop into the next gully to the north. Turn right (east) and do a descending traverse to the east, passing a pond. After the pond, continue to descend to the east northeast to Unit Lake (El 7,007 ft.). Both the pond and Unit Lake can be seen from the top of the rocky rise.

Unit Lake is the lowest lake in the Lakes Basin area. It is surrounded by thicker and larger timber than the other lakes in the area. The fishing is good for brook trout. There is plenty of firewood around Unit Lake, and it is in a more protected area than the other lakes. It is also lightly used.

Unit Lake is only 0.5 mile off the main trail, and the elevation gain and loss are only a couple hundred feet; however, some route finding is required to locate it.

9   RAZZ LAKE ROUTE

General description: A steep off-trail route of about 1.5 miles from Lakes Basin to Razz Lake.
Difficulty: Strenuous.
Trail maintenance: None.
Best season: Late July through September.
Traffic: Light.
Elevation gain: 863 feet.

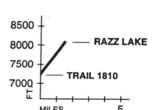

Maximum elevation: 8,103 feet.
Map: Eagle Cap Mountain USGS quad.
For more information: U.S. Forest Service at Wallowa Mountain Visitors Center, Enterprise, Oregon.
Finding the trail: The route to Razz Lake leaves Lakes Basin Trail 1810, 0.5 mile west of Lee, Lily, Horseshoe Lake Trail junction (El 7,240 ft.). See Hike 7 Lakes Basin. The point where the route leaves the trail is unmarked, but it can be found by going to the first main stream crossing, then backtracking (east) a few feet. At some times of the year there may be one or more very small streams, a foot or less wide, before reaching this point. The main stream is 5 to 10 feet wide. See map on p. 27.

0.0   Lakes Basin Trail 1810.
1.5   Razz Lake.

The trail: Turn right (north) off the main trail, and follow a faint path, steep uphill. Stay 100 to 200 feet to the right (east) of the creek, and work your way up through some rock outcroppings. At 7,500 feet elevation the route is the farthest away from the creek (to the east) that it gets. Continue to stay to the east of the creek, which is the outlet of Razz Lake, until reaching the lake (El 8,103 ft.).

The route to Razz Lake is fairly steep and requires some route finding. The total distance from the Lakes Basin Trail is 1.5 miles, and the elevation gain is 863 feet. Campsites around the lake are limited. Fishing is good most of the time, but the lake may be ice covered until late July. Golden trout were stocked here at one time.

There is a scrambling route north from Razz Lake to Ice Lake. This route is short, 1.5 miles, but is very steep and somewhat unstable. It should only be attempted by experienced mountaineers.

Above Razz Lake 0.5 mile, to the west is another small unnamed lake. To get to this higher lake, follow the stream (not the dry stream bed) which flows into the west end of Razz Lake, up and to the west. The stream has some small ponds in it. Continue past them to the lake (El 8,450 ft.).

This small lake is partly surrounded by cliffs. The area around this lake is very alpine with only a few small trees. It makes a good out of the way campsite for those of us who like such places. There are probably no fish in this lake, which may be ice covered until early August. This is big mule buck country, and there are mountain goats in the area, so keep your eyes open.

10   LEE, LILY, HORSESHOE LAKES

Trail 1821

General description: A short connecting trail in the lower Lakes Basin. Trail 1821 leaves Lakes Basin Trail 0.5 mile northeast of Douglas Lake and rejoins Lakes Basin Trail at Horseshoe Lake. Trail 1821 is slightly over 1 mile long.

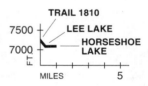

Difficulty: Easy.
Trail maintenance: Yearly.
Best season: Late June through September.
Traffic: Heavy, with heavy horse traffic.
Elevation loss: 167 feet (west to east).
Maximum elevation: 7,300 feet.
Map: Eagle Cap Mountain USGS quad.
For more information: U.S. Forest Service at Wallowa Mountain Visitors Center, Enterprise, Oregon.
Finding the trail: The Lee, Lily, Horseshoe Lakes Trail leaves the Lakes Basin Trail 1810, 0.5 mile northeast of Douglas Lake. See Hike 7 Lakes Basin. The elevation at the trail junction is approximately 7,300 feet. See map on p. 27.

0.0   Trail junction with Lakes Basin Trail 1810.
0.5   Lee Lake.
0.8   Lily Lake is a few hundred feet to the north.

1.0   Horseshoe Lake.
1.2   Trail junction with Lakes Basin Trail 1810.

The trail: Coming from Douglas Lake, turn right (southeast), and descend 0.5 mile to Lee Lake (El 7,145 ft.).

There are several campsites at Lee Lake. The north shore of the lake drops off very abruptly. This should be a good spot to try for the many fish in Lee Lake; however, it could also be quite dangerous, especially for young children, as the bottom of the lake drops off very quickly into deep water..

After leaving Lee Lake the trail leads east northeast. It passes a few hundred feet south of Lily Lake, and reaches Horseshoe Lake in 0.5 mile. Just before reaching Horseshoe Lake there is an excellent campsite by a stream. This stream is the outlet stream from Razz Lake.

There is a path completely encircling Horseshoe Lake. Trail 1821 follows the north shore and rejoins Lakes Basin Trail 1810 at the east end of the lake. See Hike 7 Lakes Basin.

11   *LAKES BASIN ALTERNATE*

Trail 1810A

General description: A 1.8 mile trail in the upper Lakes Basin, between Lakes Basin Trail at Douglas Lake and East Fork Lostine River Trail near Mirror Lake. This trail is the access to Moccasin Lake, Glacier Pass Trail, and the off trail route to Pocket Lake.

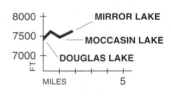

Difficulty: Easy.
Trail maintenance: Yearly.
Best season: July through September.
Traffic: Heavy, with heavy horse traffic.
Elevation gain: Approximately 445 feet. Loss: Approximately 150 feet.
Maximum elevation: 7,630 feet.
Map: Eagle Cap Mountain USGS quad.
For more information: U.S. Forest Service at Wallowa Mountain Visitors Center, Enterprise, Oregon.
Finding the trail: Trail 1810A leaves the Lakes Basin Trail 1810 at the east end of Douglas Lake (El 7,326 ft.). See Hike 7 Lakes Basin, map on p. 27.

0.0   Trail junction with Lakes Basin Trail 1810 at Douglas Lake.
0.5   Top of rise.
0.8   Trail junction with Pocket Lake Route.
1.0   Moccasin Lake and trail junction with Glacier Pass Trail.
1.6   Mirror Lake and trail junction with Trail 1810.
1.8   Trail junction with East Fork Lostine River Trail 1662.

Mirror Lake and Eagle Cap Mountain.

The trail: The trail heads southwest from the junction. It crosses the outlet of Douglas Lake and follows its shoreline for a short distance.

Soon the trail leaves the lake and climbs 0.5 mile to the top of a small rise, topping out at approximately 7,600 feet. It then drops slightly for 0.25 mile, to an unmarked trail junction. The route to Pocket Lake begins here. See Hike 12 Pocket Lake Route. Continue straight ahead (west) 0.25 mile to Moccasin Lake and lots of fish to be caught. The trail follows the north shore of Moccasin Lake.

At the west end of Moccasin Lake is another trail junction. The trail to the left (south) goes to Glacier Lake. See Hike 13 Glacier Pass. After passing the Glacier Pass Trail 1806 junction, the trail climbs a short distance, then flattens out for 0.5 mile to the junction with Lakes Basin Trail 1810, at Mirror Lake (El 7,595 ft.). A quarter mile more brings you to the junction with the East Fork Lostine River Trail 1662. See Hike 18 East Fork Lostine River.

12   *POCKET LAKE ROUTE*

General description: A fairly steep off-trail route from Lakes Basin Alternate Trail 1810A, near Moccasin Lake to Pocket Lake. The distance to Pocket Lake is approximately 1.75 miles.

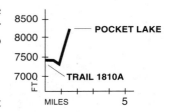

Difficulty: Strenuous.
Trail maintenance: None.
Traffic: Light, with little or no horse traffic past the meadow.
Best season: July through September.
Elevation gain: 900 feet. Loss: 100 feet.
Maximum elevation: 8,225 feet.
Map: Eagle Cap Mountain USGS quad.
For more information: U.S. Forest Service at Wallowa Mountain Visitors Center, Enterprise, Oregon.
Finding the trail: The route to Pocket Lake begins 0.25 mile east of Moccasin Lake on Lakes Basin Alternate Trail 1810A. See Hike 11 Lakes Basin Alternate, map on p. 27.

0.0	Unmarked junction with Lakes Basin Alternate Trail 1810A.
0.5	Route enters a meadow.
0.7	Route comes to pond.
1.0	Route starts up a steep valley.
1.7	Pocket Lake.

The trail: Turn south on the side trail off Lakes Basin Alternate Trail 1810A, and cross Lake Creek. Follow the side trail 0.5 mile to a large meadow with a stream in it. There is a campsite in a grove of trees in this meadow. Cross the stream and head east southeast 0.25 mile to a large pond on the north (left) side of the faint path. Then head east for 0.25 mile along the base of the cliffs. Soon a wide steep boulder-strewn valley will come into view to the right (southwest).

Head up the steep valley, staying to the right (west) of the small stream which flows down the center of it. Climb up the valley, 0.75 mile, and 900 vertical feet, to Pocket Lake (El 8,225 ft.).

The climb to Pocket Lake is strenuous, and requires considerable route finding. It should be attempted only by experienced parties in good condition.

Pocket Lake sits in a glacial cirque, with cliffs and steep mountains on three sides. It is a very alpine setting with only a few small scattered trees. There is an excellent view of the Lakes Basin area and the West Fork Wallowa River Canyon from the rise just north of the lake. Fishing for brook trout is good at Pocket Lake. Lack of firewood and the unprotected nature of the area may be limiting factors for campsite suitability, but the beauty of the area makes the hardships worth it.

Pocket Lake. *Photo by Lowell Euhus.*

13   GLACIER PASS

Trail 1806

General description: A fairly steep trail from Moccasin Lake, over spectacular Glacier Pass to Glacier Lake. This trail connects the Lakes Basin with the West Fork Wallowa River and Glacier Lake. The distance between Moccasin Lake and Glacier Lake is 3 miles.

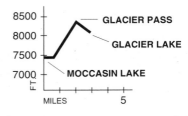

Difficulty: Moderate to strenuous.
Trail maintenance: Yearly.
Best season: July through September.
Traffic: Moderate, with moderate horse traffic.
Elevation gain: 980 feet. Loss: 310 feet.
Maximum elevation: 8,450 feet.
Map: Eagle Cap Mountain USGS quad.
For more information: U.S. Forest Service at Wallowa Mountain Visitors Center, Enterprise, Oregon.
Finding the trail: Glacier Pass Trail leaves Lakes Basin Alternate Trail 1810A at the west end of Moccasin Lake (El 7,470 ft.). See Hike 11 Lakes Basin Alternate, map on p. 27.

0.0	Trail junction with Lakes Basin Alternate Trail 1810A at Moccasin Lake.
2.0	Trail crosses Glacier Pass.
3.0	Glacier Lake.

The trail: From the junction with Lakes Basin Alternate Trail 1810A, the Glacier Pass Trail heads south and crosses the inlet of Moccasin Lake. There are stepping stones crossing the inlet stream.

After leaving Moccasin Lake, the trail goes up and down over outcroppings of glacially eroded granite. At 0.3 mile it crosses a small stream. The trail then climbs steeply in small switchbacks to another stream crossing at 7,940 feet elevation. After crossing the second stream, the trail climbs steeply for 1 more mile, then traverses the last 0.25 mile to Glacier Pass (El 8,450 ft.).

The "trees" at Glacier Pass are whitebark pine elfinwood. These small trees show the severity of the climate in this area. The view from Glacier Pass includes Eagle Cap Mountain to the west: Lakes Basin, Hurricane Creek Canyon, and Matterhorn Mountain to the north; Glacier Lake to the south; and West Fork Wallowa River Canyon to the southeast.

From Glacier Pass the trail switchbacks down the last mile to Glacier Lake (El 8,140 ft.). Here it becomes the West Fork Wallowa River Trail. See Hike 4 West Fork Wallowa River.

Glacier Lake. *Photo by Lowell Euhus.*

Glacier Pass Trail is a rewarding day hike from a camp in the Lakes Basin. It can also be used as a connecting route to make a loop trip by continuing on down the West Fork Wallowa River Trail to Wallowa Lake Trailhead.

14 HURRICANE CREEK

Trail 1807 and 1810

General description: A 12.1 mile backpack, from Hurricane Creek Trailhead, up Hurricane Creek Canyon, one of the deepest in the range, to Mirror Lake in the Lakes Basin.

Difficulty: Moderate.

Trail maintenance: Yearly.

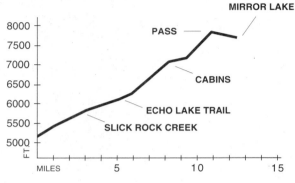

Best season: Mid-May through October to Echo Lake Trail junction, and mid-June through September past there.

Traffic: Heavy to Echo Lake Trail, then moderate to trail junction with Lakes Basin Trail 1810, and heavy again from the trail junction to Mirror Lake. Heavy horse traffic.

Elevation gain: 2,675 feet.

Maximum elevation: 7,700 feet.

Maps: Imus Geographics Wallowa Mountains Eagle Cap Wilderness, or Chief Joseph Mountain and Eagle Cap Mountain USGS quads.

For more information: U.S. Forest Service at Wallowa Mountain Visitors Center, Enterprise, Oregon.

Finding the trail: From Enterprise go 5 miles south on Hurricane Creek Road to Hurricane Creek Grange Hall. Bear right (actually straight ahead) off the paved road, and go 3 more miles south to Hurricane Creek Trailhead (El 5,025 ft.). There are stock loading facilities, an outhouse, and a few campsites at the trailhead.

0.0	Trail begins at Hurricane Creek Trailhead.
0.1	Trail junction with Falls Creek Trail.
0.2	Trail crosses Falls Creek.
0.8	Trail crosses avalanche area.
1.5	Trail crosses Deadman Creek.
3.0	Trail crosses Slick Rock Creek.
4.2	Trail crosses Granite Creek.
5.0	Trail junction with Echo Lake Trail.
5.5	Trail crosses Hurricane Creek.

6.0	Trail crosses Fullington Creek.
8.3	Cabins on the right side of the trail.
10.5	Trail goes over pass.
11.0	Trail junction with Lakes Basin Trail 1810.
12.1	Trail junction with Lakes Basin Alternate Trail 1810A, and Mirror Lake.

The trail: The trail heads south from the trailhead, passing the junction with Falls Creek Trail 1807A at 0.1 mile (El 5,105 ft.). See Hike 15 Falls Creek. A short distance farther the trail crosses Falls Creek. There is no bridge, so crossing can be a problem during periods of high water.

At 0.75 mile the trail enters an area of knocked down trees. This is the result of an avalanche. In the middle of the avalanche debris is the Eagle Cap Wilderness boundary sign (El 5,350 ft.). One and one half miles from the trailhead the trail crosses Deadman Creek. Legend has it that an early day miner dropped his .45 revolver on a rock near the mouth of Deadman Creek and shot himself dead. His friends buried him along Deadman Creek in the basin below the limestone cliffs west of Hurricane Creek Trail.

Just after crossing Deadman Creek, a cross-country route takes off to the west up through Deadman Basin (where the miner was buried) to Deadman Lake. The route to Deadman Lake takes lots of route finding skills. There is a way that can be hiked by strong hikers, but if one misses this route, roped climbing may be required. Watch for mountain goats and big horn sheep in the

Matterhorn Mountain from upper Hurricane Creek Trail. *Photo by Kerry Searls.*

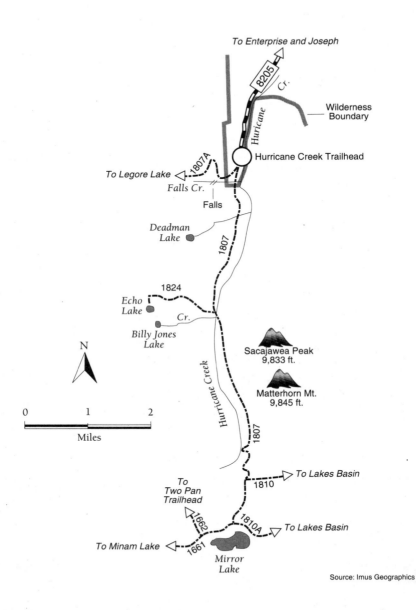

To Enterprise and Joseph

8205

Cr.

Hurricane

Wilderness
Boundary

Hurricane Creek Trailhead

1807A

To Legore Lake

Falls Cr.

Falls

*Deadman
Lake*

1807

1824

*Echo
Lake*

Cr.

*Billy Jones
Lake*

N

Sacajawea Peak
9,833 ft.

Matterhorn Mt.
9,845 ft.

Hurricane Creek

0   1   2

Miles

1807

To Lakes Basin

1810

To
Two Pan
Trailhead

1810A   To Lakes Basin

1662

To Minam Lake

1661

*Mirror
Lake*

Source: Imus Geographics

higher parts of Deadman Creek drainage. They can sometimes be seen with binoculars from Hurricane Creek Trail.

One-third mile past Deadman Creek the unmarked Thorp Creek Trail turns to the left. See Climb 11 Sacajawea Peak. At 3 miles the trail makes a switchback and climbs above a small but spectacular gorge with Hurricane Creek rushing through the bottom. Past the gorge is Slick Rock Creek crossing. This area can be very dangerous in early or late season because of snow and ice. This is also a prime avalanche area (El 5,760 ft.).

At 4.25 miles the trail crosses Granite Creek and enters a moist area, where it is held in place with logs on each side. The trail crosses another creek at 5 miles, and soon comes to the junction with Echo Lake Trail 1824 (El 6,040 ft.). See Hike 16 Echo Lake and Billy Jones Lake. Just past the junction, the trail crosses Billy Jones Creek and at 5.5 miles crosses Hurricane Creek. Neither crossing has a bridge. It will probably be impossible to cross Hurricane Creek dry footed, so take off your shoes, find a walking stick, roll up your pant legs and wade through the cold knee-deep water. There are good camp sites just before the crossing on the west side of Hurricane Creek.

At 6 miles (El 6,310 ft.) is Fullington Creek, with a sign to tell you its name. Just past Fullington Creek is a campsite on the right. The trail comes to an opening at 7.75 miles (El 6,690 ft.). Above the trail to the left is the gleaming white limestone face of 9,845 foot high Matterhorn Mountain, the highest peak in the Wallowa Mountains. This area abounds with pikas and other mountain rodents. Bears are also common here. Look for them on the open hillsides, digging grubs and also grazing.

At 8 miles the trail makes a switchback to the left. Above the switchback at 8.3 miles (El 7,100 ft.) there are two old cabins to the right of the trail. The cabins are not in good enough shape to stay in and should be left as they are. The notice that is posted on them says to please leave them as you found them. The cabins are protected by the Antiquities Act of 1906.

Past the cabins, the trail enters an area of beautiful meadows, with frogs croaking and extensive beaver dams on the creek (El 7,200 ft.). Travel on through the meadow for a mile or so, then climb on a moderate grade over a pass (El 7,700 ft.). After crossing the pass the trail drops down to the junction with Trail 1810. Lakes Basin Trail 1810 comes in from the left. At this junction (El 7,660 ft.) 11 miles from the Hurricane Creek Trailhead, the trail number of our trail changes to 1810. Continue 1.1 miles south, passing Sunshine Lake, to Mirror Lake (El 7,595 ft.) in the upper part of the Lakes Basin. Like most of the lakes in the Wallowa Mountains, Mirror Lake has good fishing for small brook trout. There are many campsites in the Lakes Basin area. See Hike 7 Lakes Basin and Hike 11 Lakes Basin Alternate.

The return trip can be made over the same trail, or a one way trip with a car shuttle can be done by using either Lakes Basin Trail or Lakes Basin Alternate Trail and West Fork Wallowa River Trail. See Hikes 7, 11, and 4 or see Hike 18 East Fork Lostine River.

15 FALLS CREEK

Trail 1807A

General description: A steep 4.0 mile mine trail, from Hurricane Creek Trail to Legore Mine, then a faint path over a 9,100 foot high pass to Legore Lake, the highest lake in the Wallowa Mountains.

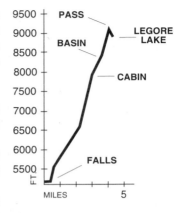

Difficulty: Strenuous.
Trail maintenance: Rare, above the falls done only by volunteers, not maintained for stock traffic.
Best season: June through October to Legore Cabin, July through September above the cabin.
Traffic: Heavy for the first 0.25 mile to the falls, light above the falls, except during late September and October hunting seasons, when traffic can be heavy.
Elevation gain: 4,000 feet. Loss: 140 feet.
Maximum elevation: 9,100 feet.
Map: Chief Joseph Mountain USGS quad.
For more information: U.S. Forest Service at Wallowa Mountain Visitors Center, Enterprise, Oregon. Don't expect too much additional information from the Forest Service or anyone else about this trail.
Finding the trail: Falls Creek Trail leaves Hurricane Creek Trail 1807, 0.1 mile south of Hurricane Creek Trailhead. See Hike 14 Hurricane Creek.

0.0	Trail junction with Hurricane Creek Trail 1807.
0.2	Path to falls.
2.2	Trail crosses side creek.
3.1	Legore cabin and mine.
3.8	Trail crosses pass.
4.0	Legore Lake.

The trail: Turn right at the sign marking Falls Creek Trail. One-fourth mile up the trail, a side trail turns to the left. This trail leads to Falls Creek Falls. The main trail bears right. It makes a long switchback and contours up Falls Creek Canyon, parallel to, but well above the creek. At 0.75 mile (El 5,520 ft.) the trail makes a switchback to the right above the point where the creek forks. This is the point where Falls Creek Ridge Route to Twin Peaks leaves the trail. See Climb 12 Twin Peaks via Falls Creek Ridge. This is the first in a series of switchbacks. The trail climbs up through open areas, then through a forest of mountain mahogany. At 6,050 feet elevation it straightens out and goes on up the canyon to the west. The trail still stays well above the creek. At 2.25 miles

(El 6,630 ft.) the trail crosses a side creek and enters a large open area. After crossing the creek, it begins another series of switchbacks and enters the timber again at the top of the clearing.

Here the trail straightens out again and continues up the canyon high above the creek. Several waterfalls are visible from the trail in this section; the one that appears to come over the ridge to the west is the outlet from Legore Lake. At 3 miles (El 7,830 ft.) the trail crosses another side creek. Directly above here on the right side of the creek are a couple of very shallow mine shafts. The trail crosses the creek and passes another mine shaft. A short climb past the mine shaft is the remains of the old Legore Cabin (El 7,950 ft.). Please don't harm what's left of the cabin. Joe Legore, the original owner of the cabin, called this the Red Cloud Mine. The trail fades out temporarily at the cabin; head west northwest.

A few feet above the cabin the trail becomes visible again. It climbs steeply to a saddle, then fades out. Head up the valley to the west on a talus slope of huge white boulders and enter a beautiful timberline basin (El 8,600 ft.). Here the trail bears left slightly. It climbs over the 9,100 foot high pass to the south and drops to Legore Lake.

Legore Lake (El 8,957 ft.) is 4 miles from Hurricane Creek Trail. This is the highest lake in the Wallowa Mountains. Legore Lake has some brook trout in it, but the extreme elevation keeps them small bodied with large heads. No firewood is available at Legore Lake. In fact, there are no trees, only some scattered whitebark pine elfinwood . There are some flat spots to camp at this isolated lake. The Falls Creek Trail is very steep, and in some places fine sand

Looking west up Falls Creek Canyon. *Photo by Gary Fletcher.*

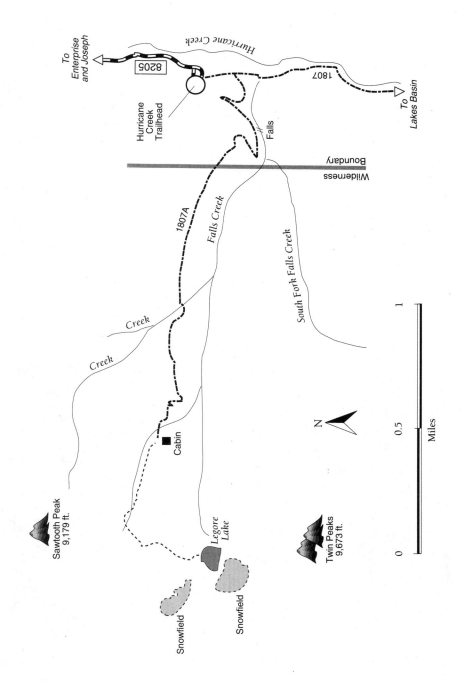

scree on the top of a hardpan trail makes for a ball bearing effect underfoot. It may be difficult for all but hardy hikers.

From the timberline basin, Sawtooth Peak to the north may be climbed quite easily. Sawtooth Peak (El 9,175 ft.) offers 360 degrees of beautiful views. There is also a chance of seeing both mountain goats and bighorn sheep. Return by retracing the trail to Hurricane Creek Trail.

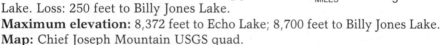

16   ECHO LAKE AND BILLY JONES LAKE

Trail 1824

General description: A backpack of 3 fairly steep miles, from Hurricane Creek Trail to Echo Lake. The total distance from Hurricane Creek Trailhead to Echo Lake is 8.0 miles.
Difficulty: Strenuous.
Trail maintenance: Infrequent and not maintained for stock.
Best season: Mid-July through September.
Traffic: Moderate.
Elevation gain: From Hurricane Creek Trail, 2,332 feet to Echo Lake; 2,640 feet to Billy Jones Lake. Loss: 250 feet to Billy Jones Lake.

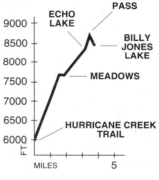

Maximum elevation: 8,372 feet to Echo Lake; 8,700 feet to Billy Jones Lake.
Map: Chief Joseph Mountain USGS quad.
For more information: U.S. Forest Service at Wallowa Mountain Visitors Center, Enterprise, Oregon.
Finding the trail: From Hurricane Creek Trailhead follow Hurricane Creek Trail 1807 for 5.0 miles south to Echo Lake Trail junction (El 6,050 ft.). See Hike 14 Hurricane Creek.

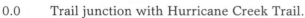

0.0	Trail junction with Hurricane Creek Trail.
3.0	Echo Lake.
3.7	Billy Jones Lake.

The trail: Echo Lake turns right (west) off Hurricane Creek Trail. There is a trail sign marking the junction. At first the trail climbs steeply in switchbacks, then it makes a traverse to the northwest to a creek crossing. (El 6,800 ft.). After crossing the creek, the trail switchbacks steeply up a ridge between two small creeks, topping out at 7,680 feet elevation. A few yards after flattening out and dropping slightly, the trail enters a small lush meadow, and then a larger one. In the larger meadow the trail crosses a stream, then heads on across the meadow in a northwesterly direction. In these swampy meadows the trail may be difficult to see for a short distance.

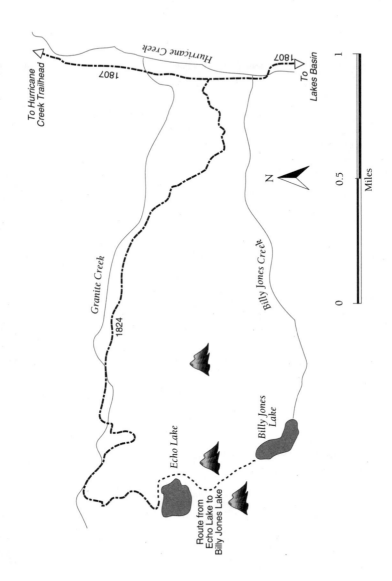

Echo Lake.

After leaving the meadows, the trail climbs steadily. Here the vegetation opens up and becomes more alpine. Whitebark pines become the dominant tree, and alpine flowers bloom along the snow line up the mountains. At 8,100 feet elevation the trail turns to the left (south) and climbs through some rock outcroppings to Echo Lake (El 8,372 ft.).

The total distance to Echo Lake from Hurricane Creek Trail is only 3 miles, but with a 2,300 foot elevation gain and an eroded, poorly maintained trail, it seems much farther. As is true with many of the steep side trails in the Wallowa Mountains, an altimeter is a better indicator of where you are than is a pedometer. The altitude gain is much more significant than the mileage. The alpine country and spectacular views around Echo Lake make the hike well worthwhile. The high ridges to the north of Echo Lake are good places to spot bighorn sheep, and large mule deer bucks abound in the area.

To go on to Billy Jones Lake, go around Echo Lake on the east side, cross the outlet, and follow a steep rough path to the saddle south of the lake (El 8,700 ft.). The faint path then drops for 250 vertical feet to Billy Jones Lake (El 8,450 ft.).

Both Echo and Billy Jones Lakes may be ice covered well into July. Until early August there may be snow covering the trail above 8,000 feet elevation. There are some usable campsites on the north side of Echo Lake, but camping spots are very limited at Billy Jones Lake. The return trip is made by using the same trail.

17   EAGLE CAP MOUNTAIN

Trail 1910 and 1805

General description: The trail to the summit of Eagle Cap Mountain is a fairly steep day hike of 2.7 miles, from Minam Lake/Mirror Lake Trail 1661.

Difficulty: Strenuous.

Trail maintenance: Yearly.

Best season: Mid-July through September. The trail may have some snow patches into early August.

Traffic: Moderate, with little or no horse traffic.

Elevation gain: 1,972 feet.

Maximum elevation: 9,572 feet.

Map: Eagle Cap Mountain USGS quad.

For more information: U.S. Forest Service at Wallowa Mountain Visitors Center, Enterprise, Oregon.

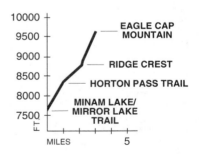

Finding the trail: Eagle Cap Mountain Trail leaves Minam Lake/Mirror Lake Trail 1661, 0.25 mile west of Mirror Lake (El 7,610 ft.). See Hike 19 Minam Lake/Mirror Lake.

0.0   Trail junction with Minam Lake/Mirror Lake Trail.
1.2   Trail junction with Horton Pass Trail, and trail number changes to 1805.
2.0   Ridge crest and trail junction with ridge path to Horton Pass.
2.7   Summit of Eagle Cap Mountain.

The trail: At the trail junction 0.25 mile west of Mirror Lake, turn left (south) off Minam Lake/Mirror Lake Trail 1661. Head around the east side of Upper Lake through the open alpine country on Trail 1910 towards Horton Pass. After following Trail 1910 for 1.2 miles, to 8,350 feet elevation, turn left (southwest) again on Trail 1805 toward Eagle Cap Mountain. Horton Pass is straight ahead if you don't turn left. See Hike 79 East Eagle Creek. Above this junction the trail switchbacks and climbs out to the ridge crest at 8,730 feet elevation. At the ridge crest a rough path turns right and drops down the ridgeline to Horton Pass. Keep on the main trail which turns left and climbs the ridge to the southeast, passing a viewpoint at 8,950 feet elevation. Above the viewpoint, the trail switchbacks up to the summit. The summit (El 9,572 ft.) is 2.7 miles from the Minam Lake/Mirror Lake Trail.

From the summit there is an unobstructed panoramic view of nearly all of the Wallowa Mountains. Whitebark pine elfinwood reaches nearly to the top, and there are usually some golden mantle ground squirrels begging for food at the summit. Eagle Cap Mountain is the only high peak in the Wallowas with an actual trail leading to its summit. Eagle Cap is more or less the center point of the Wallowa Mountains, with canyons radiating in all directions from near its summit. From the summit one can see Hurricane Creek and East Fork Lostine River flowing north, the West Fork Wallowa River flowing east, and Eagle Creek flowing south. A couple of miles to the northwest is Minam Lake, where both the West Fork Lostine and Minam Rivers begin. Minam Lake is not visible from the summit. Three miles to the southeast are the headwaters of the Imnaha River.

Eagle Cap Mountain was originally thought to be the highest peak in the Eagle Mountains, which the Wallowa Mountains were once called. Surveys have since shown several peaks in the range to be higher than Eagle Cap.

For parties wishing to make a loop hike, use the rough path you passed when the Eagle Cap Summit Trail reached the ridge line, can be used for the descent. This path is in poorer condition than the main Eagle Cap Trail, but provides a shortcut to Horton Pass (El 8,470 ft.). From the junction on the ridge line the path descends directly to Horton Pass, 0.3 mile down the northwest ridge of Eagle Cap Mountain. From Horton Pass head north on Trail 1910 to return to Mirror Lake. See Hike 79 East Eagle Creek.

At Horton Pass is the Floyd Vernon (Jack) Horton Memorial Plaque. The plaque was placed here in remembrance of this early day assistant forester who began working for the Forest Service May 10, 1913.

The 1 mile of trail from Horton Pass down (north) to the junction with Eagle Cap Summit Trail may be covered with snow and hard to find until late in the summer. This is open country and the route is not difficult to find, except in bad weather with low visibility.

17 *Eagle Cap Mountain*

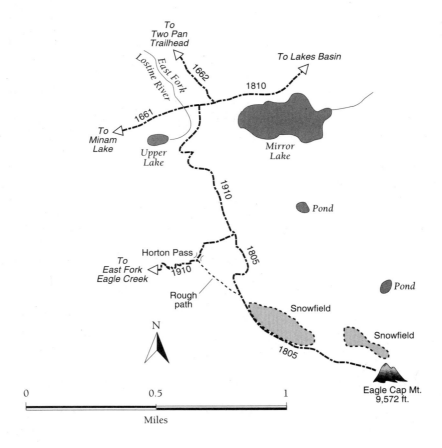

Trail 1662

General description: A day hike or back-pack of 7.3-miles from Two Pan Trailhead to Mirror Lake.
Difficulty: Moderate.
Trail maintenance: Yearly.
Best season: Late June through September.
Traffic: Heavy, with heavy horse traffic.
Elevation gain: 2,044 feet.
Maximum elevation: 7,619 feet.
Maps: Imus Geographics Wallowa Mountains Eagle Cap Wilderness, or Lostine and Eagle Cap Mountain USGS quads.
For more information: U.S. Forest Service at Wallowa Mountain Visitors Center, Enterprise, Oregon.
Finding the trail: From Lostine go 18 miles south on Lostine River Road to Two Pan Campground and Trailhead (El 5,585 ft.). There is a large parking area with a stock loading ramp on the left side of the road across from the campground, just before reaching the trailhead.

0.0   Trail begins at Two Pan Campground and Trailhead.
0.1   Trail junction with West Fork Lostine River Trail.
1.0   Trail crosses river on single log bridge.
3.2   Lost Lake.
4.7   Trail crosses East Fork Lostine River again on a bridge.
7.3   Trail junction with Minam Lake/Mirror Lake Trail.

The trail: Head south from the turnaround just south of the parking area. Follow the trail 200 yards south to the wilderness boundary and the junction with the West Fork Lostine River Trail. Another trail from the south side of the large parking area connects with the main trail just before the junction. Bear left at the junction. From here the trail climbs for 1 mile to a single log bridge crossing the East Fork of the Lostine River.

The trail continues to climb, making a couple of switchbacks on an open boulder strewn hillside, then makes a couple more switchbacks and comes out in a level area 2 miles from the trailhead. The elevation here is 6,850 feet. You get a good view of Hurricane Divide to the east from the switchbacks on the open hillside. Watch for pikas in the rocks of the switchback area, as they are common here.

The trail is level for a short distance but soon climbs again. It enters the beautiful U-shaped upper Lostine Canyon, 2.5 miles from the trailhead. The U shape is indicative of glacier-carved valleys. The elevation where the trail enters the upper valley is 7,040 feet. At this point the river forms a large pool

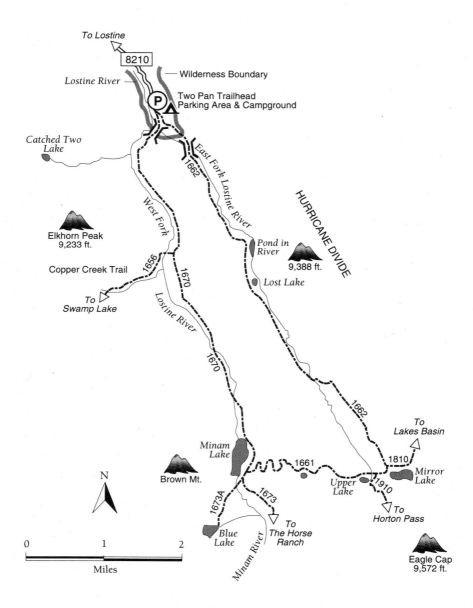

To Lostine

8210

Lostine River

Wilderness Boundary

P

Two Pan Trailhead
Parking Area & Campground

Catched Two
Lake

1662

East Fork Lostine River

HURRICANE DIVIDE

West Fork

Elkhorn Peak
9,233 ft.

Copper Creek Trail

1656

1670

Pond in
River

9,388 ft.

Lost Lake

To
Swamp Lake

Lostine River

1670

N

Minam
Lake

1661

1810

To
Lakes Basin

Brown Mt.

1673A

1673

Upper
Lake

1910

Mirror
Lake

To
Horton Pass

0   1   2

Miles

Blue
Lake

Minam River

To
The Horse
Ranch

Eagle Cap
9,572 ft.

with excellent fishing for small brook trout. The trail passes Lost Lake 0.75 mile farther along. The lake is to the east (left) of the trail. After going 1.5 miles past Lost Lake, the trail crosses a bridge over the East Fork Lostine River.

After crossing the river, the trail stays on the east side. It makes a couple of switchbacks and climbs above the canyon floor. Above the switchbacks the trail makes a gentle ascending traverse to the junction with Trail 1661. See Hike 19 Minam Lake/Mirror Lake. The elevation at the junction is 7,619 feet. Mirror Lake (El 7,590 ft.), in the upper part of the Lakes Basin, is to the left. There are many good campsites among the granite outcroppings along the north side of Mirror Lake. Be sure to camp at least 200 feet from the lake. Fishing for small brook trout is generally very good in Mirror Lake. This trail is heavily used by horse parties and may be dusty.

A loop trip can be made by combining this trail with Minam Lake/Mirror Lake Trail to Minam Lake, then heading back north on West Fork Lostine River Trail. See Hike 21 West Fork Lostine River.

East Fork Lostine River near Mirror Lake.

19 MINAM LAKE/MIRROR LAKE

Trail 1661

General description: A 3.75-mile-long connecting trail from Minam Lake, over a pass to Mirror Lake.
Difficulty: Moderate.
Trail maintenance: Yearly.
Traffic: Moderate.
Best season: Mid-July through September.
Elevation gain: 1,135 feet (west to east). Loss: 925 feet (west to east).
Maximum elevation: 8,520 feet.
Map: Eagle Cap Mountain USGS quads.
For more information: U.S. Forest Service at Wallowa Mountain Visitors Center, Enterprise, Oregon.
Finding the trail: This trail can be accessed from either the East or West Fork Lostine River Trails, or from the Lakes Basin Trail. This description goes from the West Fork Lostine Trail at Minam Lake, east to Mirror Lake. See Hike 21 West Fork Lostine River, and Hike 18 East Fork Lostine River.

0.0   Trail begins at Minam Lake.
1.5   Trail goes over pass.

Minam Lake. *Photo by Gary Fletcher.*

3.0	Upper Lake.
3.2	Trail crosses East Fork Lostine River on bridge.
3.4	Mirror Lake.

The trail: The trail begins at the southwest corner of Minam Lake. It leaves the West Fork Lostine River Trail 1670 at an elevation of 7,385 feet. The trail climbs steadily on meandering switchbacks and passes a couple of ponds. These ponds are below and to the right of the trail. The trail reaches a pass (El 8,520 ft.) 1.5 miles after leaving Minam Lake. The view from the pass is quite spectacular. Minam and Blue Lakes can be seen to the west, with Upper Lake and the rest of the Lakes Basin to the east. Eagle Cap Mountain is close by to the southeast, and the Matterhorn, with its huge white limestone cliffs forming the highest point on Hurwal Divide and in the Wallowa Mountains, is in the distance to the northeast.

From the pass the trail meanders down 1.5 miles to Upper Lake (El 7,650 ft.). The trail crosses a bridge over the East Fork of the Lostine River, 0.2 mile past Upper Lake. Just past the bridge is the junction with the Old East Fork Lostine River Trail. Mirror Lake is a short distance straight ahead. Horton Pass is to the right and the Old East Fork Trail is to the left. See Hike 17 Eagle Cap Mountain and Hike 79 East Fork Eagle Creek. Straight ahead a few yards is the East Fork Lostine River Trail 1662. See Hike 18 East Fork Lostine River. The elevation at this junction is 7,619 feet.

This trail is used to connect Minam Lake with the many attractions in the Lakes Basin area. For a loop trip see Hike 18 East Fork Lostine River.

19 *Minam Lake/Mirror Lake*

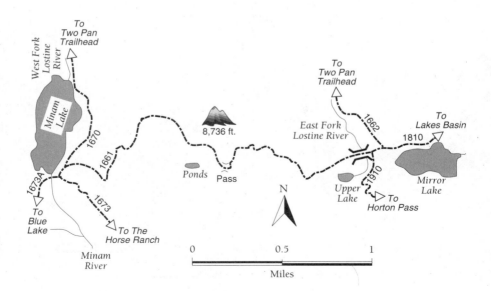

Trail 1673A

General description: A 1-mile-long trail connecting Minam Lake and Blue Lake.
Difficulty: Easy.
Trail maintenance: Yearly.
Best season: July through September.
Traffic: Moderate, with moderate horse traffic.
Elevation gain: 330 feet.
Maximum elevation: 7,730 feet.

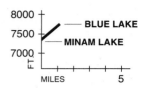

20   *Blue Lake*

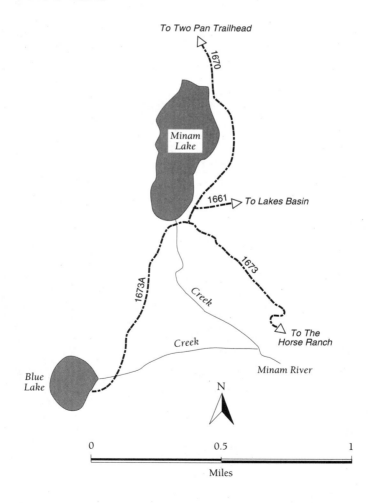

Map: Eagle Cap Mountain USGS quad.

For more information: U.S. Forest Service at Wallowa Mountain Visitors Center, Enterprise, Oregon.

Finding the trail: The trail to Blue Lake leaves the Upper Minam River Trail 1673, just south of Minam Lake. See Hike 42 Upper Minam River. The Blue Lake Trail junction is a few hundred feet south of the junction with Minam Lake/Mirror Lake Trail 1661. See Hike 21 West Fork Lostine River.

0.0	Trail junction with Upper Minam River Trail.
0.8	Trail crosses outlet of Blue Lake.
1.0	Blue Lake.

The trail: Blue Lake Trail heads west and crosses the Minam River creek bed. The Minam River is very small here and will probably be completely dry. The water that used to flow down the Minam River from Minam Lake, was diverted many years ago. It now flows north down the West Fork of the Lostine River into the Wallowa Valley.

After crossing the dry creek bed, the trail turns to the southwest and begins to climb. It climbs steadily for 0.8 mile. Here the trail crosses the outlet of Blue Lake. This stream is actually now the headwaters of the Minam River, since the water from Minam Lake has been diverted. After crossing the stream, the trail turns to the right (west), and goes the last few yards to Blue Lake (El 7,703 ft.). There are several campsites around Blue Lake and trout to be caught. The return trip is made by the same trail.

21   WEST FORK LOSTINE RIVER

Trail 1670

General description: A 6.1 mile day hike or backpack from Two Pan Trailhead to Minam Lake. This trail can be used to access Copper Creek Trail, Minam Lake/Mirror Lake Trail and the Upper Minam River Trail.

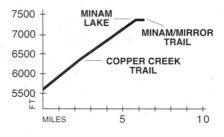

Difficulty: Moderate.

Trail maintenance: Yearly.

Best season: Mid-June through September.

Traffic: Heavy, with heavy horse traffic.

Elevation gain: 1,845 feet.

Maximum elevation: 7,430 feet.

Maps: Imus Geographics Wallowa Mountains Eagle Cap Wilderness, or Eagle Cap Mountain and Steamboat Lake USGS quads.

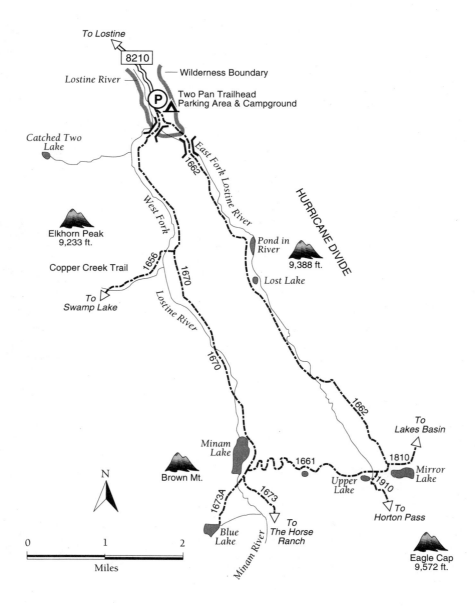

To Lostine

8210

Lostine River

Wilderness Boundary

Two Pan Trailhead
Parking Area & Campground

P

Catched Two
Lake

Elkhorn Peak
9,233 ft.

West Fork

East Fork Lostine River

1662

HURRICANE DIVIDE

9,388 ft.

Copper Creek Trail

1656

1670

Pond in
River

Lost Lake

To
Swamp Lake

Lostine River

1670

1662

To
Lakes Basin

Minam
Lake

1661

1810

Mirror
Lake

Brown Mt.

Upper
Lake

1910

N

1673A

1673

To
Horton Pass

Blue
Lake

To
The Horse
Ranch

Minam River

Eagle Cap
9,572 ft.

0   1   2

Miles

For more information: U.S. Forest Service at Wallowa Mountain Visitors Center, Enterprise, Oregon.

Finding the trail: West Fork Lostine River Trail begins at Two Pan Campground and Trailhead (El 5,585 ft.). See Hike 18 East Fork Lostine River for description.

0.0	Trail begins at Two Pan Trailhead and Campground.
2.6	Trail junction with Copper Creek Trail.
4.3	Trail crosses West Fork Lostine River.
5.5	North end of Minam Lake.
6.1	Trail junction with Minam Lake/Mirror Lake Trail.

The trail: From the trailhead follow the trail south 200 yards to the wilderness boundary and the junction with East Fork Trail 1662. Bear right at the junction. One-third mile from the junction the trail crosses the East Fork of the Lostine River on a concrete bridge (El 5,670 ft.). The unmarked turn off to Catched Two Lake is 0.7 mile past the bridge. See Hike 22 Catched Two Lake Route. This area was hit by an avalanche some years ago, leaving it quite open. A waterfall can be seen uphill and to the right. This stream starts at Catched Two Lake. The lake is about 1 mile away and nearly 2,000 feet up. The impressive north face of Elkhorn Peak is close by to the southwest at the Catched Two Lake turnoff.

The junction with Copper Creek Trail 1656 is 1.5 miles farther. See Hike 23 Copper Creek. Copper Creek Trail goes west and leads to Swamp and

West Fork Lostine River Trail. *Photo by Gary Fletcher.*

Steamboat Lakes. The West Fork Lostine River Trail continues straight ahead and crosses the river 1.75 miles past the Copper Creek Trail junction. It crosses the river again 1 mile farther along. Between the river crossings, the river flows through open meadows. Here there are several areas of slow flowing water that are full of small but beautiful brook trout that are just waiting to be caught. The elevation at the second crossing is 7,250 feet. At 5.5 miles, Minam Lake (El 7,373 ft.) comes into view on the right.

The trail goes around the east (left) side of the lake and climbs 50 feet or so above the shoreline. Other access paths follow the shore in this area. At 6.1 miles the trail comes to the junction with Trail 1661, which goes to the east to Mirror Lake and the Lakes Basin. See Hike 19 Minam Lake/Mirror Lake. The Upper Minam River Trail goes straight ahead at the junction. See Hike 42 Upper Minam River. Blue Lake Trail is a short distance south on the Upper Minam River Trail. See Hike 20 Blue Lake.

At the south end of Minam Lake there is an earthen dam. This dam prevents Minam Lake water from going down the Minam River. The water now drains north down the Lostine River to the Wallowa Valley where it is used for irrigation. There are good campsites all around Minam Lake, but make sure your camp is 200 or more feet away from the water. Fishing can be good in Minam Lake. Some of the larger trout in the Wallowas live here, but you have to be here at the right time and use the right tackle or fishing may be very slow. This timing and the bait to use is extremely variable, so each fisherman has to use his or her own ideas and take a chance.

To make a loop trip, take Minam Lake/Mirror Lake Trail to Mirror Lake and return to Two Pan Trailhead via East Fork Lostine River Trail. See Hike 18 East Fork Lostine River.

22 CATCHED TWO LAKE ROUTE

General description: A steep 1 mile off-trail climb, from West Fork Lostine River Trail to Catched Two Lake.
Difficulty: Strenuous.
Trail maintenance: None.
Best season: Mid-July through September.
Traffic: Light.
Elevation gain: 1,980 feet.
Maximum elevation: 7,980 feet.
Map: Steamboat Lake USGS quad.

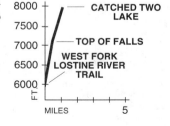

For more information: U.S. Forest Service at Wallowa Mountain Visitors Center, Enterprise, Oregon. Further information will probably be limited.
Finding the trail: The route to Catched Two Lake begins 1 mile south of the Lostine River Trailhead, on the West Fork Lostine River Trail 1670. See Hike 21 West Fork Lostine River. At the point where the route turns off the West

Fork Lostine River Trail there is a semi-open area, and a waterfall can be seen high above to the right. This waterfall is on the stream which flows out of Catched Two Lake. (Check your map.)

0.0   Route leaves the West Fork Lostine River Trail.
1.0   Catched Two Lake.

The trail: The route (there is no trail) begins by crossing the West Fork Lostine River on a log (El 6,000 ft.) or by wading the ice cold waters. After crossing the river, work your way northwest to the the right side of the stream coming down from Catched Two Lake. Keep to the right of the stream and climb to a point just above the falls (El 7,200 ft.). Above the falls follow the main fork of the stream, turn slightly to the right, and climb on up through the rock outcropping to Catched Two Lake (El 7,980 ft.).

The 1,982 foot climb to Catched Two Lake takes about 2 hours under good conditions. Catched Two Lake is far enough off the trail and a steep enough climb that it is not heavily used. There are plenty of brook trout to be caught, and this is a good area to see mule deer and elk. A good campsite is located next to the stream some distance below the lake, and there are some less desirable sites around the lake. The name Catched Two, as the story goes, comes from the fact that two early day sheep herders were caught by there boss sleeping next to the lake. He said in his broken English, "I catched two," hence the name.

This route requires some route finding and off trail skills. It should not be attempted by novice hikers.

22   *Catched Two Lake Route*

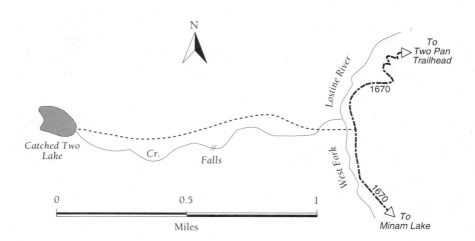

Trail 1656

General description: A long day hike or backpack of 5 miles from the West Fork Lostine River Trail to the North Minam River Trail. This trail is also the access to Granite Creek Trail and Cheval Lake Trail.

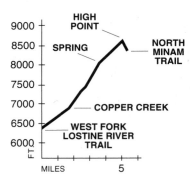

Difficulty: Moderate to strenuous.
Trail maintenance: Yearly.
Best season: July through September.
Traffic: Moderate, with moderate horse traffic.
Elevation gain: 2,175 feet. Loss: 180 feet.
Maximum elevation: 8,600 feet.
Maps: Imus Geographics Wallowa Mountains Eagle Cap Wilderness, or Eagle Cap Mountain and Steamboat Lake USGS quads.
For more information: U.S. Forest Service at Wallowa Mountain Visitors Center, Enterprise, Oregon.
Finding the trail: Copper Creek Trail leaves the West Fork Lostine River Trail 1670, 2.8 miles south of the Lostine River Trailhead. See Hike 21 West Fork Lostine River. There is a signpost at this junction (El 6,425 ft.).

0.0	Trail junction with West Fork Lostine River Trail.
0.1	Trail crosses West Fork Lostine River.
1.7	Trail crosses Copper Creek.
2.3	Trail enters alpine valley at the head of Copper Creek.
4.7	Trail comes to high point overlooking Swamp Lake.
5.0	Trail junction with North Minam River Trail.

The trail: Turn right (west) at the junction. Copper Creek Trail crosses the West Fork of the Lostine River 200 yards after leaving West Fork Lostine River Trail 1670. There is no bridge at this crossing. A few yards up river from the spot where the trail crosses is a shallower spot, which is easier to cross for people who are on foot. After crossing the river, the trail crosses a couple of small side streams, then begins to climb.

At 1.75 miles the trail crosses Copper Creek (El 6,900 ft.). After crossing Copper Creek the trail climbs steadily through thinning forest. One-half mile farther (El 7,320 ft.) is another crossing of Copper Creek. After crossing the creek, the trail flattens out and enters the beautiful subalpine valley at the head of Copper Creek. The trail crosses Elkhorn Creek and heads on up the valley for 0.3 mile before turning to the right and beginning to climb again in switchbacks. There are several nice campsites in the subalpine valley.

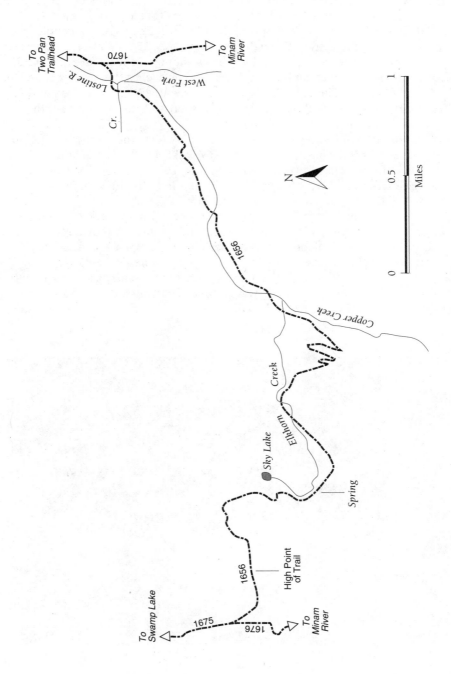

The trail climbs out of the valley and crosses Elkhorn Creek at 7,800 feet elevation and enters a small alpine valley. The trail soon crosses Elkhorn Creek again and goes on up the valley for 0.25 mile, where it makes a couple of switchbacks. Above the switchbacks the trail makes an ascending traverse to the northwest, passing a good spring (El 8,110 ft.). Sky Lake is a couple hundred yards off the trail to the right (northwest), 0.25 mile after passing the spring. After the traverse the trail works its way up through rounded granite outcroppings and small alpine meadows until it reaches the top of a rounded ridge (El 8,510 ft.). This ridge top is 4.5 miles from the West Fork Lostine River Trail. After reaching the ridge, the trail turns left and climbs to the southwest 0.25 mile to its high point (El 8,600 ft.).

From this point Swamp Lake can be seen below to the northwest. A quarter-mile farther is the junction with Trail 1675 (El 8,420 ft.). North Minam River Trail 1675 turns right and goes down to Swamp Lake and North Minam Meadows. See Hike 43 North Minam River. To the left Granite Creek Trail 1676 heads for the Minam River. See Hike 46 Granite Creek.

The area around this junction is very alpine, with only a few small trees. The country is typical of ridge top areas in the western Wallowa Mountains. Many alpine flowers bloom in this timberline area as soon as the snow melts. This is big buck mule deer country, and also has quite a few elk.

An extended loop trip is possible by combining Copper Creek Trail with North Minam River Trail, Upper Minam River Trail and the West Fork Lostine River Trail. See Hike 43 North Minam River for a description of this extended trip.

Swamp Lake from the high point of Copper Creek Trail. *Photo by Gary Fletcher.*

Trail 1674

General description: A 4 mile day hike or backpack, from Maxwell Lake Trailhead on the Lostine River Road, to Maxwell Lake.
Difficulty: Moderate.
Trail maintenance: Yearly.
Best season: July through September.
Traffic: Moderate.
Elevation gain: 2,350 feet. Loss: 61 feet.
Maximum elevation: 7,790 feet.

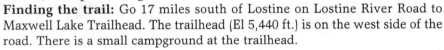

Map: North Minam Meadows USGS quad.
For more information: U.S. Forest Service at Wallowa Mountain Visitors Center, Enterprise, Oregon.
Finding the trail: Go 17 miles south of Lostine on Lostine River Road to Maxwell Lake Trailhead. The trailhead (El 5,440 ft.) is on the west side of the road. There is a small campground at the trailhead.

0.0	Maxwell Lake Trailhead, cross Lostine River.
0.2	Trail crosses creek.
3.0	End of reconstructed trail.
3.7	Trail crosses pass.
4.0	Maxwell Lake.

The trail: The trail heads west from the trailhead, and crosses the Lostine River on a bridge. Seventy-five feet after crossing the river is the Eagle Cap Wilderness Boundary sign. At 0.2 mile there is a major creek crossing (El 5,470 ft.). This crossing may be difficult during periods of heavy runoff. There are boulders a few feet below the trail that can be used to aid in the crossing. After crossing the creek, the trail makes several switchbacks, crossing a couple of small creeks several times. At 2.75 miles (El 6,600 ft.) there is a good view of Eagle Cap Mountain to the south, directly up the East Fork Lostine Canyon.

   At 3 miles the trail becomes very rocky and steep. The trail below this point has been reconstructed, but above here it has not been. The trail climbs steeply to a small meadow at 3.5 miles, where it may disappear for a short distance. The trail follows the right (north) side of the meadow and climbs slightly to a pass (El 7,790 ft.) then descends to Maxwell Lake (El 7,729 ft.). Maxwell Lake, 4 miles from the trailhead, has excellent fishing for the usual small brook trout. Campsites are not plentiful at the lake, but can be found on the north side. Be sure to camp at least 200 feet from the lake. The setting of Maxwell Lake near the top of a ridge is well worth the hike. Return via the same trail.

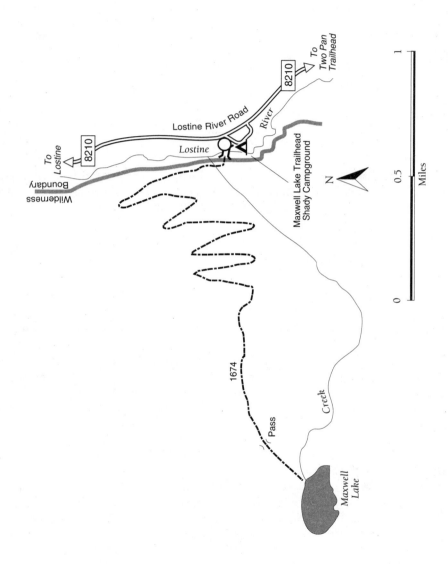

Trail 1663

General description: A long day hike or backpack of 9 miles from the Lostine River Road over a pass to Frances Lake.

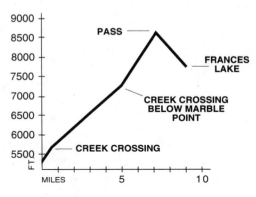

Difficulty: Moderate. This trail is never very steep, but it is a long 9 percent grade.

Trail maintenance: Yearly.

Best season: Mid-July through September.

Traffic: Moderate, with moderate horse traffic.

Elevation gain: 3,300 feet. Loss: 905 feet.

Maximum elevation: 8,610 feet.

Maps: Imus Geographics Wallowa Mountains Eagle Cap Wilderness, or North Minam Meadows and Chief Joseph Mountain USGS quads.

For more information: U.S. Forest Service at Wallowa Mountain Visitors Center, Enterprise, Oregon.

Finding the trail: From Lostine go 15 miles south on Lostine River Road to Frances Lake Trailhead (El 5,280 ft.). There is a parking area and stock loading ramp at the trailhead, which is on the east side of the road.

0.0	Trail begins at Frances Lake Trailhead.
0.7	Trail crosses creek.
5.0	Trail crosses creek below Marble Point.
7.0	Trail crosses pass.
9.0	Frances Lake.

The trail: The trail heads east from the trailhead and starts the climb immediately. The trail passes Eagle Cap Wilderness boundary 200 feet from the trailhead. It then switches back continually at an even, easy, grade. The trail crosses a creek at 0.75 mile (El 5,690 ft.). At 5 miles it comes to an open area and another creek crossing (El 7,260 ft.) below Marble Point. There are many flowers in this open area.

Above the creek crossing the trail makes a long switchback to the north. It then switches back south again, just below the ridge dividing Lake Creek drainage and the Lostine Canyon. At 7 miles the trail crosses the pass (El 8,610 ft.). From the top of the ridge the view is impressive, with the dark brown spires of 9,673 foot high Twin Peaks to the east, and Frances Lake below, to the southeast.

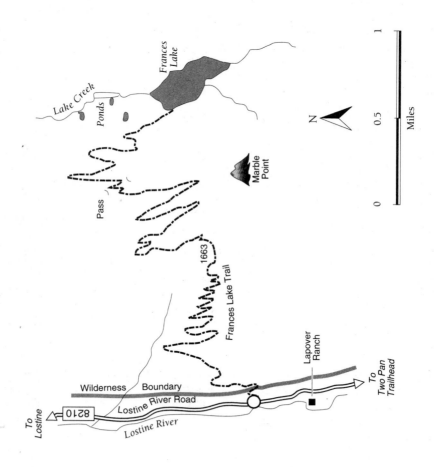

After crossing the pass, the trail descends the last 2 miles to Frances Lake (El 7,705 ft.). At Frances Lake the vegetation looks much like that of the mountainous areas of Alaska. There are a few stunted trees, alpine willows, and a lot of tundra and exposed rock. This is one of the best areas in the Wallowa Mountains to see mountain goats and bighorn sheep. Look for them with binoculars to the east on Hurricane Divide. The entire 9 mile trail, to Frances Lake is an even grade. While it is quite long, it is not difficult. There are many campsites around Frances Lake. The ponds in Lake Creek below the lake are known for their large trout, and there are lots of fish in Frances Lake itself. Return to the trailhead by going back down the same trail.

26   BOWMAN

Trail 1651

General description: A 9.8 mile backpack from Bowman Trailhead, on the Lostine River Road, to North Minam Meadows.
Difficulty: Moderate.
Trail maintenance: Yearly.
Best season: July through September.
Traffic: Heavy to Chimney Lake Trail, and moderate past there, with moderate to heavy horse traffic.

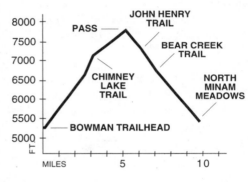

Elevation gain: 2,520 feet. Loss: 2,300 feet.
Maximum elevation: 7,740 feet.
Map: North Minam Meadows USGS quad.
For more information: U.S. Forest Service at Wallowa Mountain Visitors Center, Enterprise, Oregon.
Finding the trail: From Lostine go 14.5 miles south on the Lostine River Road to Bowman Trailhead (El 5,220 ft.). There is a small parking area at the trailhead. A stock loading ramp and truck parking area is available 0.5 mile farther south at Frances Lake Trailhead.

0.0   Trail begins at Bowman Trailhead.
3.8   Trail junction with Chimney Lake Trail.
5.3   Trail crosses pass.
6.3   Trail junction with John Henry Lake Trail.
7.3   Trail junction with Bear Creek Trail.
9.8   North Minam Meadows and trail junction with North Minam River Trail.

The trail: From Bowman Trailhead, head west on the trail and cross the Lostine River on a concrete bridge. At 0.1 mile (El 5,250 ft.) the trail crosses Bowman Creek. A footbridge is located just upstream from the trail. After crossing the footbridge, the trail makes a long switchback, coming back again to Bowman Creek in 0.9 mile. It then switches back south again, and climbs through mixed timber and open hillsides. Near the end of this switchback, Lapover Ranch can be seen far below to the south. The mountain across the canyon to the east is Marble Point, near Frances Lake.

The trail crosses Bowman Creek again, which has three channels at this point, at 2.75 miles (El 6,670 ft.). After the crossing it makes a jog to the north, then continues up Bowman Creek. Soon a meadow comes into view below the trail to the left. This beautiful alpine meadow and the slopes around it is Brownie Basin. There are several good campsites in Brownie Basin.

At 3.8 miles is the junction with the Chimney Lake Trail 1659 (El 7,240 ft.). See Hike 27 Chimney Lake. At this point, the trail is a couple hundred feet above the floor of Brownie Basin. Looking south from the junction, there is a good view of upper Brownie Basin and Flagstaff Point.

The trail contours along the west side of Brownie Basin, then makes two switchbacks and climbs to a pass (El 7,740 ft.) 1.5 miles from the Chimney Lake Trail junction. The pass is on the ridge dividing the Lostine River drainage and the North Minam River drainage. Look down to the west to see Wilson Basin, with John Henry Lake on its far (west) side.

The trail makes a hard right turn at the pass, then drops steadily for 1 mile to the unmarked junction with John Henry Lake Trail (El 7,200 ft.). The John

North Minam Meadows. *Photo by Gary Fletcher.*

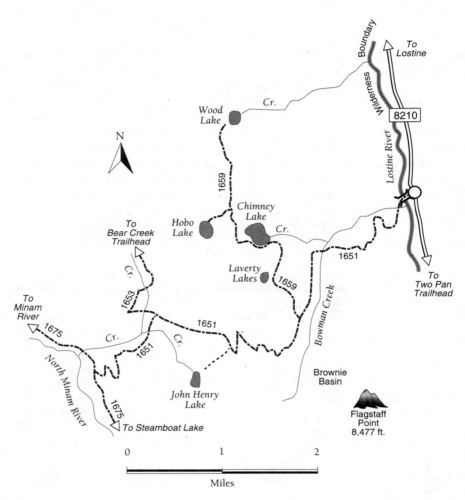

N

To
Lostine

Boundary

Wilderness

8210

Lostine River

Cr.

Wood
Lake

1659

Chimney
Lake

Hobo
Lake

Cr.

To
Bear Creek
Trailhead

Laverty
Lakes

1659

1651

To
Two Pan
Trailhead

Cr.

1653

To
Minam
River

1675

Cr.

1651

1651

Cr.

Bowman Creek

North Minam River

1675

John Henry
Lake

Brownie
Basin

To Steamboat Lake

Flagstaff
Point
8,477 ft.

0   1   2

Miles

Source: Imus Geographics

Henry Lake Trail is a poor side trail that leads straight ahead to John Henry Lake from one of the switchbacks on the Bowman Trail. The junction with this side trail is just above the floor of the basin. Don't take the side trail unless you want to go to John Henry Lake. The elevation of John Henry Lake is 7,168 feet. At the junction, John Henry lake is 0.5 mile to the southwest. There are several side trails in Wilson Basin. Be careful to stay on the main trail, which is much more well traveled than the others.

The trail continues to descend slowly through Wilson Basin to the junction with Bear Creek Trail 1653. Bear Creek Trail junction is 7.3 miles from the Bowman Trailhead. The altitude at the junction of Bear Creek and Bowman Trails is 6,750 feet. Bear Creek Trail heads to the north. See Hike 32 Bear Creek. From here the Bowman Trail winds down 2.5 miles to North Minam Meadows (El 5440 ft.) and the junction with North Minam River Trail 1675. See Hike 43 North Minam River. North Minam Meadows is large and lush, with the North Minam River flowing through it. It is common to see elk feeding in the meadow in the morning and late afternoon. There are many campsites around the edge of North Minam Meadows, and plenty of firewood.

A loop trip is possible by using Hikes 43, 23 and 21, in addition to Hike 26. This loop requires a short car shuttle to Two Pan Trailhead, or a walk back down the Lostine River Road. See Hike 43 North Minam River, Hike 23 Copper Creek, and Hike 21 West Fork Lostine River.

27 CHIMNEY LAKE

Trail 1659

General description: A 3.6 mileside trail from Bowman Trail in Brownie Basin to Wood Lake. This trail also goes to Chimney and Hobo Lakes.

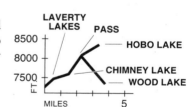

Difficulty: Moderate.
Trail maintenance: Yearly.
Best season: Mid-July through September.
Traffic: Heavy to Chimney Lake, moderate to Wood and Hobo Lakes, with moderate horse traffic.
Elevation gain: To Chimney Lake 364 feet; to Hobo Lake, 1,140 feet; to Wood Lake, 940 feet. Add another 2,020 feet of gain if coming all the way from Bowman Trailhead on the Lostine River Road. Loss: To Wood Lake, 842 feet.
Maximum elevation: 8,060 feet at Wood Lake and 8,380 feet at Hobo Lake.
Map: North Minam Meadows USGS quad.
For more information: U.S. Forest Service at Wallowa Mountain Visitors Center, Enterprise, Oregon.
Finding the trail: The Chimney Lake Trail is reached by going 3.6 miles west up the Bowman Trail from the Bowman Trailhead. The trailhead is 14.5 miles south of Lostine, on the Lostine River Road. See Hike 26 Bowman.

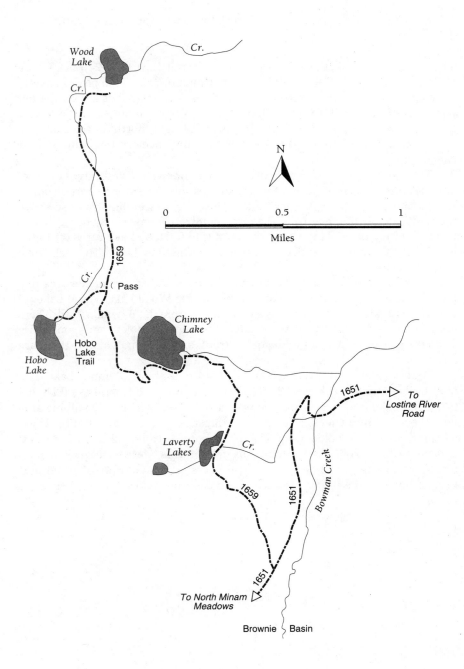

0.0	Trail junction with Bowman Trail in Brownie Basin.
0.5	Laverty Lakes.
1.3	Chimney Lake.
2.2	Trail crosses pass and trail junction with Hobo Lake Trail.
3.6	Wood Lake.

The trail: At the junction with the Bowman Trail 1651 (El 7,240 ft.), Chimney Lake Trail turns off to the right (north). Chimney Lake Trail passes Laverty Lakes (El 7,450 ft.) 0.5 mile from the junction. Laverty Lakes are on the left (west) side of the trail. Chimney Lake (El 7,604 ft.) is another 0.75 mile past Laverty Lakes. There are good campsites to the right (north) of the trail, just before reaching Chimney Lake. There is an abundance of trout waiting to be caught in Chimney Lake.

The trail goes around the south side of Chimney Lake and leaves the lake at its southwest corner. At first the trail climbs southwest for a short distance. It then makes a sharp right turn, and begins a long ascending traverse above the west side of Chimney Lake. The trail climbs to a pass (El 8,060 ft.) 1 mile from Chimney Lake. At the pass, the faint trail to Hobo Lake turns off to the left. Up to this point, the trail can be seen from Chimney Lake. (To reach Hobo Lake see below.)

From the pass the trail drops through tundra and an avalanche area to a meadow. Go along the right side of the meadow to Wood Lake. Wood Lake (El 7,338 ft.) is 1.4 miles from the pass and 3.6 miles from the Bowman Trail. There are several good campsites at Wood Lake. Fishing for brook trout is good here. The lake was once stocked with golden trout, as was Hobo Lake. If there are any of them left, they are very rare.

To reach Hobo Lake, turn left at the pass 1 mile above Chimney Lake. The faint trail crosses a creek at 8,180 feet, then goes on up to Hobo Lake (El 8,369 ft.). Hobo Lake is 0.7 mile from the pass. Hobo Lake is in an open alpine area near the ridge line. There are plenty of campsites at Hobo Lake, but firewood is scarce and should not be used. Fishing is spotty at Hobo Lake. Golden trout, a native to the Sierra Nevada Mountains in California, were once stocked here, but they have not been seen in several years and have probably died out. Legend has it that a hobo was once found camping at Hobo Lake, hence, its name.

Return trip is made via the same trail.

General description: A 3.5 mile trail from an obscure trailhead on Lime Quarry Road to Silver Creek, via Murray Saddle, aka Murray Gap or The Gap. This is not a horse trail.

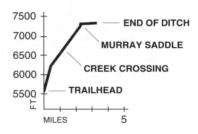

Difficulty: Moderate to strenuous to Murray Saddle, and easy past there.

Trail maintenance: Infrequent, as it is done by volunteers. However, the trail is usually in fairly good condition. This trail is not suited or maintained for horse traffic. If you have horses, please do not use this trail. The switchbacks are too small and branches are not cleared more than 5 feet above the ground. Horses cause much damage to this trail. Horse traffic should use the Old Murray Saddle Trail described within the text below.

Best season: Mid-June through October.

Traffic: Moderate, except during early October deer hunting season, when it can be heavy.

Elevation gain: 1,740 feet.

Maximum elevation: 7,320 feet.

Maps: Enterprise and Chief Joseph Mountain USGS quads cover the area, but the trail is not shown on these maps.

For more information: Wallowa Lake General Store in the resort area at Wallowa Lake is the best place for information on this trail. U.S. Forest Service at Wallowa Mountain Visitors Center, Enterprise, Oregon. Further information from the forest service will probably be limited.

Finding the trail: From the south end of Enterprise, on State Highway 82, take Hurricane Creek Road. Hurricane Creek Road goes straight ahead (south) at the last 90 degree corner the highway makes in Enterprise. Go 2 blocks south on Hurricane Creek Road to Fish Hatchery Road. Turn

Young hiker next to Silver Creek Ditch.
Photo by Gary Fletcher.

right on Fish Hatchery Road and follow it 1.2 miles to Alder Slope Road. Turn left on Alder Slope Road and follow it 1.7 miles to Black Marble Lane. Black Marble Lane is a gravel road that goes straight ahead at a corner on Alder Slope Road. Take Black Marble Lane for 1.8 miles, then turn left on Lime Quarry Road. Follow Lime Quarry Road for 2.1 miles, passing several poor side roads, to a wide spot with room for a couple of vehicles to park. At the parking spot there is the number nine painted on a rock on the right side of the road. There is a small sign marking the trail on a tree, also on the right side of the road.

0.0	Trail begins at trailhead.
0.5	Trail comes to the top of a ridge and starts to follow a stock driveway.
1.5	Trail crosses a stream.
2.5	Murray Saddle.
3.5	Trail comes to the upper end of the ditch and Silver Creek.

The trail: From the trailhead (El 5,580 ft.) the trail, known locally as Bill George Trail, heads west up a gully. After going steeply up the gully for 100 yards, it makes a switchback to the right. The trail climbs steeply for 0.5 mile, through transitional zone forest to the top of a ridge, making twenty-one switchbacks along the way. Once it reaches the ridge, the trail heads on up to the west southwest. This ridge was once cleared for use as a stock driveway; it still remains mostly open today. After climbing 0.25 mile, the ridge and trail turn to the southwest (El 6,289 ft.). Another 0.2 mile and the trail crosses a large log that has been partly chopped out by hand to make way for the trail. After crossing the log, the trail goes slightly to the left of the ridge line as it continues to climb. It makes several small switchbacks and soon regains the top of the ridge (El 6,580 ft.). There is a wet area in the trail 150 yards after reaching the top of the ridge. A hundred yards or so to the right of the trail at the wet area is a small pond. The pond cannot be seen from the trail. Just past the wet area, the ridge you have been climbing merges with the main ridge (Sheep Ridge). The trail continues to climb, making three switchbacks, then it heads southeast and drops a few feet to a creek crossing. After crossing the creek, the trail climbs a short distance and enters an opening. It makes a tiny switchback as it works along the bottom of the opening, then climbs, rounding a point (El 6,780 ft.). From the point the Seven Devils Mountains across Hells Canyon can be seen in the distance to the east.

After rounding the point, the dark brown cliffs and ridges of Ruby Peak come into view to the southeast. From here on the country is more open and alpine, and the view gets better the farther you climb. Past the point the trail continues to climb steeply, making several more small switchbacks as it works its way up toward the red brown wall of Upper Sheep Ridge. About 150 yards below the cliffs, the trail traverses south to the junction with the Old Murray Saddle Trail (El 7,260 ft.). See description below. One hundred yards past the junction is Murray Saddle.

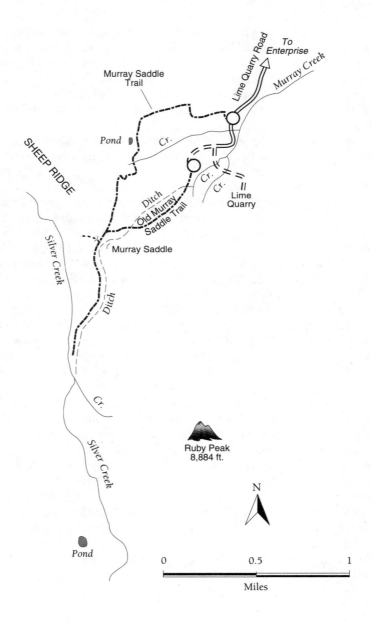

Murray Saddle (El 7,290 ft.) is a beautiful spot with the knife ridge of Ruby Peak to the southeast and the equally steep and rugged spire of Sheep Ridge to the northwest. Silver Creek Canyon and Traverse Ridge are to the southwest, and most of the Wallowa Valley can be seen to the northeast. Most of the time there is a breeze blowing through Murray Saddle; sometimes, mainly during spring, it is more like a hurricane. Watch for bighorn sheep on the ridges above the saddle. From the saddle a trail drops down to the southwest 100 yards to a nice campsite. This trail is the old Silver Creek pack trail. It is seldom used any more and very difficult to follow after about 0.5 mile. There are some springs a short distance past the campsite on the old pack trail. A climbing route for Ruby Peak leaves the trail in the saddle. See Climb 13 Ruby Peak from the Gap.

At the saddle, bear left and head along the right ditch bank of Silver Creek Ditch. This ditch was built by the CCC in the Great Depression. Please do not take horses along this ditch bank. They tear it up and cause the ditch to leak and erode. If you have horses, please take them up the bottom of the ditch in the water. After going 0.25 mile, there is a wooden gate in the ditch. Cross the gate on the boards and continue on. A small stream enters the ditch on the other side 0.1 mile past the gate. After another 0.2 mile is another gate in the ditch bank, and 150 yards farther another stream enters the ditch. There is yet another gate in the ditch bank 0.1 mile past the stream and another creek bed 150 yards farther along. One hundred fifty yards past this creek is Silver Creek and the beginning of Silver Creek Ditch (El 7,320 ft.) 1 mile from the saddle. All along the ditch bank from the saddle is a lush flower garden in July.

At the upper end of the ditch is a faint trail heading up Silver Creek to the southeast. Two climbing routes to Ruby Peak take off from this path. See Climb 14 and Climb 15 Ruby Peak. There is a meadow with a good campsite next to it a short distance up Silver Creek from the end of the ditch. Return to the saddle along the ditch.

From the junction 100 yards north of Murray Saddle it is possible to take the Old Murray Saddle Trail back down to the trailhead. This trail crosses private land and is very steep. It gets very little maintenance and was in poor condition as of 1995. This is, however, the trail to take if you have horses, as the trail described above is not suitable for stock. It is 1 mile down the old trail to a logging road, and in that distance the trail drops 1,310 vertical feet with many sharp steep switchbacks. At the road, turn left and head down for 0.2 mile to Lime Quarry Road. The trailhead described above is 0.35 mile back down Lime Quarry Road from the junction. This trail has been used by the public for many years, but it doesn't hurt to get permission. For permission check at the last house on Lime Quarry Road. It is very important that horse parties use this trail.

WESTERN REGION

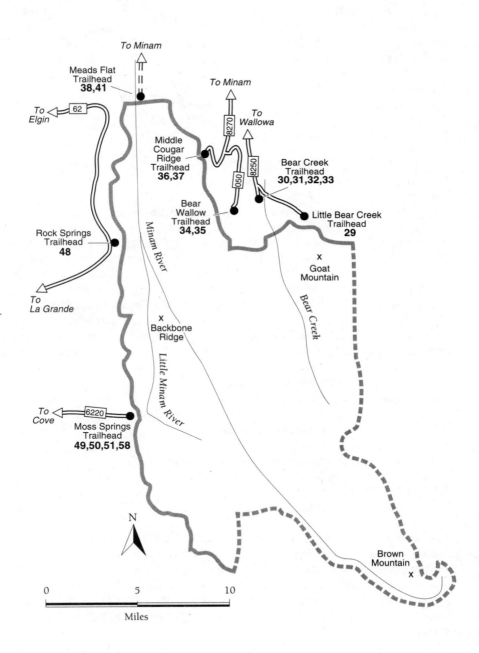

To Minam

Meads Flat
Trailhead
38,41

To
Elgin
62

To Minam

8270

To
Wallowa

Middle
Cougar
Ridge
Trailhead
36,37

Bear Creek
Trailhead
30,31,32,33

050

8250

Bear
Wallow
Trailhead
34,35

Rock Springs
Trailhead
48

Little Bear Creek
Trailhead
29

Minam River

x
Goat
Mountain

To
La Grande

Bear Creek

x
Backbone
Ridge

Little Minam River

To
Cove
6220

Moss Springs
Trailhead
49,50,51,58

N

Brown
Mountain
x

0   5   10

Miles

Trail 1667 and 1689

General description: An 8.5 mile backpack from Little Bear Creek Trailhead to Little Storm Lake.

Difficulty: Moderate, but requires some route finding.

Trail maintenance: Rare.

Best season: Mid-June through October.

Traffic: Light, except during October and November hunting season, with moderate horse traffic in the fall.

Elevation gain: 2,600 feet. Loss: 500 feet.

Maximum elevation: 7,860 feet.

Maps: Imus Geographics Wallowa Mountains Eagle Cap Wilderness, or Lostine and North Minam Meadows USGS quads.

For more information: U.S. Forest Service at Wallowa Mountain Visitors Center, Enterprise, Oregon. Further information will probably be limited.

Finding the trail: From Wallowa take Bear Creek Road, Forest Road 8250, 9 miles south to Little Bear Creek Road, which is also Forest Road 8250. Turn left on Little Bear Creek Road. Go east approximately 7 miles to the saddle that divides Bear Creek drainage and the Lostine River drainage. To the right (south) of the road is a logged area. Follow the logging road (trail) to the south a short distance to reach Little Bear Creek Trailhead and Huckleberry Mountain Trail.

0.0	Little Bear Creek Trailhead.
2.0	Trail junction with Baker Trail.
2.2	Old Huckleberry Mountain Lookout site.
3.7	Trail junction with Goat Creek Trail.
4.7	Trail comes to spring.
6.0	Trail crosses saddle at the head of Goat Creek.
7.2	Trail crosses bottom of little valley.
7.5	Trail crosses saddle.
8.5	Little Storm Lake.

The trail: From Little Bear Creek Trailhead (El 5,600 ft.) the trail heads south and soon crosses Little Bear Creek (El 5,660 ft.). Get your water here, as there may be none for the next 4 miles. Above the creek the trail climbs fairly steeply with some switchbacks. At 2 miles the trail tops a ridge at 7,330 feet elevation and enters Eagle Cap Wilderness. At the ridge top, Baker Trail leads to the right (northwest) down to Bear Creek. See Hike 30 Baker. Huckleberry Mountain Trail turns left (southeast) and continues to climb a bit around the left side of a rock outcropping to the top of the ridge. Upon regaining the ridge, look to

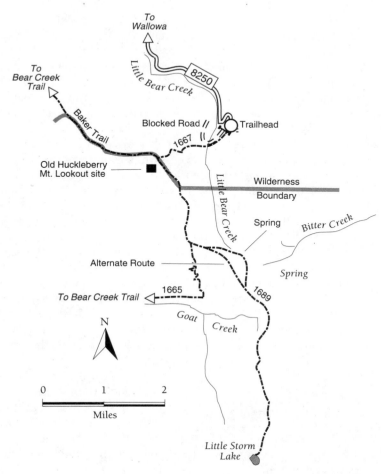

To
Wallowa

To
Bear Creek
Trail

Little Bear Creek

8250

Baker Trail

Blocked Road // Trailhead

1667 ||

Old Huckleberry
Mt. Lookout site

Little Bear Creek

Wilderness
Boundary

Spring   Bitter Creek

Alternate Route

Spring

To Bear Creek Trail ◁

1665

1689

N

Goat Creek

0   1   2

Miles

Little Storm
Lake

Source: Imus Geographics

the right for a faint path which leads to the site where Huckleberry Mountain Lookout used to be. The elevation at the old lookout site is 7,551 feet.

From the site of Huckleberry Mountain Lookout, the trail follows the ridge of Huckleberry Mountain, southeasterly. After going another 1.5 miles, the junction with Goat Creek Trail 1665 is reached (El 7,600 ft.). See Hike 31 Goat Creek. Goat Creek Trail junction is marked only with a rock pile and a post, no sign. The ridgeline between the lookout and Goat Creek Trail junction is the hydrological divide between Goat Creek and Little Bear Creek. From the lookout site up to this point the trail has only minor ups and downs. It may be difficult to see in some spots, but when in doubt, follow the ridge. This ridge-top country is mostly open grassland. There may be many wildflowers in July along the ridge. This is big game country. Watch for mule deer and elk grazing along the fringes of the timber. There are also a few bighorn sheep in the area, and bears are fairly common, as are cougars and coyotes.

After passing Goat Creek Trail junction, the trail climbs slightly for 0.25 mile, then descends 0.75 mile to a spring and campsite. Here the trail disappears completely. Go straight ahead across a small meadow to pick up the trail again. Past the campsite the trail climbs slightly for 0.1 mile to the southeast, to the ridge dividing Goat Creek and Lostine River drainages. Once on the ridge, the trail heads south. In the next 0.4 mile, the trail climbs to an elevation of 7,860 feet. At this point the trail is above the head of Bitter Creek, which is a tributary of the Lostine River.

Another route can be taken from Goat Creek Trail junction to the point above Bitter Creek. The route is more direct, but misses the water source at the spring. To take this route, bear to the right 0.25 mile southeast of Goat Creek Trail junction. This is where the main trail begins to descend. Stay high, just to the left of the ridgeline. There is a large rock outcropping on the ridgeline. The route is on the left (northeast) side of the outcropping, about 50 yards downslope. Once past the outcropping, the route follows the somewhat flattened ridge top for 0.5 mile to where it rejoins the main trail above the head of Bitter Creek.

The trail continues south, contouring around to the right (west) side of a high point on the ridge. It then drops slightly to a saddle near the head of Goat Creek. At this saddle is a wilderness boundary sign. Five hundred yards past the wilderness boundary sign, the faint trail bears southeast to the ridgeline. Drop over the ridgeline to the left (east) a few feet, staying just below the crest, and head south. Soon the trail will show up again.

The trail drops below some cliffs, and then drops some more in steep switchbacks to the bottom of a little valley (El 7,450 ft.). After getting to the bottom of the valley, the trail heads south. It soon climbs to a saddle at the head of the valley (El 7,540 ft.), then drops down to a spring and campsite.

A few feet below the spring the trail disappears in an open, marshy area. Go straight across the open area; the trail will appear again on the other side. To the right the cliffs above have a large red rock band. From here the

Backpacker on Huckleberry Mountain.
Photo by Gary Fletcher.

trail heads south past another spring and goes through another meadow. In a few hundred yards it reaches Little Storm Lake (El 7,610 ft.). The total distance to Little Storm Lake is 8.5 miles. This trail requires quite a bit of route finding ability.

The area is typical of the Western Wallowa Mountains. It is mostly transition and Canadian zone forests with a small amount of Hudsonian zone plants and trees on the highest ridges. There is also much open grassland. Like much of the Western Wallowas, water may be scarce in places. There are probably no fish in Little Storm Lake, but there are plenty of good campsites and lots of firewood.

Return trip can be made via the same trail.

30 BAKER

General description: A 6 mile long connecting trail from Bear Creek Trail to Huckleberry Mountain Trail.
Difficulty: Strenuous.
Trail maintenance: Rare.
Best season: June through October.
Traffic: Light.
Elevation gain: 3,240 feet.
Maximum elevation: 7,320 feet.
Maps: Fox Point and Lostine USGS quads.
For more information: U.S. Forest

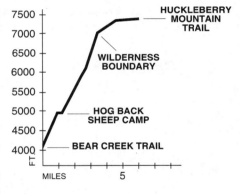

Service at Wallowa Mountain Visitors Center, Enterprise, Oregon. Further information will probably be very limited.
Finding the trail: The unmarked Baker Trail leaves Bear Creek Trail 1653, 1.75 miles south of Bear Creek Trailhead. See Hike 32 Bear Creek. The trail junction is 0.25 mile past Baker Gulch. There is a sign marking Baker Gulch. The elevation at the junction is 4,080 feet.

0.0   Trail junction with Bear Creek Trail.
1.0   Trail crosses saddle, and Hog Back Sheep Camp.
2.7   Trail reaches ridge line.
3.5   Eagle Cap Wilderness Boundary.
6.0   Trail junction with Huckleberry Mountain Trail.

The trail: Baker Trail turns to the left (east) off Bear Creek Trail. At first it climbs through the open forest as a faint path, which becomes more evident in a short distance. The trail makes a long switchback to the left, then to the right, and comes to a saddle at the top of a ridge. The last 200 yards before the saddle may be overgrown with grass. Go straight ahead and look for a large ponderosa pine with a white insulator on it. This insulator was used for the old telephone line to the now nonexistent Huckleberry Lookout. The pine is at the point where the trail crosses the ridge. This saddle (El 4,980 ft.) is 1 mile from Bear Creek Trail. Cross the saddle and drop slightly to Hog Back Sheep Camp. There is a sign marking the camp.

At the sheep camp the trail forks; take the trail on the right. Past the sheep camp the trail climbs fairly steeply up the creek bed, then makes a switchback and comes out on a ridge at 2.75 miles (El 6,140 ft.). From here, the trail generally follows the ridge, sometimes going a little to the left side.

At 3.5 miles is the Eagle Cap Wilderness Boundary sign. From here to the Huckleberry Mountain Lookout site the wilderness boundary almost follows the trail. Past the sign, continue up the ridge to the point where it flattens out at 4.75 miles (El. 7,250 ft.). Here the trail is faint. Go a few yards southeast and the trail appears again, following the ridgeline. After following the ridgeline a short distance, the trail goes off to the right side to avoid climbing a high point. It soon comes back to the ridge, in a saddle. This saddle (El 7,320 ft.) is 6 miles from Bear Creek Trail. The Baker Trail meets the Huckleberry Mountain Trail 1667 in this saddle. See Hike 29 Huckleberry Mountain.

30   Baker

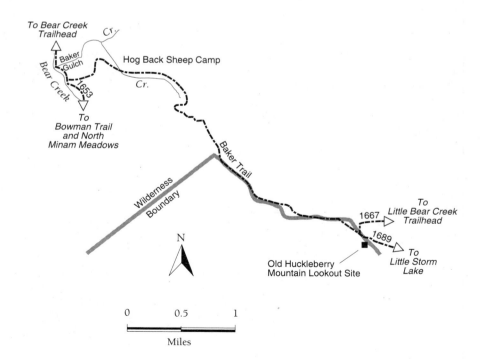

There may be no water on this trail, so carry some along. There may be many deer, elk, and bear in the area. This trail requires some route finding skills. An alternate return trip may be made by turning left (northeast) on Huckleberry Mountain Trail, and dropping down the 2 miles to Little Bear Creek Trailhead. This loop requires an 8 mile car shuttle.

31   GOAT CREEK

Trail 1665

General description: A 5.2 mile connecting trail between Bear Creek Trail and Huckleberry Mountain Trail.
Difficulty: Moderate to strenuous.
Trail maintenance: Rare.
Best season: June through October.
Traffic: Light.
Elevation gain: 3,200 feet.
Maximum elevation: 7,600 feet.
Maps: Imus Geographics Wallowa Mountains Eagle Cap Wilderness, or Fox Point and Lostine USGS quads.
For more information: U.S. Forest Service at Wallowa Mountain Visitors Center, Enterprise, Oregon. Further information will probably be very limited.

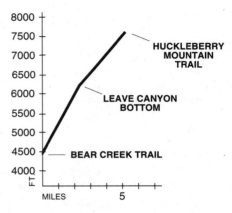

Finding the trail: Goat Creek Trail leaves Bear Creek Trail, 4 miles south of Bear Creek Trailhead at 4,400 feet elevation. See Hike 32 Bear Creek.

0.0	Trail junction with Bear Creek Trail.
3.5	Trail starts to climb out of the canyon bottom.
5.2	Trail junction with Huckleberry Mountain Trail.

The trail: Goat Creek Trail turns left (east) off of Bear Creek Trail. The trail climbs gently at first, then steepens and makes a switchback. Look up Goat Creek Canyon from the switchback to see Goat Creek Falls. After 1 mile the grade of the trail becomes more moderate. It continues up Goat Creek Canyon for another 2.5 miles. It then switches back to the top of Huckleberry Mountain (El 7,600 ft.) and the junction with Huckleberry Mountain Trail 1689, 5.2 miles from Bear Creek Trail. See Hike 29 Huckleberry Mountain. Watch for bighorn sheep on Goat Mountain to the south of the trail. Mule deer, elk and bear are also common in this area.

To make a loop hike, turn left (northwest) on Huckleberry Mountain Trail and follow it 1.7 miles to the junction with Baker Trail. See Hike 30 Baker.

31 *Goat Creek*

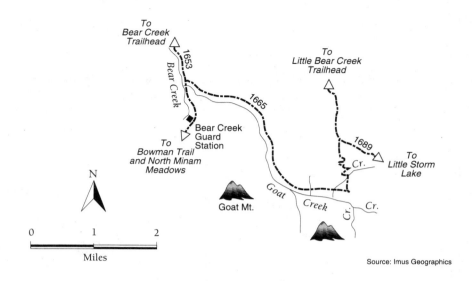

To
Bear Creek
Trailhead

1653

Bear Creek

To
Little Bear Creek
Trailhead

1665

Bear Creek
Guard
Station

To
Bowman Trail
and North Minam
Meadows

1689

Cr.

To
Little Storm
Lake

N

Goat Mt.

Goat

Creek

Cr.

Cr.

0   1   2

Miles

Source: Imus Geographics

Take Baker Trail back to Bear Creek Trail. This loop requires some route finding skill on Baker Trail. Be sure you have enough water to complete the trip, as water is scarce on this loop.

---

32 BEAR CREEK

Trail 1653

General description: A 19.2 mile backpack along Bear Creek, from Bear Creek Trailhead to the Bowman Trail. This trail gives access to Baker Trail, Goat Creek Trail, Dobbin Creek Trail, Washboard Trail and the Bowman Trail. It also passes a short distance from Bear Lake.
Difficulty: Easy to moderate, but long.
Best season: April through November, up to Dobbin Creek Trail; mid-June through October past there.
Trail maintenance: Yearly.
Traffic: Heavy to Bear Creek Guard Station, and moderate beyond there, except in October and November hunting season, when it can be heavy all the way. Moderate to heavy horse traffic, heaviest in the fall.
Elevation gain: 3,980 feet. Loss: 950 feet.
Maximum elevation: 7,700 feet.
Maps: Imus Geographics Wallowa Mountains Eagle Cap Wilderness, or Fox Point, Jim White Ridge and North Minam Meadows USGS quads.

For more information: U.S. Forest Service at Wallowa Mountain Visitors Center, Enterprise, Oregon.

Finding the trail: To reach Bear Creek Trailhead, take Bear Creek Road (FR 8250), south from the town of Wallowa. Eight miles south of town the road forks. Keep right (south) and go 1 mile farther to Bear Creek Trailhead (on FR 040). Boundary Campground is located near the trailhead, and there is a stock loading ramp.

0.0	Trail begins at Bear Creek Trailhead.
0.2	Trail crosses bridge over Bear Creek.
1.5	Trail crosses Baker Gulch.
1.7	Trail junction with Baker Trail.
3.3	Eagle Cap Wilderness Boundary.
4.0	Trail junction with Goat Creek Trail and bridge.
4.3	Bear Creek Guard Station.
5.0	Trail junction with Dobbin Creek Trail.
10.6	Trail crosses Granite Creek.
16.8	Trail crosses Bear Creek, and Bear Lake is a short distance to the left (east).
17.1	Trail crosses saddle, and trail junction with Washboard Trail.
19.2	Trail junction with Bowman Trail.

The trail: From the trailhead (El 3,720 ft.) Bear Creek Trail heads south, up Bear Creek. At 0.25 mile the trail crosses a bridge over Bear Creek. Three-quarters of a mile farther, is an open view point on the right side of the trail. Looking to the south, the high point is Fox Point. Fox Point is at the end of a side ridge, extending northeast from Standley Ridge. There is a trail which reaches Fox Point from Standley Ridge. See Hike 35 Standley Ridge, Hike 33 Dobbin Creek, and Hike 34 Fox Point.

At 1.5 miles the trail crosses Baker Gulch. A quarter-mile farther the unmarked Baker Trail turns off to the left (east) (El 4,080 ft.). See Hike 30 Baker. Continue south on the main trail. At 3.3 miles (El 4,300 ft.) the trail enters Eagle Cap Wilderness. The junction with Goat Creek Trail 1665 is 0.7 mile past the

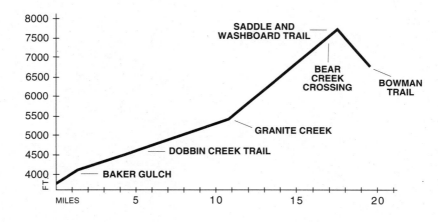

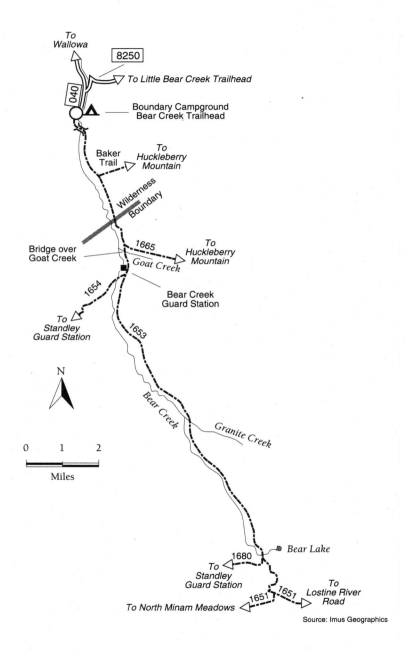

To
Wallowa

8250

To Little Bear Creek Trailhead

040

Boundary Campground
Bear Creek Trailhead

Baker
Trail

To
Huckleberry
Mountain

Wilderness
Boundary

1665

To
Huckleberry
Mountain

Bridge over
Goat Creek

Goat Creek

1654

Bear Creek
Guard Station

To
Standley
Guard Station

1653

N

Bear Creek

Granite Creek

0   1   2

Miles

Bear Lake

1680

To
Standley
Guard Station

To
Lostine River
Road

1651   1651

To North Minam Meadows

Source: Imus Geographics

wilderness boundary. Goat Creek Trail goes left (east). See Hike 31 Goat Creek. One hundred yards past Goat Creek Trail is Goat Creek Bridge. There are good campsites to the right of the trail just past the bridge. Fishing for fairly large trout is sometimes good in this section of Bear Creek.

Bear Creek Guard Station is 0.3 mile up Bear Creek Trail from Goat Creek Bridge. The old guard station is a short distance to the right (west) of the trail. To reach it turn right off the main trail and go past the outhouse, which can be seen from the main trail. The guard station is made of square-cut logs and is in quite good condition. It is locked and not available for public use. Many campsites are available in the timbered fringes of the beautiful meadows near the guard station.

Bear Creek Trail continues on to the south. Seven-tenths of a mile south of the guard station, Dobbin Creek Trail 1654 turns to the right (west) at a poorly marked junction. See Hike 33 Dobbin Creek. Bear Creek Trail heads on south past Dobbin Creek Trail another 5.8 miles to Granite Creek crossing (El 5,540 ft.). The last 2 miles below Granite Creek may be quite dry, as there are no major creek crossings and the trail is some distance form Bear Creek. Extra water should be carried in this section during dry weather.

Above Granite Creek the trail continues up Bear Creek Canyon, remaining on the east side of Bear Creek. It occasionally climbs up and away from the creek bed in switchbacks. At 6.25 miles above Granite Creek crossing, the trail has climbed nearly to the head of Bear Creek Canyon. It crosses Bear Creek for the last time (El 7,600 ft.). Bear Creek is a small stream at this point. The head of Bear Creek is only 0.5 mile upstream at Bear Lake. This area is much more open and alpine than the lower parts of Bear Creek Canyon. The trees are mostly subalpine fir, and the sloping meadows are teeming with alpine wildflowers.

Above the crossing, the trail continues to climb for 0.25 mile to the saddle (El 7,700 ft.) dividing Bear Creek drainage and the North Minam drainage. At the saddle, Washboard Trail 1680 goes to the right (west). See Hike 39 Washboard. The path to Bear Lake goes to the left from the saddle. Bear Lake (El 7,905 ft.) is 0.5 mile to the northeast on this path. The trail may not be visible for a few yards in the grassy area just below the saddle. However, it soon becomes evident again. The saddle area is subalpine in character, and is typical of the ridge tops in the western part of the Wallowa Mountains.

After crossing the saddle, the trail begins its descent towards Wilson Basin. One and one fourth miles below the saddle North Minam Meadows come into view in the canyon far below. The junction with the Bowman Trail 1651 is 0.5 mile farther at the lower end of Wilson Basin (El 6,750 ft.). The junction with the Bowman Trail is 19.2 miles from Bear Creek Trailhead. See Hike 26 Bowman. Return by the same trail or make a one way trip, which requires a car shuttle on the Bowman Trail, to Bowman Trailhead on the Lostine River Road.

33 DOBBIN CREEK

Trail 1654

General description: A 4.1 mile connecting trail, from Bear Creek Trail to Standley Ridge Trail. Do not confuse this with Hike 59 which is also Dobbin Creek, but is in the Little Minam River drainage. The area along the upper 1.5 miles of this trail was burned in the 1994 Fox Point Fire.

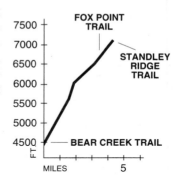

Difficulty: Strenuous.
Trail maintenance: Infrequent.
Best season: Mid-June through October.
Traffic: Light, except during October and November hunting season, with moderate horse traffic in the Fall.
Elevation gain: 2,590 feet.
Maximum elevation: 7,060 feet.
Map: Fox Point USGS quad.
For more information: U.S. Forest Service Service at Wallowa Mountain Visitors Center, Enterprise, Oregon.
Finding the trail: Dobbin Creek Trail begins 0.7 mile south of Bear Creek Ranger Station on Bear Creek Trail 1653 (El 4,470 ft.). See Hike 32 Bear Creek.

0.0	Trail junction with Bear Creek Trail.
0.1	Trail crosses Bear Creek.
1.5	Trail crosses Dobbin Creek.
3.7	Trail junction with Fox Point Trail.
4.1	Trail junction with Standley Ridge Trail.

The trail: Dobbin Creek Trail turns right off Bear Creek Trail. After leaving Bear Creek Trail, the path becomes faint for a short distance through a grassy area. The trail fords Bear Creek 0.1 mile from Bear Creek Trail. After crossing Bear Creek the trail becomes obvious again.

After crossing Bear Creek, the trail is level for a short distance, then it climbs steeply with many switchbacks. At 1.5 miles (El 5,560 ft.) the trail crosses Dobbin Creek. It continues to climb steeply to about 6,000 feet elevation. Above 6,000 feet the trail becomes more gentle. The trail enters the burn area of the Fox Point Forest Fire at approximately 6,300 feet elevation. At 3.25 miles (El 6,600 ft.) the trail crosses another creek in a completely charred forest. It then climbs 0.4 mile farther, flattens out for 0.1 mile, then climbs again to the junction with Fox Point Trail (El 6,850 ft.). See Hike 34 Fox Point. The unmarked junction with Fox Point Trail can be very difficult to see. It is 50 yards up the trail to the west from the point where the trail leaves a flat area and begins its final ascent to Standley Ridge Trail junction. Another 0.4 mile, brings you to the junction with Standley Ridge Trail 1677 (El 7,060 ft.). See Hike 35 Standley Ridge. Standley Guard Station is 1 mile to the south on Standley Ridge Trail. This may be the best way to reach Standley Guard Station early in the season when Standley Ridge Road and Trail are still blocked with snow.

A one way trip is possible by taking Standley Ridge Trail north from the junction, 3.8 miles to Bear Wallow Trailhead. This involves a car shuttle. See Hike 35 for directions to Bear Wallow Trailhead. If you are going to make a one way trip, it is easier to start at Bear Wallow Trailhead and end at Bear Creek Trailhead.

33 *Dobbin Creek*
34 *Fox Point*

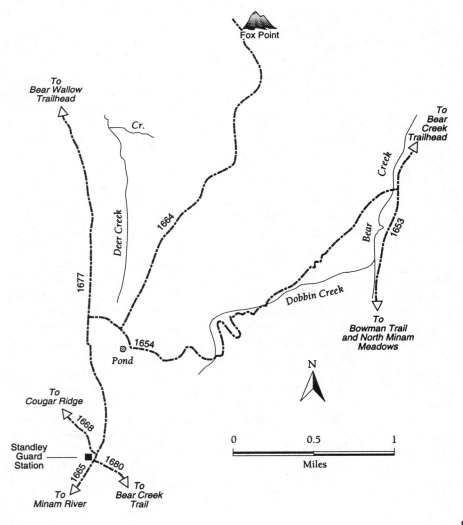

Trail 1664

General description: A short hike of slightly over 2 miles from Dobbin Creek Trail to Fox Point.
Difficulty: Easy.
Trail maintenance: Rare. This trail is no longer maintained by the forest service.
Best season: Mid-June through Mid-November, barring early snow.
Traffic: Light, except during hunting season, with moderate horse traffic in October and early November.
Elevation gain: 225 feet. Loss: 240 feet.
Maximum elevation: 7,085 feet.
Map: Fox Point USGS quad.
For more information: U.S. Forest Service at Wallowa Mountain Visitors Center, Enterprise, Oregon.
Finding the trail: The trail begins 0.4 mile east of Standley Ridge Trail on Dobbin Creek Trail. See Hike 33 Dobbin Creek and Hike 35 Standley Ridge.

0.0	Trail junction with Dobbin Creek Trail.
0.7	Top of the ridge.
2.0	Ranger Camp.
2.3	Fox Point.

The trail: A large portion of the area along this trail was burned in the September 1994 Fox Point Forest Fire. The trail turns northeast off Dobbin Creek Trail about 50 yards above (west of) the point where Dobbin Creek Trail flattens out for the first time after leaving Standley Ridge Trail (El 6,860 ft.). The unmarked junction can be difficult to find in this nearly completely burned area. At first the trail crosses a small flat area through the scorched woods. Soon it begins to contour along a hillside. After traversing along nearly level for 0.5 mile, the trail turns up hill to the east for a short distance and climbs to the top of the ridge (El 7,060 ft.). From here the trail generally follows the top of the ridge, heading northeast. There is a fire line cut to the west of the trail 0.75 mile after reaching the ridge top. This fire line may look like a trail, but it is not. Continue along the ridge to the north 2 miles from Dobbin Creek Trail to a place called Ranger Camp (El 6,880 ft.). The area around Ranger Camp is mostly burned and the sign identifying the spot is now gone.

The trail may be hard to follow when it goes through open areas, but it never disappears for long. There are good views of Bear Creek Canyon to the east in this area; also, there is a good chance of seeing wildlife.

From Ranger Camp the trail follows the open ridge heading northwest and soon leaves the burned area. It then drops slightly to Fox Point (El 6,850 ft.).

There is an old sign here that says Fox Point Telephone, but there is no telephone. For good views of lower Bear Creek Canyon and the lower Wallowa Valley, follow the ridge another 200 yards north to an open point.

When I hiked this trail, I stepped over a fallen log and nearly stepped right on a new born fawn. There is no water on Fox Point Trail. Fox Point Trail is like several other trails in the Western Wallowas, it doesn't go to any real particular place, but the scenery, wildlife, flowers and solitude along the way make the hike well worth the effort. To follow this trail requires some route finding and map reading skill. Return via the same trail.

35 STANDLEY RIDGE

Trail 1677

General description: A 4.8 mile day hike from Bear Wallow Trailhead to Standley Guard Station, or a backpack to a base camp there. Standley Guard Station is the trail hub for the area between Bear Creek and the Minam River. From here trails head out in all directions. Most of this trail follows an abandoned roadbed which is reverting nicely to a trail. A

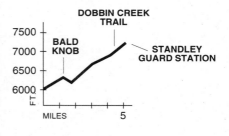

large section of this trail goes through the burn area of the September 1994 Fox Point Forest Fire.

Difficulty: Easy.

Trail maintenance: Yearly.

Best season: June through early November.

Traffic: Light to moderate, except in fall hunting seasons when it is heavy. This trail may have heavy horse traffic from the last weekend in September through early November.

Elevation gain: 1,200 feet.

Maximum elevation: 7,220 feet.

Map: Fox Point USGS quad.

For more information: U.S. Forest Service at Wallowa Mountain Visitors Center, Enterprise, Oregon.

Finding the trail: The trail begins at Bear Wallow Trailhead. To reach Bear Wallow Trailhead, turn south off State Highway 82, 1 mile east of Minam, on Big Canyon Road 8270. Follow FR 8270 for 10.4 miles to the junction with FR 050. Turn left (southeast) and follow FR 050 for 6.8 miles to Bear Wallow Trailhead. Take a National Forest map along, to make finding the trailhead easier. The trailhead is on top of a ridge. A few yards to the east of the trailhead parking area is an open area that allows an excellent view of Bear Creek Canyon. The Big Canyon Road is also used to reach Middle Cougar Ridge Trailhead. Bear Wallow Trailhead is not the same place as Bear Creek Trailhead.

0.0	Bear Wallow Trailhead.
1.0	Bald Knob.
2.8	Trail crosses Eagle Cap Wilderness Boundary.
3.8	Trail junction with Dobbin Creek Trail.
4.8	Standley Guard Station.

35 *Standley Ridge*

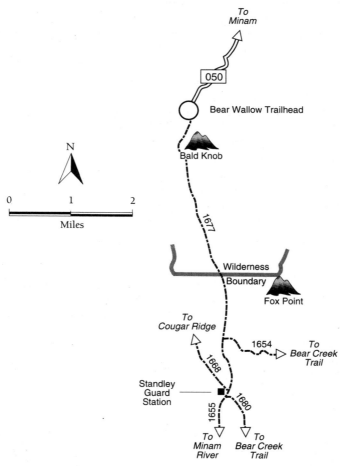

Source: Imus Geographics

The trail: The trail begins at the southeast corner of the parking area (El 6,020 ft.) at Bear Wallow Trailhead. The trail, which is actually an abandoned road-bed in places, goes south along the east side of a logged area. There may be a lot of blown down trees across the trail for the first 0.25 mile or so if there has been a wind storm since the trail was last maintained, but this problem lasts only a short distance.

One mile from the trailhead the trail comes into a more open area near the top of Bald Knob. Where the trail enters this opening, it forks. The main trail bears right (south), going around the highest part of Bald Knob. The trail to the left that was an old jeep road, goes directly over the top and rejoins the main trail on the other side at 1.25 miles (El 6,340 ft.).

Past Bald Knob the trail follows the ridge south, entering the burn area at 1.9 miles. Most of the burn area is on the left (east) side of the trail, but the burn did cross over the trail in places. After heading on south for 0.9 mile through mostly burned timber along the ridge, the trail enters Eagle Cap Wilderness (El 6,780 ft.). The trail continues along the ridge through mostly burned trees, for 0.9 mile more, then goes for 0.1 mile through green trees to the junction with Dobbin Creek Trail 1654 (El 7,060 ft.). See Hike 33 Dobbin Creek. Standley Guard Station (El 7,220 ft.) is 1 mile through the timber and open ridge top meadows, past the junction 4.8 miles from Bear Wallow Trailhead.

The Standley Guard Station cabin is in good condition, but is not for public use. It is protected by the Antiquities Act and should be left as it was found. There is an outhouse and developed spring here which are available for public use.

Standley Guard Station is the hub for trails connecting the Minam River, North Minam River and Bear Creek. So many trails going in all directions from here, makes this an excellent place to camp and explore the western part of the Wallowa Mountains. See Hike 36 Cougar Ridge, Hike 38 Murphy Creek, Hike 40 Minam River/Standley Guard Station, and Hike 39 Washboard.

The Standley Guard Station area is a site where range studies were conducted in the early 1900s to evaluate the grazing potential, mostly for sheep, of the area. Herders grazed their sheep on these ridge top meadows until recently.

Remember that most of the ridges are dry in summer, so carry water with you. Standley Ridge has no water between Bear Wallow Trailhead and Standley Guard Station. Mosquitoes can be problem in the marshy meadows around Standley Guard Station during early summer months of June and July. Return by the same trail, or use one of the other trails mentioned above to make a one way trip, requiring a car shuttle. See Hikes 33, 36 and 38.

Trail 1649 and 1668

General description: A backpack of 13.7 miles from the Minam River Trail to Standley Guard Station. The upper and lower portions of this trail may be hiked separately by using Middle Cougar Ridge Trailhead.

Difficulty: Strenuous for lower part, but easy for the upper part.

Trail maintenance: Infrequent.

Best season: Late May through early November for the lower portion, and mid-June through October for the upper portion.

Traffic: Light, except during fall hunting seasons, with light horse traffic.

Elevation gain: 4,200 feet for full trail; 2,880 feet for lower portion and 1,320 feet for the upper portion above Middle Cougar Ridge Trailhead.

Maximum elevation: 7,220 feet.

Maps: Imus Geographics Wallowa Mountains Eagle Cap Wilderness, or Mount Moriah and Fox Point USGS quads.

For more information: U.S. Forest Service at Wallowa Mountain Visitors Center, Enterprise, Oregon.

Finding the trail: Cougar Ridge Trail leaves Minam River Trail 1673, 1 mile up river from Meads Flat Trailhead. The elevation at the junction is 3,020 feet. See Hike 41 Lower Minam River. This trail can also be reached at a point 5 miles from the Minam River at Middle Cougar Ridge Trailhead. To reach this trailhead take Big Canyon Road off Oregon Highway 82, 1 mile east of Minam. Turn south on Big Canyon Road and go 10 miles to the junction with FR 8270. This is the junction for Bear Wallow Trailhead. Do not turn left, but go straight ahead on FR 8270 to its end at the trailhead, approximately 6 miles.

0.0   Trail junction with Minam River Trail.
1.5   Saddle.

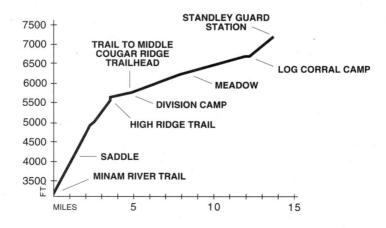

4.2	Trail junction with High Ridge Trail.
5.0	Trail junction with Middle Cougar Ridge Trailhead.
5.1	Division camp.
7.2	Meadow with red digger colony.
11.9	Log Corral Camp.
13.7	Standley Guard Station.

The trail: Cougar Ridge Trail turns left (east) off the Minam River Trail, when coming from Meads Flat Trailhead. Initially, the trail switchbacks up, to get on a finger of lower Cougar Ridge. The trail reaches the top of this rounded finger 0.25 mile after leaving The Minam River Trail. It then heads up the finger to the east northeast through open timber. There may be blow downs in this area. The trail continues up the finger through the timber for 0.5 mile. It then climbs a grassy slope with steep switchbacks for 0.25 mile more. Elevation at the top of the switchbacks is 3,990 feet.

At the top of the switchbacks the trail turns to the right (southeast). This is the beginning of a 0.5 mile long ascending traverse. The traverse heads southeast to a saddle on Cougar Ridge (El 4,210 ft.).

Above the saddle the trail heads up the ridgeline to the southeast. One hundred fifty yards above the saddle the trail goes off to the left side of the ridge, slightly, for 200 yards, then gets back on top. Three hundred fifty yards beyond is a small switchback in open woods (El 4,460 ft.). Above the switchback, the trail stays on the ridgeline for 0.9 mile, climbing to 4,920 feet elevation. Many types of flowers bloom along this ridgeline in June. As the trail climbs higher, the horizon broadens to include sweeping views of much of the Western Wallowa Mountains.

At 4,920 feet elevation the trail goes to the right side of the ridgeline and continues to climb, staying about 50 vertical feet below the ridgeline for 0.25 mile. After 0.25 mile on the right side, the trail crosses the ridgeline (El 5,060 ft.) and continues up the left side for 250 yards where it regains the ridge.

A quarter mile after regaining the ridge the trail passes some rock outcroppings. The trail can be difficult to see in this area. Continue on up the ridge 0.5 mile more, and the trail then bears left (El 5,280 ft.) and climbs to the east for 0.3 mile to the junction with High Ridge Trail. For the last 150 yards before reaching the junction the trail can be difficult to see. By going up to the east northeast it will soon show up again. This junction can be especially difficult to find when descending. If you are going back down this trail, take note of where the junction is.

At the unmarked junction with High Ridge Trail (El 5,620 ft.), turn right (southeast). See map of Middle Cougar Ridge Trailhead area and Hike 37 High Ridge. Follow the trail for 700 yards southeast to an unmarked junction with a logging "cat trail," at the upper edge of a clear cut.

After passing the "cat trail," Cougar Ridge Trail continues along the top of the clear cut 650 more yards to another unmarked junction. Here it meets the trail coming up from Middle Cougar Ridge Trailhead. This is the only logged area along this trail. After leaving the clear cut area, another 250 yards of trail brings us to Division Camp (El 5,760 ft.). There is yet another trail here going back to Middle Cougar Ridge Trailhead.

One and eight-tenths miles past Division Camp is a campsite on the left side of the trail (El 5,920 ft.). One-third mile farther is a rocky opening with a view to the right of Trout Creek Canyon. Another 0.9 mile past the viewpoint, the trail enters a grassy meadow (El 6,200 ft.). There is a path to the left (northeast) here, but Cougar Ridge Trail crosses the meadow and continues to head southeast. There is a red digger colony in this meadow.

Past the meadow, the trail stays fairly close to the ridgeline. It goes through alternating areas of timber and open places. A couple of miles past the meadow

36   *Cougar Ridge*
37   *High Ridge*
38   *Murphy Creek*

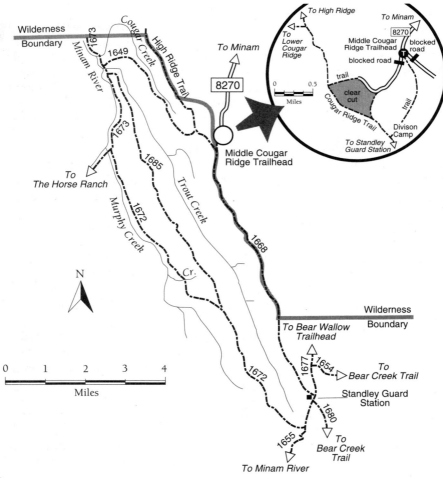

at about 6,500 feet elevation, the timber begins to become more alpine in nature. Log Corral Camp (El 6,770 ft.) is reached 4.5 miles past the meadow. Past Log Corral Camp the trail climbs steadily but gently for 1.5 miles to Standley Guard Station and Standley Spring (El 7,220 ft.). The junction with Trail 1677, coming from Bear Wallow Trailhead, is at Standley Guard Station. See Hike 35 Standley Ridge.

Cougar Ridge Trail, below the junction with High Ridge Trail, is quite steep in places. It is also difficult to find in spots. Above High Ridge Trail junction, it is gentle and easy to see. There is no water on Lower Cougar Ridge; however, there is a spring on High Ridge Trail 0.3 mile from its junction with Cougar Ridge Trail. On Upper Cougar Ridge there is no water adjacent to the trail. There is water at Standley Springs. As is true with most surface water, it should be treated, filtered or boiled to make it safe to drink.

It is 13.7 miles from the Minam River Trail to Standley Springs and 4,200 feet of elevation gain. This trail can be done in two sections, from the Middle Cougar Ridge Trailhead (see map). Some route finding skills may be required to follow this trail, especially the lower part. There is a lot of wildlife along Cougar Ridge. Keep your eyes open for mule deer and elk. You might also see a bear. There is the possibility of a rattlesnake on the lower part of this trail. Watch where you step and especially where you place your hands when climbing.

Standley Guard Station is a good place to make camp and explore the area. Hikes 35, 39, and 40 all meet at Standley Guard Station, and Hikes 33, 34, and 38 are only a short distance away.

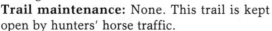

37   HIGH RIDGE

General description: A 2.9 mile day hike along High Ridge, from Cougar Ridge Trail to a jeep road and campsite on High Ridge. Add 0.9 mile if coming from Middle Cougar Ridge Trailhead.
Difficulty: Easy to moderate, but requires route finding.
Trail maintenance: None. This trail is kept open by hunters' horse traffic.

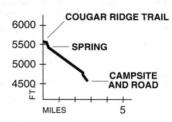

Best season: June through October.
Traffic: Light, with light horse traffic in the fall.
Elevation loss: 1,050 feet, add 200 feet if coming from Middle Cougar Ridge Trailhead.
Maximum elevation: 5,620 feet.
Map: Mount Moriah USGS quad.
For more information: U.S. Forest Service at Wallowa Mountain Visitors Center, Enterprise, Oregon. Further information may be limited.

Finding the trail: High Ridge Trail leaves Cougar Ridge Trail 1649, 0.9 mile below (north northwest) Division Camp. See Hike 36 Cougar Ridge for the Middle Cougar Ridge Trailhead area map and directions to Middle Cougar Ridge Trailhead. The elevation at the junction is 5,620 feet. At this junction High Ridge Trail, rather than Cougar Ridge Trail, appears to be the main trail.

0.0 Trail junction with Cougar Ridge Trail.
0.3 Spring.
2.6 Trail begins to drop steeply.
2.9 Jeep road and campsite.

The trail: High Ridge Trail heads north northwest from the junction. One-third mile from the junction is a spring (El 5,440 ft.). Past the spring, the trail is not always easy to see. Watch for blazes on the trees. A quarter mile past the spring the trail reaches the ridgeline of High Ridge. For the next 2 miles the trail generally follows the ridgeline, dropping about 600 vertical feet in elevation. The trail goes through alternating open and wooded areas along the ridge. There is quite a bit of both blue and yellow lupine blooming in June and July along High Ridge.

Two and one-fourth miles past the spring the trail begins to drop steeply and becomes braided. After dropping for 0.25 mile, the trail comes to a National Forest boundary sign and a jeep road. This is the end of High Ridge Trail. There are campsites at the end of the trail but no visible water. Elevation here is 4,570 feet. There is no water on High Ridge Trail between the spring at 5,440 feet and the campsite at the lower end. Route finding skills may be needed to follow this trail.

Return by the same trail, and watch for mule deer and elk.

38 MURPHY CREEK

Trail 1672 Alternate Trail 1685

General description: A 10 mile trail from Minam River/Standley Guard Station Trail to Minam River Trail.
Difficulty: Strenuous.
Trail maintenance: Infrequent.
Best season: Mid-June through October.
Traffic: Very light, except during October and November hunting seasons, when it can be moderate.
Elevation loss: 3,860 feet.
Maximum elevation: 6,940 feet.
Maps: Imus Geographics Wallowa Mountains Eagle Cap Wilderness, or Jim White Ridge, Fox Point and Mount Moriah USGS quads. The Big Sheep Ridge alternate route is shown on the Imus Geographics map but not on the USGS maps.

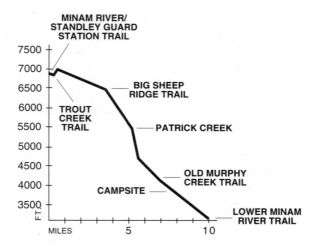

For more information: U.S. Forest Service at Wallowa Mountain Visitors Center, Enterprise, Oregon.

Finding the trail: The trail begins at the junction with Minam River/Standley Guard Station Trail 1655, 1 mile south of Standley Guard Station. See Hike 40 Minam River/Standley Guard Station. See map on p.98.

0.0   Trail junction with Minam River/Standley Guard Station Trail.
0.2   Trail junction with abandoned Trout Creek Trail.
0.9   Trail junction with now abandoned Old Murphy Creek Trail.
4.0   Trail junction with Big Sheep Ridge Trail.
5.4   Trail drops off Mahogany Ridge.
5.9   Trail crosses Patrick Creek.
6.6   Trail junction with Old Murphy Creek Trail.
7.4   Campsite.
10.0   Trail junction with Minam River Trail.

The trail: From the junction with Minam River/Standley Guard Station Trail 1655, Murphy Creek Trail heads to the northwest. There is a trail sign at this junction (El 6,930 ft.). The trail drops slightly through the timber for 0.2 mile, to the unmarked junction with the now abandoned Trout Creek Trail. The junction is in a swampy meadow. Trout Creek Trail is difficult to spot. After passing the junction, the trail climbs slightly. It generally follows the ridge top for the next 0.7 mile to an unmarked junction (El 7,020 ft.). Just before the junction the trail goes through a burn area. The path to the left (west) is the now abandoned Old Murphy Creek Trail. Murphy Creek Trail bears to the right (northwest) and heads down Big Sheep Ridge. Past the fork the trail gradually descends through forest and openings. For the next 2 miles it generally follows the broad ridge top. The trail is a bit difficult to see in the open areas but never disappears for long. After the 2 miles the ridge narrows. The trail stays close to the top of the ridge for the next mile to the junction with Big

Sheep Ridge Trail 1685. This junction (El 6,440 ft.) is 4 miles from the junction with Minam River/Standley Guard Station Trail. The trail to the right (northwest) follows Big Sheep Ridge to the Minam River Trail. See the alternate trail description below.

At the junction Murphy Creek Trail bears left (west northwest) and descends through thinning timber for 1.4 miles to a saddle on Mahogany Ridge (El 5,450 ft.). The open slopes along Mahogany Ridge may be covered with balsamroot, paintbrush, and lupine in late June and early July. At the saddle the trail turns right (north) and begins to descend steeply towards Patrick Creek. It makes eleven switchbacks as it drops the 0.5 mile to the creek crossing. The trail crosses Patrick Creek in the last switchback (El 4,720 ft.). After the crossing the trail descends along Patrick Creek, crossing it a couple of times, for 0.7 miles to the lower junction with Old Murphy Creek Trail (El 4,160 ft.). Old Murphy Creek Trail, which is now abandoned, turns to the left and crosses Patrick Creek. There is a sign at this junction, which points up Patrick Creek to Standley.

Turn right at the junction and head down Murphy Creek Trail. There is a good campsite on the left side of the trail next to Murphy Creek 0.8 mile after passing Old Murphy Creek Trail junction. For the next 2.6 miles, from the campsite to the Minam River Trail junction, Murphy Creek Trail drops gently through the forested canyon bottom. The trail generally stays on the right side of Murphy Creek, but it does cross to the left side for a short time. This section of the trail is more difficult to follow because of the many blowdowns and the infrequent maintenance. At the junction with Lower Minam River Trail 1673 (El 3,080 ft.) there is a trail sign, and a few yards to the left (south) on the Minam River Trail is a bridge across Murphy Creek. See Hike 41 Lower Minam River.

Author Heading down Big Sheep Ridge. *Photo by Gary Fletcher.*

Alternate trail: From the junction with Murphy Creek Trail, Big Sheep Ridge Trail 1685 heads on down Big Sheep Ridge to the northwest. The path which is Big Sheep Ridge Trail generally follows the ridgeline, keeping slightly to the left of the top and staying mostly in the open for 7 long miles. It then turns to the left and drops, making thirteen steep switchbacks in the last 0.3 mile to the unmarked junction with the Minam River Trail. While this route is more scenic than the Murphy Creek Trail, it is a very long way, without any water at all. It is next to impossible for anyone not familiar with this trail to find this junction, while on the Minam River Trail 1673. See Hike 41 Lower Minam River. However, finding the junction, which is 2.3 miles north of the Murphy Creek Trail junction on the Minam River Trail, is no problem, when coming down Big Sheep Ridge. There are several possible dry campsites in the saddles along Big Sheep Ridge.

Murphy Creek Trail and the alternate route on Big Sheep Ridge require considerable route finding skills to follow safely. Watch for mule deer, elk, and bear that are common along the ridges and canyons in the western Wallowas. Along the lower parts of these trails, mostly below 4,000 feet elevation, keep an eye on the ground ahead for an occasional rattlesnake. Carry plenty of water as there is none available along Murphy Creek Trail above Patrick Creek and none at all if you head down Big Sheep Ridge. A gallon per person may not be too much on a warm day.

For the ambitious hiker who is skilled in route finding and doesn't mind lots of elevation loss and gain, taking the alternate Big Sheep Ridge Trail down and coming back up Murphy Creek Trail makes a great hike. To do this it is best to allow 2 days from Standley Guard Station and to camp at either the Minam River or the campsite 2.6 miles up Murphy Creek Trail from the Minam River.

39   WASHBOARD

Trail 1680

General description: A 9.7 mile backpack from Standley Guard Station, along the jagged crest of Washboard Ridge, to Bear Creek Trail.

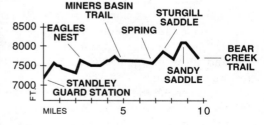

Difficulty: Moderate to strenuous.

Trail maintenance: Infrequent, but this trail is mostly in open country, so downed logs are not much of a problem.

Best season: Mid-July through October.

Traffic: Light, except during fall hunting seasons when it can be moderate to heavy. Much of the traffic is horse traffic.

Elevation gain: 2,050 feet. Loss: 1,570 feet.

Maximum elevation: 8,100 feet.

Maps: Imus Geographics Wallowa Mountain Eagle Cap, or Jim White and North Minam Meadows USGS quads.

For more information: U.S. Forest Service at Wallowa Mountain Visitors Center, Enterprise, Oregon.

Finding the trail: The trail begins at Standley Guard Station, 4.6 miles south of Bear Wallowa Trailhead. See Hike 35 Standley Ridge.

0.0	Standley Guard Station and spring.
0.7	Ridge narrows.
2.0	Saddle above Blowout Basin.
2.2	Eagles Nest.
4.7	Trail junction with Miners Basin Trail.
7.3	Sturgill Saddle.
8.5	Sandy Saddle.
9.7	Trail junction with Bear Creek Trail.

The trail: The Washboard Trail junction is unmarked at Standley Guard Station. If you stand in front (east side) of the old guard station cabin and look east southeast, a path can be seen heading through the small timber. This path is the Washboard Trail. Fill your water bottles at Standley Spring, or from the creek just southeast of the cabin. There is no water along the trail for the first 4.6 miles. Be sure to treat, boil, or filter the water.

At first, the trail climbs gently to the southeast through small timber. Soon it flattens out and crosses a ridge top meadow heading generally south. Seven-tenths mile from Standley Guard Station , the ridge narrows (El 7,560 ft.) and the view to the south opens up. China Cap is the prominent peak to the south across the Minam River drainage, but many other, mostly unnamed, peaks can also be seen.

As the ridge narrows the trail drops slightly to the right of the ridgeline and heads down and southeast to a saddle. It then traverses the phlox and lupine covered slope on the right side of the ridgeline for 0.3 mile before reaching another saddle. In this saddle the trail follows the ridge for a couple hundred yards, then traverses along the slope on the right side again. One third mile into this traverse the trail is on a rock ledge for 100 yards or so, and 0.1 mile farther it follows another ledge for 75 yards. This is very steep and rugged country, and not well suited to inexperienced horses or horsemen. It is no problem for hikers however.

After leaving the second ledge, the trail comes to another saddle (El 7,310 ft.) with a sign pointing out Blowout Basin which is to the left. In the saddle the trail crosses to the left side of the ridge for the first time, and climbs steeply for a few yards before crossing back to the right side of the ridge. The trail reaches a rugged notch called Eagles Nest 0.2 mile after leaving Blowout Basin Saddle. There is a sign at Eagles Nest. The most difficult part of the trail for horse traffic is a short distance past Eagles Nest. Here the trail is chipped

39 *Washboard*

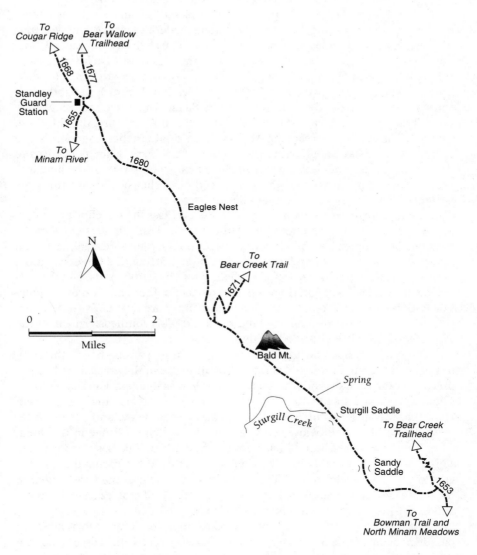

To Cougar Ridge

To Bear Wallow Trailhead

1668

1677

Standley Guard Station

1655

To Minam River

1680

Eagles Nest

To Bear Creek Trail

1671

N

0   1   2
Miles

Bald Mt.

Spring

Sturgill Saddle

Sturgill Creek

To Bear Creek Trailhead

Sandy Saddle

1653

To Bowman Trail and North Minam Meadows

Source: Imus Geographics

out of a rock face as it climbs steeply to another saddle. Several horse wrecks have happened at this difficult spot.

After passing the difficult section, the trail makes a left turn in the saddle (El 7,640 ft.). Another 10 yards and the trail turns right again, as it drops steeply off the left side of the ridgeline. Soon the grade moderates, as the trail descends to a meadow in a broad saddle on the ridgeline. The trail stays on the left side, but very close to the ridgeline, for 0.7 mile, then it crosses back to the right side, where it begins an ascending traverse to yet another ridgeline crossing. The trail crosses the ridgeline at 7,800 feet elevation then drops slightly as it starts to traverse around the head of Miners Basin. The junction with Miners Basin Trail 1671 (El 7,640 ft.) is reached 0.3 mile after crossing the ridgeline. A short distance before reaching Miners Basin Trail junction there are some springs some distance below the trail to the left. Miners Basin Trail turns to the left (northeast) and descends 2.7 miles to Bear Creek Trail. At the junction, Washboard Trail heads straight ahead to the southeast and continues its traverse around the head of Miners Basin.

The trail traverses below a rocky bluff then crosses the ridgeline again 0.25 mile after passing the junction with Miners Basin Trail. It stays close to the ridgeline for another 0.25 mile, then traverses on the right side again. The trail enters an area with no vegetation 0.5 mile after starting this traverse. In the bare area head southeast, descending slightly for about 100 yards, and the trail will soon reappear as it enters a grass covered slope. From here on to the junction with Bear Creek Trail, the trail and the country are much less rugged then than were back towards Standley Guard Station. This southeastern end of the Washboard Trail is well suited to horse traffic.

The trail traverses the grassy slope for 0.4 mile, passing below the summit of Bald Mountain, then becomes difficult to see in the grass. Head southeast, dropping slightly, and pick up the trail again as it enters some small trees. The trail rounds a small sub-ridge and continues its traverse to the southeast. Here the lush meadow of Sturgill Basin can be seen below and to the southwest. The trail is well below the ridgeline of Washboard Ridge in this area. After traversing above Sturgill Basin for 0.4 mile, the trail passes a good spring. The spring is a few feet below the trail to the right. At the spring the trail begins to get into thicker timber. The trail forks 0.2 mile past the spring. Bear to the left to stay on the main trail. After the fork, the trail crosses a small stream and begins its 0.3 mile climb to Sturgill Saddle (El 7,820 ft.).

The trail crosses the saddle and drops through thin timber to a meadow, passing a campsite next to a stream along the way. The trail crosses a stream (El 7,590 ft.) as it enters the meadow and another stream as it is about to leave the meadow. Upon leaving the meadow, the trail climbs slightly to the south southeast, through a rocky area. Watch for cairns marking the trail. The trail passes a couple of prospect holes 0.25 mile after leaving the meadow. There is lots of quartz which was dug from these holes laying on the ground here. The trail crosses a smaller meadow after passing the prospect holes, then climbs a ridge made of gray tan granite sand. At the top of the small ridge the trail turns to the left and climbs a short distance more to the main ridgeline. On the ridgeline the trail heads southeast for a short distance. This area of the ridgeline is known as Sandy Saddle, and at 8,100 feet elevation it is the highest point reached on the Washboard Trail. The ridge is thinly timbered here, with white bark pine and subalpine fir.

After following the nearly level ridgeline for 400 yards, the trail begins to descend. It winds its way down, sometimes steeply, through the thin but occasionally large whitebark pine timber for 0.7 mile to the top of the broad open meadow in the saddle at the head of Bear Creek. As the trail enters the meadow, a rock pile with a post in it comes into view. This is the first of three such markers, showing the way down to the junction with Bear Creek Trail. The trail crosses a small stream between the second and third posts. The junction with Bear Creek Trail 1653 (El 7,700 ft.) is on the divide between Bear Creek and the North Minam River drainages.

At the junction, Bear Creek is to the left (north), Bowman Trail and North Minam Meadows are to the right (south), and Bear Lake is straight ahead to the east. There are several campsites available near the junction. See Hike 32 Bear Creek. A return trip can be made to Standley Guard Station by retracing the same trail, or one can head down Bear Creek 13.6 miles to Dobbin Creek Trail and climb back out 3.6 miles on Dobbin Creek Trail , to Standley Ridge Trail one mile north of Standley Guard Station. See Hike 33 Dobbin Creek. This loop is best done in two long or three short days using the campsites along Bear Creek.

40 MINAM RIVER/STANDLEY GUARD STATION

Trail 1655

General description: A 4.4 mile connecting trail from the Upper Minam River Trail, 1.6 miles south of the Horse Ranch, to Standley Guard Station.
Difficulty: Strenuous.
Trail maintenance: Yearly.
Best season: Mid-June through October.
Traffic: Light, with light horse traffic, except during the fall hunting season when horse traffic can be moderate.
Elevation gain: 3,420 feet.
Maximum elevation: 7,220 feet.
Maps: Jim White Ridge and Fox Point USGS quads.

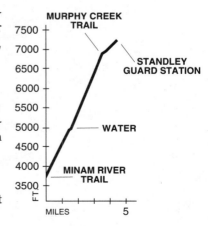

For more information: U.S. Forest Service at Wallowa Mountain Visitors Center, Enterprise, Oregon.
Finding the trail: Minam River/Standley Guard Station Trail 1655 leaves Upper Minam River Trail 1673, 300 yards east southeast of Wallowa Creek,

which is marked with a sign. This junction is 1.6 miles up river from Moss Springs Trail junction and The Horse Ranch. The elevation at the junction with Minam River Trail is 3,800 feet. See Hike 42 Upper Minam River.

0.0   Trail junction with Upper Minam River Trail.
1.5   Side trail to water.
3.4   Trail junction with Murphy Creek Trail.
4.4   Standley Guard Station.

40   *Minam River/Standley Guard Station*

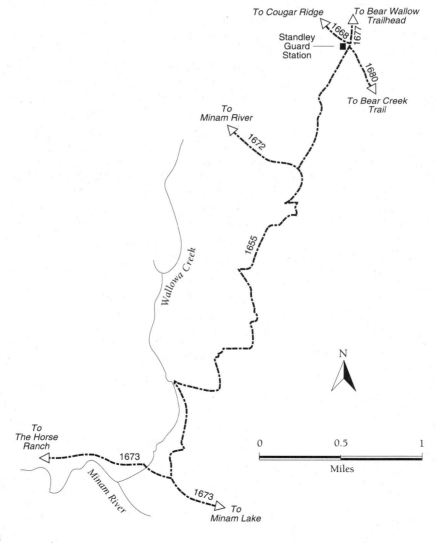

The trail: At the marked junction, Minam River/Standley Guard Station Trail turns north off the Minam River Trail. It works its way up through medium-aged transitional zone forest and granite outcroppings to 4,500 feet elevation where the first basalt outcroppings appear. Basalt rock generally overlays granite in this area.

At 1.5 miles (El 5,030 ft.) a side trail leads 50 feet to the left to a creek where water may be obtained. There is a large ponderosa pine with an arrow cut into its side, marking the spot where this side trail leaves the main trail.

The trail continues to climb, with some switchbacks, to the top of a ridge (El 5,460 ft.). Here the view opens up, with views of the Minam River Canyon below and Standley Ridge above. The trail climbs the top of the ridge for a time, then traverses to the right. At 6,460 feet elevation the trail crosses a small seasonal stream and continues to climb to the junction with Murphy Creek Trail 1672. See Hike 38 Murphy Creek. The elevation at this junction is 6,930 feet. The junction is 3.4 miles from Minam River Trail. From the junction with Murphy Creek Trail, Standley Guard Station (El 7,220 ft.) is 1 mile ahead to the north. See Hike 35 Standley Ridge .

Between the seasonal stream and Murphy Creek Trail junction is a game trail which takes off to the left (west). This game trail could be mistaken for the main trail, especially when coming down. Be careful not to take it.

The ridge top area above Murphy Creek Trail junction is mostly open subalpine in nature. It is typical of ridge top areas in the western Wallowas. There are campsites at Standley Guard Station, which is the trail hub of the area.

41   LOWER MINAM RIVER

Trail 1673

General description: A long gentle backpack down the Minam River from the Horse Ranch to Meads Flat Trailhead, and possibly then on to the town of Minam on Oregon Highway 82. The distance from the Horse Ranch to Meads Flat Trailhead is 14.5 miles, to Minam it is 24.5 miles.
Difficulty: Easy, but long.
Trail maintenance: Yearly to Meads Flat, seldom on the trail portion past there, down river.
Best season: April through November.

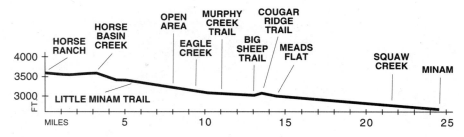

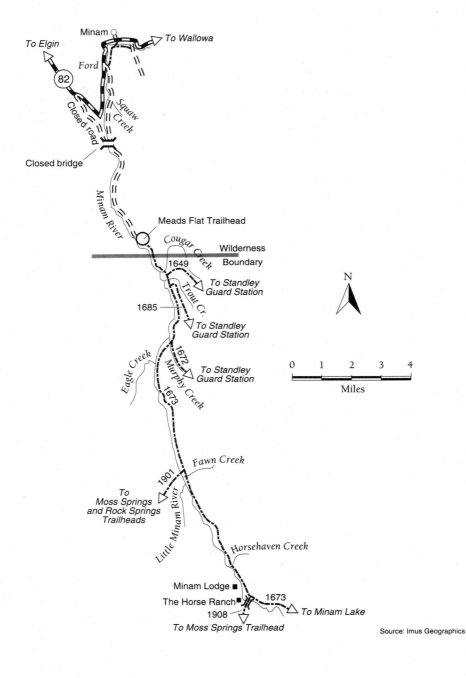

Minam

To Wallowa

To Elgin

Ford

82

Squaw Creek

Closed road

Closed bridge

Minam River

Meads Flat Trailhead

Cougar Creek

Wilderness Boundary

1649

To Standley Guard Station

Trout Cr.

1685

To Standley Guard Station

Eagle Creek

1672

Murphy Creek

To Standley Guard Station

1673

N

0 1 2 3 4

Miles

Fawn Creek

1901

To Moss Springs and Rock Springs Trailheads

Little Minam River

Horsehaven Creek

Minam Lodge

The Horse Ranch

1673

1908

To Minam Lake

To Moss Springs Trailhead

Source: Imus Geographics

Traffic: Moderate, with moderate horse traffic.

Elevation loss: 670 feet to Meads Flat, 340 feet more to Minam.

Maximum elevation: 3,600 feet.

Maps: Imus Geographics Wallowa Mountains Eagle Cap Wilderness, or Mount Fanny and Mount Moriah USGS quads.

For more information: U.S. Forest Service at Wallowa Mountain Visitors Center, Enterprise, Oregon. For a flight to the Horse Ranch, locally called Red's, call Spence Air Service in Enterprise, Oregon.

Finding the trail: The Lower Minam River Trail begins at the junction of Minam River Trail 1673 and Moss Springs Trail 1908, 100 yards east of the Horse Ranch (El 3,600 ft.). The Horse Ranch can be reached by flight from LaGrande or Enterprise, or by hiking from Moss Springs Trailhead. See Hike 51 Moss Springs/Horse Ranch. There are several other ways to get there, but they involve longer hikes. Meads Flat may be reached by a poor road from Minam. Inquire locally before trying to reach Meads Flat by car (four-wheel-drive).

0.0	Trail junction with Moss Springs/Horse Ranch Trail and the Horse Ranch.
5.6	Trail junction with Little Minam River Trail.
9.2	Open area with red digger colony.
10.8	Trail junction with Murphy Creek Trail.
13.5	Trail junction with Cougar Ridge Trail.
14.5	Meads Flat Trailhead.
21.5	Squaw Creek crossing.
24.5	Minam.

The trail: From the junction 100 yards east of the Horse Ranch the trail heads down river to the north northwest. One-half mile from the junction the trail enters Eagle Cap Wilderness. A quarter mile farther between the river and the trail is a good campsite. From the campsite, a small sawmill, which is part of the Minam Lodge operation, can be seen across the river to the west. There is a small stream just below the campsite. The trail in this area is apparently an old roadbed. There is a stream crossing at 1.5 miles (El 3,570 ft.). At 1.75 miles the trail splits, with the left trail going to a beautiful riverside campsite. After passing the campsite, the side trail rejoins the main trail 0.25 mile from where it forked off. The northern down river end of the side trail is, however a bit difficult to find.

After the trails join back together 2 miles from the Moss Springs Trail junction, the trail gets farther away from the Minam River. It stays away from the river for about 1.5 miles, crossing Horse Basin Creek. After coming closer to the river again, the trail continues on to a trail junction, at 4.75 miles (El 3,470 ft.). The trail to the left, which is an alternate for the Little Minam River Trail, fords the river and heads west. The Lower Minam River Trail goes straight ahead.

Three hundred yards past the junction the trail passes the mouth of the Little Minam River. The Little Minam River joins the Minam River from the west, the opposite side from the trail. Another 0.4 mile and the trail crosses Fawn Creek, and 0.25 mile farther is the junction with the Little Minam River Trail 1901 (El 3,430 ft.). See Hike 49 Lower Little Minam River. Crossing the Minam River here to get to the Little Minam River Trail is very dangerous, and without a horse can be difficult to impossible in the spring and early summer. There is no bridge.

At the junction with the Little Minam River Trail there is an excellent campsite. The campsite is located across the flower covered meadow to the west of the main trail near the river. The canyon bottom in this area is mostly covered with well diversified transitional zone forest. The coniferous trees include Douglas-fir, true fir, tamarack, lodgepole, and ponderosa pine. In addition to these needle leaf trees are aspen, native hawthorn, and some cottonwood. Plants include lots of lupine and wild strawberries.

After passing the Little Minam River Trail junction, the Minam River Trail continues on down river, crossing a couple of streams in the next 2.6 miles, before coming to a semi-open area. This area was logged many years ago. There is a red digger colony here. These ground squirrels can be fun to watch. This is also a nice camping area (El 3,240 ft.). Eagle Creek flows into the Minam River from the southwest 1.5 miles past the open area. It flows in on the opposite side of the river from the trail.

The bridge over Murphy Creek is 1.25 miles below Eagle Creek. Just past the bridge is the junction with Murphy Creek Trail 1672 (El 3,040 ft.). See Hike 38 Murphy Creek. Two and two-thirds miles past Murphy Creek Trail junction is the junction with Big Sheep Trail 1685 (El 2,940 ft.). This junction is unmarked and very difficult to find. It is 200 yards before Trout Creek crossing. Another 0.1 mile brings you to Trout Creek crossing, and 0.3 mile more is the junction with Cougar Ridge Trail 1649 (El 3,020 ft.). See Hike 39 Cougar Ridge.

One mile below Cougar Ridge Trail junction is the National Forest Boundary, also Eagle Cap Wilderness Boundary, and Meads Flat. There is an old foundation on the east side of the trail just before reaching Meads Flat. Meads Flat (El 2,930 ft.) is 14.5 miles from the Horse Ranch. It maybe possible to get to Meads Flat by a jeep road from the town of Minam. Check locally for road conditions and directions.

The hike from Meads Flat to OR 82 is about 10 miles over jeep roads and a poor trail. If you are going to walk it, follow the road for 7 miles north, staying on the east side of the river, to Squaw Creek. Then follow the trail 3 more miles down river, until you hit a road in a side canyon. Turn left on the road, go down a short distance, and cross the bridge over the Wallowa River. Here the road meets OR 82. You are now at the town of Minam.

The river may be forded 1.5 miles before reaching the road in the side canyon. The ford leads to a parking area a short distance off OR 82, 1 mile south of Minam. Do this ford only in times of low water.

The hike from the Horse Ranch to Minam is long, but it is gentle, and goes through beautiful canyon country filled with forests, flowers, and animals.

Meadow in the Minam River Canyon near the mouth of the Little Minam River.

Fishing anywhere on the Minam River is likely to get you a trout dinner. Check Angling Synopsis for special regulations. During the warmer months keep a watch out for rattlesnakes. I was once stalked by a cougar while walking this trail.

A one way trip can be made from Moss Springs Trailhead to Minam by combining this trail with Moss Springs/Horse Ranch. See Hike 51 Moss Springs/Horse Ranch. This requires a car shuttle. One can also fly in to the Horse Ranch and then hike down the Minam River to Minam.

42   UPPER MINAM RIVER

Trail 1673

General description: A long but easy backpack of 26.4 miles, from Minam Lake, down the Minam River to the Horse Ranch. This is a main trail through the western part of Eagle Cap Wilderness. Many other trails connect with the Upper Minam River Trail.
Difficulty: Easy, but long.
Trail maintenance: Yearly or more often if needed.
Best season: Mid-June through October.
Traffic: Moderate, except heavy during fall hunting seasons, with moderate horse traffic.
Elevation loss: 3,780 feet.
Maximum elevation: 7,380 feet.
Maps: Imus Geographics Wallowa Mountains Eagle Cap Wilderness, or Eagle Cap Mountain, Steamboat Lake, China Cap, and Jim White Ridge USGS quads.
For more information: U.S. Forest Service at Wallowa Mountain Visitors Center, Enterprise, Oregon.
Finding the trail: The Upper Minam River Trail begins at the south end of Minam Lake. It starts at the junction of the Minam Lake/Mirror Lakes Trail 1661 and the West Fork Lostine River Trail. See Hike 19 Minam Lake/Mirror Lake. This junction is 6 miles south of Two Pan Trailhead. The elevation at the junction is 7,380 feet. See Hike 21 West Fork Lostine River.

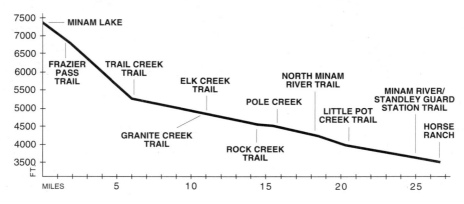

0.0	Minam Lake and trail junction with West Fork Lostine River Trail.
2.0	Trail junction with Frazier Pass Trail.
6.1	Trail junction with Trail Creek Trail.
10.4	Trail junction with Granite Creek Trail.
10.5	Trail junction with Elk Creek Trail.
13.0	Trail crosses Last Chance Creek.
14.6	Trail junction with Rock Creek Trail.
15.9	Trail crosses Pole Creek.
18.6	Trail junction with North Minam River Trail.
20.6	Trail junction with Little Pot Creek Trail.
24.9	Trail junction with Minam River/Standley Guard Station Trail.
26.4	Trail junction with Moss Springs/Horse Ranch Trail and the Horse Ranch.

The trail: From the junction the trail heads south a few yards to the junction with Blue Lake Trail 1673A. See Hike 20 Blue Lake. Blue Lake Trail turns off to the right (west). A small stream runs down the trail for a short distance 0.3 mile past Blue Lake Trail junction. There is another small creek crossing with a bridge 0.8 mile from the junction. The trail crosses another creek 325 yards after crossing the bridge. In 0.25 mile the trail crosses the Minam River. There is no bridge here, but there is a log jam on which to cross just below the trail crossing. The elevation here is 6,880 feet. After crossing the Minam River, the trail heads down the right (west) side of the river 0.7 mile to the junction with Frazier Pass Trail 1947. Frazier Pass Trail turns left (east) at the junction (El 6,750 ft.). See Hike 81 Frazier Pass. There is a large meadow to the left (east)

Upper Minam Trail near Frazier Pass Trail junction. *Photo by Gary Fletcher.*

of the trail at the junction. Around the fringes of the meadow are several camp-sites. This meadow and the campsites around it are often used by parties with stock, as there is grazing available here. The meadow areas along the Upper Minam River are heavily used by elk as summer range.

After passing Frazier Pass Trail junction, the trail crosses several small streams and makes a few switchbacks as it makes its way, dropping gently to the junction with Trail Creek Trail 1922. The Trail Creek Trail junction (El 5,320 ft.) is 4.1 miles from the junction with Frazier Pass Trail and 6.1 miles from Minam Lake. See Hike 76 Trail Creek. By the time we get to this junction the forest has changed from the canadian zone forest we saw at Minam Lake to transitional zone forest. Here the trees are fir, tamarack, spruce, and some ponderosa pine. The direction which the trail is heading has also changed. After leaving Minam Lake, the trail was heading southeast; now at Trail Creek Trail junction it has turned around and is going northwest.

There is a good campsite to the left of the trail next to the river, 3.3 miles past the Trail Creek Trail junction. The junction with Granite Creek Trail 1676 (El 4,920 ft.) is 250 yards past the campsite. See Hike 46 Granite Creek. Granite Creek Trail turns off to the right (north). After passing Granite Creek Trail, Elk Creek Trail junction is 200 yards farther down the Minam River Trail. Elk Creek Trail 1944 turns to the left (south) and crosses the Minam River. See Hike 67 Elk Creek. Elk Creek Trail junction is 10.4 miles from Minam Lake.

After passing Elk Creek Trail, our trail crosses four streams in the 2.6 miles to Last Chance Creek. Some of the area between Elk Creek and Last Chance Creek looks like it was logged many years ago. There are old stumps, and the trail is quite wide in places. There is no bridge at Last Chance Creek, but there are logs across it a short distance upstream.

The junction with Rock Creek Trail 1905 is 1.6 miles past Last Chance Creek. There are good campsites on Rock Creek Trail across the river from the junction, but there is no bridge. This crossing is easy during times of low water but could be dangerous during times of heavy run-off. Rock Creek Trail junction (El 4,590 ft.) is 14.6 miles from Minam Lake. See Hike 56 Rock Creek. The trail crosses Pole Creek 1.3 miles past Rock Creek Trail junction. There is no bridge over Pole Creek either. The elevation is 4,470 feet at Pole Creek crossing. In the next 1.3 miles the trail crosses three small streams. After the third stream crossing the trail goes through a stand of yew trees, for about 0.25 mile. Yew is not very common in Eastern Oregon; it is generally found in wetter climates. About 1 mile past the small yew stand is the bridge over North Fork Minam River (El 4,220 ft.). Just past the bridge is the junction with the North Minam River Trail 1675. This junction is 18.6 miles from Minam Lake. See Hike 43 North Minam River.

Just past the junction, there are two large stream crossings without bridges. The trail climbs to a saddle 0.9 mile past the streams. This climb is to avoid the steep terrain next to the river. After crossing the saddle, the trail drops down and crosses two small streams. The junction with Little Pot Creek Trail 1919 (El 4,080 ft.) is 1.1 miles past the saddle. See Hike 55 Little Pot Creek.

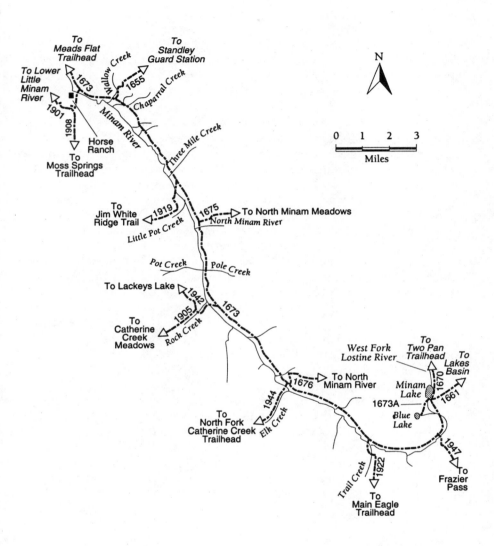

N

0   1   2   3
Miles

To Meads Flat Trailhead

To Standley Guard Station

To Lower Little Minam River

Wallow Creek

1673

1655

Chaparral Creek

1901

1908

Minam River

Horse Ranch

To Moss Springs Trailhead

Three Mile Creek

To Jim White Ridge Trail

1919

1675

To North Minam Meadows

North Minam River

Little Pot Creek

Pot Creek

Pole Creek

To Lackeys Lake

1942

1673

To Catherine Creek Meadows

1905

Rock Creek

West Fork Lostine River

To Two Pan Trailhead

To Lakes Basin

To North Minam River

1676

Minam Lake

1670

1661

1673A

Blue Lake

1944

Elk Creek

To North Fork Catherine Creek Trailhead

1947

To Frazier Pass

Trail Creek

1922

To Main Eagle Trailhead

Source: Imus Geographics

117

The area around this junction is known as Big Burn. There are many flowers in the meadow at Big Burn. Native hawthorn trees with their white flowers or red berries, depending on the season, are common here also. There is a red digger colony here too.

One-half mile past Little Pot Creek Trail junction, the trail crosses Three Mile Creek. It crosses an unnamed creek 1.25 miles past Three Mile Creek. Garwood Creek crossing is 0.5 mile farther, and another 0.25 mile is Whoopee Creek. One and one fourth miles past Whoopee Creek is Chaparral Creek. The junction with Trail 1665 is 0.5 mile past Chaparral Creek. Trail 1665 turns to the right (north), and goes up to Standley Guard Station. See Hike 40 Minam River/Standley Guard Station.

After going 300 yards past the junction, the trail crosses Wallowa Creek. It is another 1.5 miles from Wallowa Creek to the junction with Moss Springs/Horse Ranch Trail 1908. This junction (El 3,600 ft.) is 26.4 miles from Minam Lake. Just before reaching the junction, there is a pond on the left side of the trail. Watch for muskrats in the pond. See Hike 51 Moss Springs/Horse Ranch. For the rest of the Minam River Trail see Hike 41 Lower Minam River section in this book.

The Horse Ranch is 100 yards west of the junction on the Moss Springs/Horse Ranch Trail. There is an air strip here, as well as a lodge and some cabins which now belong to the Forest Service. If you follow the trail across the airstrip and go a short distance farther, the trail to Minam Lodge turns off to the right. Minam Lodge is a short distance down the side trail. It is possible to fly in or out of here. Check with Spence Air Service in Enterprise, Oregon. There are many possible campsites in the area around the Horse Ranch. However, there is some private land in this area; probably the best campsites are east of the Minam River on forest service land upstream from the bridge. Do not camp on or near the airstrip.

Fishing can be good all along the Minam River. Check the current fishing regulations, as there may be some special regulations for this river. There are many more campsites than I have mentioned. The entire area abounds with wildlife, big and small, and the meadows are covered with flowers in spring and early summer, and all summer near Minam Lake. The Minam River Trail is the main trunk trail in the western Wallowa Mountains. The possible side and loop trips off of it are too numerous to name here. See Hikes 43, 46, 55, 56, 57 and 81.

Trail 1675

General description: A backpack of 13.5 miles from the Minam River Trail to Copper Creek Trail.
Difficulty: Moderate to strenuous.
Best season: Mid-July through September.
Trail maintenance: Yearly.
Traffic: Moderate, with moderate horse traffic.
Elevation gain: 4,200 feet.
Maximum elevation: 8,420 feet.
Maps: Imus Geographics Wallowa Mountain Eagle Cap Wilderness, or Jim White Ridge, North Minam Meadows and Steamboat Lake USGS quads.
For more information: U.S. Forest Service at Wallowa Mountain Visitors Center, Enterprise, Oregon.
Finding the trail: North Minam River Trail begins at the junction with Minam River Trail 1673. This junction is 7.8 miles upstream from The Horse Ranch and the junction with Moss Springs/Horse Ranch Trail, or 18.6 miles down river from Minam Lake. See Hike 42 Upper Minam River. The elevation at the junction is 4,220 feet.

0.0	Trail junction with Upper Minam River Trail.
1.1	Trail crosses Sturgill Creek.
3.6	Falls in Little Minam River.
4.2	Trail junction with Green Lake Trail.
4.3	North Minam Meadows.
4.5	Trail junction with Bowman Trail.

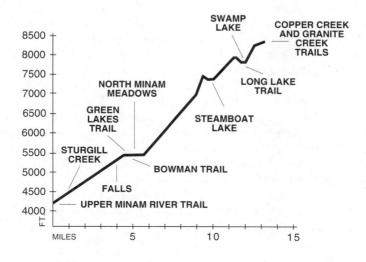

9.8   Steamboat Lake.
11.0   Pass.
11.3   Trail junction with Long Lake Trail.
12.8   Trail junction with Copper Creek and Granite Creek Trails.

The trail: The North Minam River Trail turns east off the Upper Minam River Trail. It fords a large stream, which is part of the North Minam River, 100 yards from the junction. After crossing the stream, the trail climbs steeply. It crosses Sturgill Creek 1.1 miles from the junction. The elevation at Sturgill Creek crossing is 4,580 feet. There is no bridge here either.

The trail crosses seven, small to very small streams in the next 2.5 miles as it climbs to the falls in the North Minam River. The falls (El 5,360 ft.) are a short distance to the right of the trail. One-third mile past the falls the trail crosses another small stream. Here there is an open area with a campsite to the right of the trail. After crossing the open area for 0.25 mile, the trail goes back into the woods. A few yards into the woods is the junction with Green Lake Trail 1666. Green Lake Trail turns to the right (southwest). This junction is 4.2 miles from the Minam River Trail. See Hike 44 Green Lake. Just past the junction , the trail enters North Minam Meadows (El 5,440 ft.).

After passing Green Lake Trail junction, the trail crosses two streams in the 0.3 mile to the junction with the Bowman Trail 1651. The Bowman Trail turns to the left (northeast). See Hike 26 Bowman. There are lots of campsites here along the edge of North Minam Meadows. Watch for elk feeding in the meadows early and late in the day.

The trail is fairly flat for the first mile past the Bowman Trail junction, but then it begins to climb. The trail is badly eroded in places in this area. It crosses a small stream 0.6 mile after it starts to climb. Seventy-five yards after crossing the stream, the trail makes a switchback to the left. There was a bear here in 1994 when we hiked this trail. The trail makes seven switchbacks, and crosses the small streams several times in the next 2 miles. It also climbs about 1,000 feet elevation in these switchbacks. The switchback area is mostly open slope with only scattered trees.

After going 200 yards past the last switchback, the trail crosses a very small stream (El 6,990 ft.). It then goes up through and around the head of a small alpine valley. One hundred fifty yards up the valley it crosses the same small stream again. In the next mile the trail crosses several small streams, then it comes to a larger one (El 7,140 ft.). Just past the larger stream crossing there is a view back down to North Minam Meadows. The trail then makes a switchback to the left. There is another stream crossing 0.25 mile past the switchback. Two hundred yards past the stream crossing, there is a pond 100 yards to the right of the trail. The trail crosses nine more small streams in the next 0.8 mile, to where Steamboat Lake comes into view. Along the way to the lake it climbs 100 vertical feet above the lake level, then drops back down. Before reaching the lake the trail goes around some granite outcroppings. On these outcroppings scratch marks can be seen. These were made when the

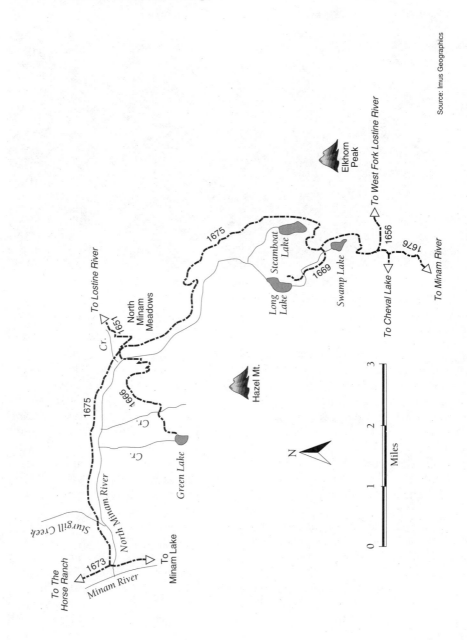

Source: Imus Geographics

Elkhorn Peak

To West Fork Lostine River

1675

1656

1676

To Minam River

Steamboat Lake

To Lostine River

North Minam Meadows

1651

Cr.

Long Lake

1669

Swamp Lake

To Cheval Lake

1675

1666

Cr.

Hazel Mt.

Cr.

Green Lake

N

Miles

3

2

1

0

Sturgill Creek

North Minam River

To The Horse Ranch

1673

Minam River

To Minam Lake

Steamboat Lake. *Photo by Gary Fletcher.*

glaciers dragged rocks beneath them over exposed bedrock. Steamboat Lake (El 7,363 ft.) is 9.8 miles from the Minam River Trail.

There are several campsites and lots of fish at Steamboat Lake. The trail goes around the left (east) side of Steamboat Lake and crosses the open, lush, green, marshy meadow at its head. There are several small streams in the meadow. At the upper (south) end of the meadow it crosses a larger stream, and then begins to climb. The trail crosses three more small streams. It climbs along the hillside temporarily heading north. In the next 0.5 mile the trail makes six switchbacks as it climbs the ridge southwest of Steamboat Lake. Above these switchbacks the trail heads north northwest for 300 yards. It then switchbacks to the left again. A few yards past this switchback the trail turns to the right and soon flattens out at 7,680 feet elevation.

After going 125 yards on fairly flat ground there are some ponds to the right of the trail. After passing the ponds, the trail heads southwest and slightly up for 250 yards, to a pass (El 7,960 ft.). The trail crosses the pass and drops for 0.25 mile to the junction with Long Lake Trail 1669. See Hike 45 Long Lake. After passing Long Lake Trail junction, the trail goes south around the left (east) side of Swamp Lake (El 7,837 ft.). Swamp Lake, 11.4 miles from the Minam River Trail, sits at the head of a magnificent glacial valley. The area is very open and alpine with snow drifts lasting late into the summer. There are lots of fish and several campsites available here.

The trail crosses the meadow at the south end of Swamp Lake. It then switchbacks up the ridge to the west nearly to the top. Here the trail levels out a bit (El 8,320 ft.) and heads south. It then climbs slightly for 0.5 mile to the junction with Copper Creek Trail 1656 and Granite Creek Trail 1676. The elevation at the junction is 8,420 feet. See Hike 23 Copper Creek and Hike 46 Granite Creek.

This trail may be difficult to follow above Swamp Lake before late summer because of the snow. In early July 1994 when we hiked this trail there was still quite a bit of snow, and that was a fairly light snow year. The surrounding high alpine plateau may be covered with a variety of flowers in August. Finding your way over this open plateau area can be a problem during times of snow and poor visibility. For a loop trip this trail can be combined with Hikes 21, 42, 23.

This extended trip can be done by combining North Minam River Trail with West Fork Lostine River Trail, from Two Pan Trailhead to Minam Lake, then taking Upper Minam River Trail to the junction with North Minam Trail. Then follow the North Minam Trail as described above. At the junction of North Minam Trail and Copper Creek Trail, take Copper Creek Trail back down to the east to West Fork Lostine River Trail. Follow West Fork Lostine Trail for 2.6 miles north back to Two Pan Trailhead. This makes a 47.4 mile loop with only 2.6 miles of the trail that is hiked twice. Allow at least three days to make this loop, but four or five days is better.

44 GREEN LAKE

Trail 1666

General description: A day hike or short backpack of 4 miles, from a camp at North Minam Meadows to Green Lake.
Difficulty: Moderate.
Trail maintenance: Yearly.
Best season: Mid-June through October.
Traffic: Moderate, with moderate horse traffic.
Elevation gain: 1,570 feet.
Maximum elevation: 7,000 feet.

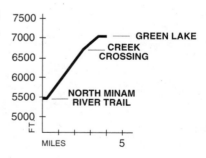

Map: North Minam Meadows USGS quad.
For more information: U.S. Forest Service at Wallowa Mountain Visitors Center, Enterprise, Oregon.
Finding the trail: The Green Lake Trail leaves North Minam Trail 1675 just north of the north end of North Minam Meadows. The elevation here is 5,430 feet. This junction is 4.2 miles up the North Minam Trail from Minam River Trail. See Hike 43 North Minam and Hike 42 Upper Minam River.

0.0	North Minam Meadows, and trail junction with North Minam River Trail 1675.
3.2	Trail enters burned area.
4.0	Trail ends at the south end of Green Lake.

The trail: Green Lake Trail heads west off the North Minam Trail and crosses the North Minam River on a bridge 100 yards from the junction. In the first 1.9 miles after crossing the bridge the trail makes seven switchbacks. In these switchbacks it crosses the same stream several times and gains 800 feet in elevation. Above the switchbacks, the trail flattens out and rounds a point. It soon begins to climb gently again. The trail crosses a creek (El 6,700 ft.) 0.7 mile past the last switchback. It comes to a small burn area 0.5 mile past the creek crossing. The trail makes another switchback 0.25 mile, past the burn area. Green Lake is 300 yards past this switchback. The elevation of Green Lake is 6,999 feet.

There is a campsite on a small rise at the north end of the lake. The trail goes around the east side of the lake to a meadow on the south end. There is another campsite 100 yards south of the lake at the edge of this lush green meadow. There are fish, brook trout, for the taking in Green Lake. The comparatively low elevation makes for denser forest than is found at most of the lakes in the Wallowas. As usual watch for animals; the rock slide at the head of the lake has some pikas in it. In the summer these little "rock rabbits" will

44   *Green Lake*

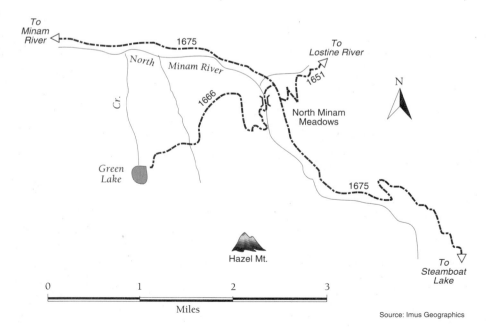

Source: Imus Geographics

Green Lake. *Photo by Gary Fletcher.*

be drying hay on top of the boulders and making their high pitched calls to announce your presence. These little animals do not hibernate and need the hay to survive the long harsh winter. In July 1994, when we hiked this trail, a yearling bear ran across in front of us and quickly scrambled up the nearest tree when he became aware we were there. We also saw elk along this trail. The return trip is made by the same trail.

45   LONG LAKE

Trail 1669

General description: A short hike of 1.3 miles from a camp on the North Minam River Trail near Swamp Lake to Long Lake.
Difficulty: Strenuous but short, with route finding required.
Trail maintenance: Seldom to none.
Best season: July through September.
Traffic: Light.
Elevation loss: 732 feet.
Maximum elevation: 7,840 feet.
Map: Steamboat Lake USGS quad.

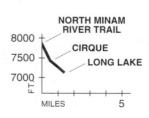

For more information: U.S. Forest Service at Wallowa Mountain Visitors Center, Enterprise, Oregon.

Finding the trail: Long Lake Trail begins at the junction with North Minam Trail 1675 (El 7,840 ft.), a short distance north of Swamp Lake. See Hike 43 North Minam River.

0.0	Trail junction with North Minam River Trail.
0.5	Bottom of cirque.
1.3	Long Lake.

The trail: The Long Lake Trail heads west from the junction with North Minam Trail. At first it drops through small, green meadows and smooth, glacier-carved, light gray, granite outcroppings. The trail crosses a couple of streams then drops to the bottom of a pretty little glacial cirque with a stream flowing through it. The trail is very badly eroded, where it drops steeply into the cirque. There are two possible paths just before getting to the bottom. One crosses the steam and the other doesn't. From above the trail can be seen in

45   Long Lake

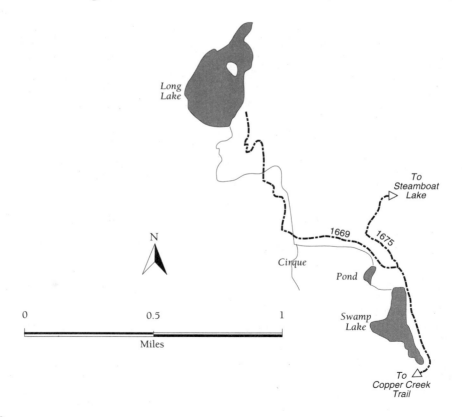

the grassy area in the bottom of the cirque. The elevation at the bottom of the cirque is 7,410 feet.

The trail crosses the stream at the north end of the cirque. It stays on the left side of the stream for about 0.3 mile. It then crosses the stream and heads north northwest to Long Lake (El 7,117 ft.).

The part of the trail below the cirque is braided and not well maintained. It is difficult to tell which path is the right one. Remember that the stream that flows out of the cirque flows into Long Lake. So one can follow it if need be.

This is a steep trail and requires some route finding. The distance to Long Lake is only a little over 1 mile, but it may seem much farther. There are campsites at the south end of Long Lake, and the fishing can be quite good. The return trip is made by the same trail.

46   GRANITE CREEK

Trail 1676

General description: A steep 5 mile connecting trail from the junction of Copper Creek and North Minam Trails to the Upper Minam River Trail.
Difficulty: Strenuous.
Trail maintenance: Infrequent.
Best season: Mid-July through September.
Traffic: Light, with light horse traffic.
Elevation loss: 4,500 feet, if going south.
Maximum elevation: 8,420 feet.
Map: Steamboat Lake USGS quad.
For more information: U.S. Forest Service at Wallowa Mountain Visitors Center, Enterprise, Oregon.
Finding the trail: Granite Creek Trail begins at the junction of North Minam Trail

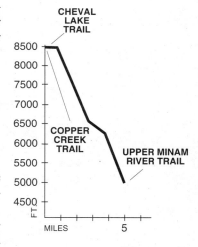

1675 and Copper Creek Trail 1656. See Hike 23 Copper Creek and Hike 43 North Minam River. This junction is on a plateau, above and south of Swamp Lake. The elevation at the junction is 8,420 feet.

0.0	Trail junction with Copper Creek and North Minam River Trails.
0.3	Trail junction with Cheval Lake Trail.
2.9	Beginning of long traverse.
3.8	End of long traverse.
5.0	Trail junction with Minam River Trail.

The trail: The area around the junction where Granite Creek Trail begins is open timberline country. There are granite boulders and a few groves of small alpine trees. From the junction, Granite Creek Trail heads south 0.3 mile to the unmarked junction with Cheval Lake Trail (El 8,420 ft.). Cheval Lake Trail turns to the right (west). See Hike 47 Cheval Lake Trail. After passing Cheval Lake Trail, Granite Creek Trail crosses several stream beds that were dry in September when we walked this trail. About 250 yards past the Cheval Lake Trail junction the trail starts to drop towards the Minam River. The trail makes a switchback to the left. It then winds its way down through granite outcroppings and meadows. There are some stream beds in the meadows. These were all dry in September.

46   *Granite Creek*
47   *Cheval Lake*

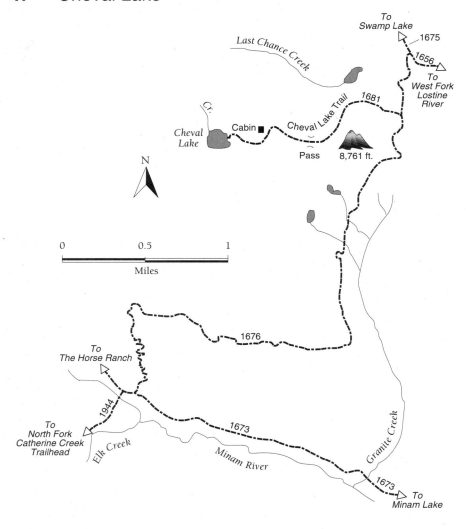

After going 0.6 mile from Cheval Lake Trail junction, the trail begins to traverse on the west side of Granite Creek Canyon, also known as Granite Gulch. The elevation at the beginning of the traverse is about 8,000 feet. After traversing for 0.3 mile, the trail starts to switch back again. It makes eight switchbacks in the next 0.25 mile to where there are a couple of dry (in September) stream crossings. The trail winds down through open woods for 325 yards. It then makes four more switchbacks and comes to a small spring which is on the left side of the trail.

After going 0.3 mile past the spring, the trail begins another series of switchbacks. It makes six switchbacks in the next 0.25 mile. This area is open forest with large open areas. The first ponderosa pines on this trail start to show up at the bottom of the last switchbacks. As usual, the upper limit for ponderosa pine is about 6,500 feet elevation.

The trail makes a long traverse after the last switchback. After traversing for 0.9 mile, there is a small stream crossing. The traverse ends with a switchback to the left 200 yards past the stream crossing. The elevation here is about 6,200 feet.

After the traverse the trail makes twenty-three switchbacks in the 1.2 miles to the junction with the Upper Minam River Trial 1673 (El 4,920 ft.). It also drops 1,280 feet in this distance at a grade of about 10 percent. See Hike 42 Upper Minam River.

This trail is easy to follow most of the way. There were several dry stream crossings which would likely have water earlier in the summer. Heading north from the Minam River Trail to the junction with Copper Creek Trail is a steep climb.

47   CHEVAL LAKE

Trail 1681

General description: A 1.7 mile hike from Granite Creek Trail to Cheval Lake.
Difficulty: Strenuous.
Trail maintenance: Seldom to none. This trail is no longer maintained by the forest service.
Best season: Mid-July through September.
Traffic: Very light.
Elevation gain: 540 feet. Loss: 1,157 feet.
Maximum elevation: 8,730 feet.

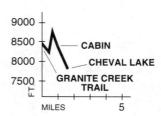

Maps: Older Eagle Cap Wilderness maps. Steamboat Lake USGS quad covers the area, but the trail is not shown on this map.
For more information: U.S. Forest Service at Wallowa Mountain Visitors Center, Enterprise, Oregon.

Finding the trail: Cheval Lake Trail turns west off Granite Creek Trail 1676, 0.3 mile south of the junction with Copper Creek Trail. The elevation at the unmarked junction with Granite Creek Trail is 8,420 feet.

0.0	Unmarked trail junction with Granite Creek Trail.
0.3	Meadow.
0.6	Top of main ridge.
0.7	Pass.
1.0	Ahalt cabin.
1.7	Cheval Lake.

The trail: At the junction with Granite Creek Trail, Cheval Lake Trail heads west. It drops 230 feet in the first 0.25 mile, to a meadow. The trail crosses two streams in the meadow. There is a pond on the left of the trail at the second stream crossing. After crossing the meadow, the trail climbs to the top of a spur ridge (El 8,320 ft.).

The trail goes southwest up the spur ridge for 0.3 mile to the top of the main ridge (El 8,590 ft.). This ridge divides Last Chance Creek and Minam River drainages. Here the trail turns right and climbs for 300 yards to a pass (El 8,730 ft.). It makes five switchbacks before reaching the pass. From here Cheval Lake can be seen far below to the west. The peak a few yards north of this pass is a good viewpoint. From the peak Last Chance Creek Canyon is below and to the north. You can also see the lake at the head of Last Chance Creek. This is a good place to see elk.

Cheval Lake and Ahalt Cabin. *Photo by Lowell Euhus.*

The trail descends to the northwest for 0.25 mile. It then drops off to the left. After going 125 yards more, there is a cabin on the right side of the trail. This cabin was built by a miner and part-time hermit named Harold Ahalt. It is very small, only 6 x 8 feet. The cabin is in fairly good condition and has a stove inside. The elevation at the cabin is 8,360 feet. There is a mine above and east of the cabin. Please do not disturb the cabin.

Below the cabin the trail makes three switchbacks. It then drops into a small meadow about 50 yards wide. The trail is difficult to see in the meadow. Bear slightly to the left and look for blazes on the trees on the far side. Cross the meadow and stream bed, which was dry in September 1994, and then begin to drop steeply down. Watch for cairns. After dropping 300 yards, the trail climbs slightly 15 feet to the right. It then drops steeply again, making 4 switchbacks, before reaching Cheval Lake (El 7,801 ft.). There is a nice camp-site on the east side of the lake. Cheval Lake is 1.7 miles from Granite Creek Trail and is a very isolated place to camp. It is possible to camp here for some time without seeing another party.

The trail is difficult to see just above the lake. There are several possible routes to take in the last 150 vertical feet. Much of the trail is steep and rocky. Some route finding skills are required to get to Cheval Lake. Return by using the same trail.

48   ROCK SPRINGS

Trail 1928

General description: A 3.5 mile hike one way, from Rock Springs Trailhead to the Little Minam River. This trail reaches The Little Minam River near its confluence with the Minam River.

Difficulty: Moderate to strenuous.
Trail maintenance: Infrequent.
Best season: June through October.
Traffic: Light, with light horse traffic.
Elevation loss: 2,270 feet, heading east.
Maximum elevation: 5,850 feet.
Map: Mount Moriah USGS quad.
For more information: U.S. Forest Service at Wallowa Mountain Visitors Center, Enterprise, Oregon.
Finding the trail: Rock Springs begins at Rock Springs Trailhead. Rock Springs Trailhead can be reached from Oregon Highway 82 by turning south on Hindman Road 9.4 miles west of the town of Minam. Head south on Hindman Road for 7.2 miles. At this point Hindman Road becomes Minam Rim Road, Forest Road 62. Go 11 miles more on FR 62 to Rock Springs Trailhead. The elevation at the trailhead is 5,850 feet.

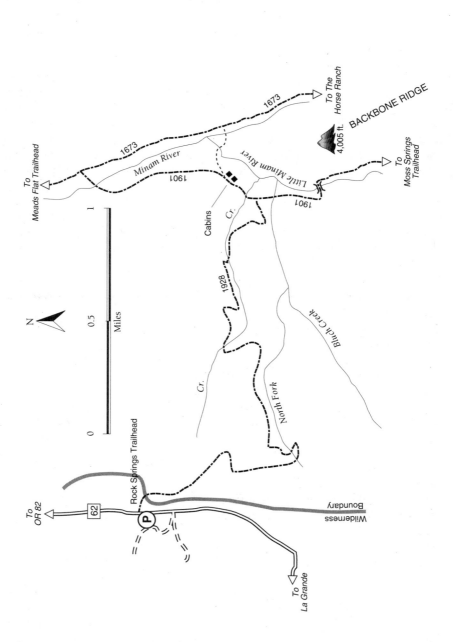

0.0	Trail begins at Rock Springs Trailhead.
1.1	Trail crosses North Fork Bluch Creek.
1.9	Trail crosses ridge line.
3.5	Trail junction with Little Minam River Trail.

The trail: From the parking area at Rock Springs, walk back north for 80 yards on FR 62 to where the trail heads east from the road. From this point the trail heads down into the canyon.

Head down the trail (east) past the wilderness boundary signs. There were two signs when I hiked this trail in June 1994. The first sign is 60 yards down, and the second is in an open area (El 5,720 ft.) with a view of the Minam and Little Minam River Canyons. The rugged dark brown ridge visible between the Minam and Little Minam Canyons is Backbone Ridge. From here the trail goes down a ridge another 125 yards then drops off to the right.

The trail crosses the North Fork of Bluch Creek (El 5,100 ft.) 1.1 miles from the trailhead. One hundred seventy-five yards past the creek crossing is a switchback. The trail crosses the North Fork of Bluch Creek again in another 120 yards.

At 1.9 miles, the trail crosses a ridgeline (El 4,550 ft.). It crosses another stream 350 yards after crossing the ridgeline. Three-fourths mile after crossing the ridgeline, the trail makes a couple of switchbacks. One hundred twenty yards past the switchbacks, the trail crosses the same stream again. One-fourth mile past the last creek crossing, the trail makes another switchback, very close to, but not crossing, Bluch Creek (El 3,680 ft.). The junction with the Little Minam Trail 1901 (El 3,580 ft.) is 175 yards farther.

Trail 1928 is easy to follow; however, it does lose quite a bit of elevation. The total distance from Rock Springs to the Little Minam River Trail is 3.5 miles. See Hike 49 Lower Little Minam River. Watch for mule deer, elk and bear along this trail. The fishing is usually pretty good in the Little Minam River.

---

49   LOWER LITTLE MINAM RIVER

Trail 1901

General description: A 6.3 mile backpack, along the Little Minam River from the Moss Springs/Horse Ranch Trail to the confluence of the Little Minam and Minam Rivers, and the Lower Minam River Trail.

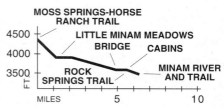

Difficulty: Easy.

Trail maintenance: Yearly.

Best season: May through October, although access to the trail from the Moss Springs and Rock Springs Trailheads may be blocked by snow until mid-June.

For early season trips you may need to hike up the Minam River, or fly into The Horse Ranch. The best time for the flowers is June.

Traffic: Light, except during fall hunting seasons, with light to moderate horse traffic.

Elevation loss: 900 feet.

Maximum elevation: 4,330 feet.

Maps: Imus Geographics Wallowa Mountains Eagle Cap Wilderness, or Mount Fanny and Mount Moriah USGS quads.

For more information: U.S. Forest Service at Wallowa Mountain Visitors Center, Enterprise, Oregon. For flying in contact Spence Air Service in Enterprise, Oregon.

Finding the trail: The Little Minam River Trail leaves the Moss Springs/Horse Ranch Trail 1908, 1 mile south of The Horse Ranch (El 4,330 ft.). See Hike 51 Moss Springs/Horse Ranch.

49   *Lower Little Minam River*

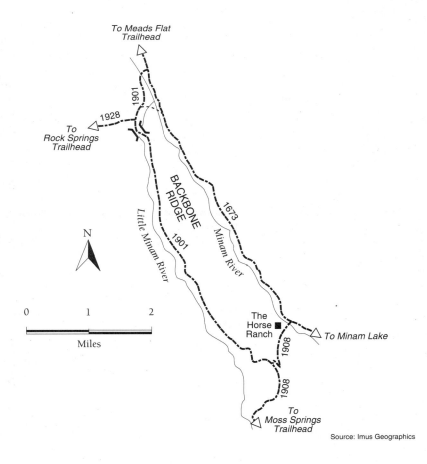

Source: Imus Geographics

0.0	Trail begins at the junction with Moss Springs/Horse Ranch Trail.
1.0	Little Minam Meadows.
5.3	Trail junction with Rock Springs Trail.
6.3	Trail crosses Minam River and trail junction with Lower Minam River Trail.

The trail: From the junction with Moss Springs/Horse Ranch Trail the trail traverses to the northwest and drop slightly. When we walked this section of the trail in early summer there was a bear ripping apart a log below the trail. The bear was looking for grubs in the rotten wood and left at our approach. After about 1 mile of traversing along the west side of Backbone Ridge, the trail drops into Little Minam Meadows.

Little Minam Meadows is a semi-open area 1 mile long at 3,850 feet elevation. There are many campsites and plenty of firewood in Little Minam Meadows. There are also plenty of mule deer in the area. The trail stays along the right side of the opener meadow area.

After passing Little Minam Meadows, the trail stays east of the Little Minam River along the bottom of Backbone Ridge. There is very little water along this section of trail. You can drop down to the Little Minam River, but this can be quite a climb in places.

Three miles below Little Minam Meadows the trail crosses the Little Minam River on a bridge (El 3,550 ft.). It crosses Bluch Creek 0.25 mile past the bridge. One hundred seventy-five yards past Bluch Creek is the junction with Rock Springs Trail 1928 (El 3,580 ft.). Trail 1928 comes down from Rock Springs, Trailhead on the Minam Rim Road FR 62. See Hike 48 Rock Springs.

One hundred twenty-five yards past the junction the trail enters a meadow. Here there are some old cabins a short distance to the right of the trail. There is also the remains of some old farm machinery and a colony of red diggers (ground squirrels) in the meadow. The trail forks 100 yards past the cabins. Take the left (north) fork. The right fork is a shortcut for parties that are going up the Minam River. One-third mile past the cabins is an old wood fence. The trail crosses the Minam River 0.4 mile past the fence. Crossing the Minam River is very dangerous during high water. People have drowned, even on horseback. It is generally better not to try to cross the Minam River here on foot except during low water times. The area between the cabins and the river crossing is a great place to camp, watch the wildlife, look at the flowers, fish in the Minam and Little Minam Rivers, and relax.

After crossing the river, the trail goes 300 yards through an open area to the junction with the Lower Minam River Trail 1673 (El 3,430 ft.), The flowers in this area are excellent in June and July, but the rivers are high and dangerous. There is an excellent campsite on the east side of the Minam River between the river and the Lower Minam River Trail. See Hike 41 Lower Minam River.

A return trip can be made to the Horse Ranch via the Lower Minam River Trail during times of low water for crossing the Minam River. From the Horse Ranch it is only 1 mile back to the start of the Lower Little Minam River Trail via Moss Springs/Horse Ranch Trail. See Hikes 41 and 51.

Trail 1942

General description: A day hike or backpack in the Upper Little Minam River Canyon. This trail is 7.8 miles long, from Moss Springs Trailhead to the junction with Jim White Ridge, Cartwheel Ridge and Lackeys Hole Trails.

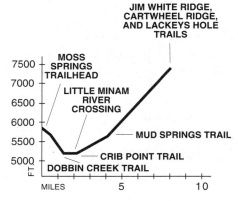

Difficulty: Moderate.
Trail maintenance: Yearly.
Best season: Mid-June through October.
Traffic: Moderate, with moderate horse traffic. Traffic is heaviest during October and November hunting seasons.
Elevation gain: 2,180 feet. Loss: 580 feet.
Maximum elevation: 7,400 feet.
Maps: Imus Geographics, Wallowa Mountains Eagle Cap Wilderness, or Mount Fanny, Jim White Ridge and China Cap USGS quads.
For more information: U.S. Forest Service at Wallowa Mountain Visitors Center, Enterprise, Oregon.
Finding the trail: To reach Moss Springs Trailhead, take Mill Creek Road, east from the town of Cove. Go 8 miles on Mill Creek Road (FR 6220) to Moss Springs Trailhead.

0.0	Trail begins at Moss Springs Trailhead.
2.0	Trail junction with Dobbin Creek Trail.
2.1	Trail crosses Little Minam River.
3.4	Trail junction with Mud Springs cut off Trail (unmarked).
7.8	Trail junction with Jim White Ridge, Lackeys Hole and Cartwheel Ridge Trails.

The trail: Upper Little Minam River Trail 1942 begins at Moss Springs Trailhead (El 5,800 ft.). At the start the Moss Springs/Horse Ranch Trail and Upper Little Minam River Trail are the same trail for a short distance. The trails fork 100 yards from the trailhead. At the fork the Upper Little Minam River Trail is to the right (southeast). From here the wide trail descends into the Little Minam River Canyon through a forest of lodgepole pine, fir and tamarack (western larch) trees.

Slightly more than 0.5 mile down, the trail makes a switchback to the left (El 5,600 ft.). The trail makes two more switchbacks in the next 0.75 mile to

Crossing the Little Minam River.

where it reaches the river bottom (El 5,200 ft.). Bears are common along this trail, especially in the first 2 miles.

A few yards after reaching the river bottom, the trail crosses Fireline Creek, then heads up the river to the southeast 0.75 mile more to the unmarked (as of August 1994) junction with Dobbin Creek Trail 1913 (El 5,250 ft.). See Hike 59 Dobbin Creek. Dobbin Creek Trail heads to the right (south). Keep on the main trail, which heads east. Past this junction the trail drops a few feet and crosses Dobbin Creek. A few yards past the creek crossing is the junction with Crib Point Trail 1909. See Hike 60 Crib Point. Crib Point Trail heads to the right (southeast). Just past the junction with Crib Point Trail, the Upper Little Minam Trail crosses the Little Minam River (El 5,220 ft.). A few yards upstream is a log on which to cross. The distance to the river crossing is 2.1 miles from the Moss Springs Trailhead.

After crossing the Little Minam River, the trail heads east up the Little Minam Canyon. It gradually gets farther away from the river, the farther up it goes. Six-tenths mile above the crossing, a path goes down to the right to a campsite. There is another campsite 0.3 mile farther along, also below the trail to the right. Between the campsites there are a couple of stream crossings. Four-tenths mile past the second campsite, the unmarked Mud Springs Cut-off Trail, heads up hill to the left (north). See Hike 53 Mud Springs Cut-off. There is another path to the left 300 yards before the Mud Springs Cut-off Trail. But this path fades out quickly. It may be just a game trail. The Mud Springs Cut-off

50   *Upper Little Minam River*

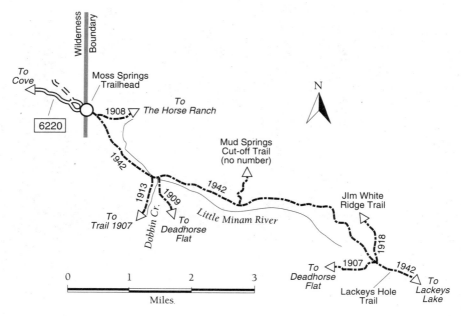

Source: Imus Geographics

Trail junction (E. 5,600 ft.) is 1.3 miles from the Little Minam River crossing and 3.4 miles from Moss Springs Trailhead.

The trail enters a burn area 1.1 miles past Mud Springs Cut-off Trail junction. The fire in this area, like most forest fires, did not burn all the timber. It left some patches of green trees. Watch for goldenrod in the burned area. After entering the burn area, the trail climbs with some switchbacks through fairly open country. There are many small stream beds in this area; however, most of them are dry in late summer. This semi-open area is excellent range for mule deer and elk.

Three and eight-tenths miles after passing the Mud Springs Cut-off Trail, in a saddle on the ridge dividing the Minam River and Little Minam River drainages, is the junction with Jim White Ridge, Lackeys Hole and Cartwheel Ridge Trails (El 7,400 ft.). See Hike 54 Jim White Ridge, Hike 57 Lackeys Hole, and Hike 61 Cartwheel Ridge. None of these trails are marked; however, there is a sign pointing back to the Little Minam River and ahead to Rock Creek on Lackeys Hole Trail. This junction is 7.8 miles from Moss Springs Trailhead. From the saddle and junction a loop can be made by turning right (southwest) and following Cartwheel Ridge Trail to Deadhorse Flat, then taking Crib Point Trail down to the Little Minam River Trail and returning to Moss Springs on the Little Minam River Trail. Other longer loops are possible. Check your map and the other trails mentioned above for the possibilities.

51 MOSS SPRINGS/HORSE RANCH

Trail 1908

General description: A 7.5 mile day hike from Moss Springs Trailhead to the Horse Ranch, or a starter for an extended backpack in the western Wallowa Mountains. This trail accesses Ben Point, Jim White Ridge, Lower Little Minam River, as well as the Upper and Lower Minam River Trails.

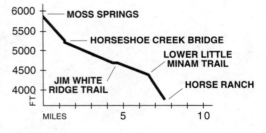

Difficulty: Easy to moderate.
Trail maintenance: Yearly.
Best season: June through October.
Traffic: Moderate to heavy, heaviest during fall hunting seasons, with moderate to heavy horse traffic.
Elevation Loss: 2,200 feet.
Maximum elevation: 5,800 feet.
Map: Mount Fanny USGS quad.

For more information: U.S. Forest Service at Wallowa Mountain Visitors Center, Enterprise, Oregon.

Finding the trail: Moss Springs/Horse Ranch Trail begins at Moss Springs Trailhead. For directions to the Moss Springs Trailhead, see Hike 50 Upper Little Minam River Trail.

0.0	Trail begins at Moss Springs Trailhead.
0.5	Trail junction with Ben Point Trail (unmarked).
1.5	Trail crosses bridge over Horseshoe Creek.
4.4	Trail crosses Little Minam River and trail junction with Jim White Ridge Trail.
6.5	Trail junction with Lower Little Minam River Trail.
7.5	Horse Ranch and trail junction with Minam River Trail.

The trail: From Moss Springs Trailhead (El 5,800 ft.) the Moss Springs/Horse Ranch Trail heads east. It forks 100 yards from the trailhead at the Eagle Cap Wilderness boundary. The right fork is the Upper Little Minam River Trail 1942. See Hike 50 Upper Little Minam River. Take the left fork and begin to descend to the east on mostly open grass-covered slopes into the Little Minam Canyon. The trail passes the unmarked Ben Point Trail 0.5 mile past the wilderness boundary. Watch for bears in this area, especially in late August and September when they may be chowing down on the abundant huckleberries.

At 1.5 miles the trail crosses a bridge over Horseshoe Creek (El 5,130 ft.). Just past the bridge, the rushing Little Minam River is close to the right (east)

The Horse Ranch.

side of the trail. One mile after crossing the bridge there is a campsite on the right between the trail and the river (El 4,950 ft.). One-half mile from the first campsite, is another campsite (El 4,870 ft.) with a path leading down to it. This campsite is also on the right side of the trail.

One and four-tenths more miles brings us to the ford across the Little Minam River. Between the last campsite and the ford there are several small stream crossings. There are also some groves of small yew trees, which are not common in Eastern Oregon. The trail forks just before the ford. Take the right (east) fork. There is a campsite here next to the river (El 4,560 ft.). This ford, through the icy cold waters of the Little Minam River, can be difficult in times of heavy runoff, but it is usually not a problem.

51   *Moss Springs/Horse Ranch*

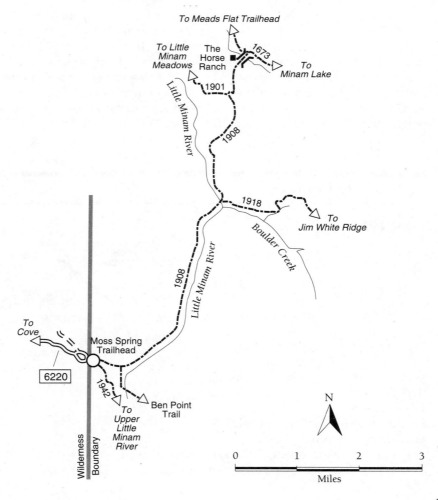

After crossing the river, the trail heads east for 100 yards to the junction with Jim White Ridge Trail 1918. See Hike 54 Jim White Ridge. The Moss Springs/Horse Ranch Trail turns left (north) at the junction. For the next 2.1 miles between the Jim White Ridge Trail junction and the Lower Little Minam River Trail 1901 junction the trail stays nearly level, except for the last 0.25 mile where it descends slightly. See Hike 49 Lower Little Minam River. The Lower Little Minam Trail junction (El 4,330 ft.) is in the saddle where Jim White Ridge and Backbone Ridge merge. The Moss Springs/Horse Ranch Trail bears right (north) at the junction.

Past the Lower Little Minam Trail junction the trail makes a few switchbacks and drops, through thick timber for 1 mile to the Horse Ranch (El 3,600 ft.). The trail crosses the airstrip and passes the ranch house. Past the buildings, the trail goes through a gate and over a small rise. It then crosses the Minam River on a bridge. Just after crossing the river is the junction with the Minam River Trail 1673. See Hike 41 Lower Minam River and Hike 42 Upper Minam River.

There are plenty of campsites along the Minam River near the Horse Ranch. However, there are a few sections of private land that must be respected. Please don't camp on or near the airstrip. It is best to camp on the east side of the Minam River above the bridge. This area is a great place for a base camp when exploring the many trails in the western Wallowa Mountains. Fishing is good in both the Minam and Little Minam Rivers. Return via the same trail or use Hikes 41 or 42 to make an extended backpack. It may also be possible to fly in and out of the Horse Ranch. Check with Spence Air Service in Enterprise, Oregon.

52   BEN POINT

Trail 1929

General description: A steep 5.4 mile "trail" connecting the Moss Springs/Horse Ranch Trail, with the Jim White Ridge Trial, via Mud Springs.

Difficulty: Strenuous, with much route finding required.

Trail maintenance: None, but a large part of this trail is in open country, so down logs are not much of a problem.

Best season: Mid-June through October.

Traffic: Light.

Elevation gain: 2,290 feet. Loss: 170 feet.

Maximum elevation: 7,590 feet.

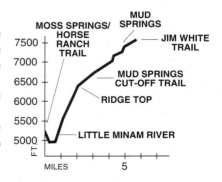

For more information: U.S. Forest Service at Wallowa Mountain Visitors Center, Enterprise, Oregon. Further information will probably be very limited.

Maps: Mount Fanny and Jim White Ridge USGS quads cover the area, but this trail is not shown on newer USGS quads or USFS maps. Trail is shown on old Eagle Cap maps, but they are hard to find.

Finding the trail: The Ben Point Trail starts at an unmarked junction (El 5,370 ft.) on the Moss Springs/Horse Ranch Trail 1908, 0.5 miles from the Moss Springs Trailhead. See Hike 51 Moss Springs/Horse Ranch.

0.0	Trail junction with Moss Springs/Horse Ranch Trail.
0.5	Trail crosses Little Minam River.
1.9	Top of ridge near Ben Point.
3.4	Trail junction with Mud Springs Cut-off Trail.
4.8	Mud Springs.
5.4	Trail junction with Jim White Ridge Trail.

The trail: The Ben Point Trail turns right (southeast) off the Moss Springs/ Horse Ranch Trail and switchbacks its way down to the Little Minam River, crossing four small muddy streams on the way. At 0.3 mile it reaches the Little Minam River. The trail heads up stream (south) for 300 yards crossing five more small streams to where it fords the calf deep Little Minam River. There is a path which bears right just before the crossing and heads up the river on the west side. This path connects with the Upper Little Minam River Trail but is unmaintained and becomes difficult to find in a short distance.

52   Ben Point
53   Mud Springs Cut-off

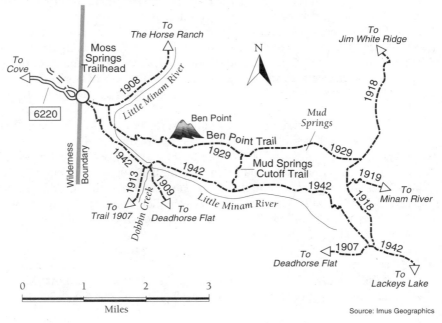

Source: Imus Geographics

After crossing the river, there is a campsite on the right side of the trail. The trail makes a switchback to the left 250 yards past the crossing. At the switchback there is a path going straight ahead up the river (southeast). This path fades out in a short distance, so be sure to turn left (northeast) at the switchback. The trail makes seventeen switchbacks in the next 1.4 miles as it works its way up to the top of the ridge near Ben Point (El 6,440 ft.). Up to the top of the ridge, the trail is steep, climbing through open forest of mostly Douglas-fir and ponderosa pine. On the ridge, subalpine fir trees start to appear.

The trail turns right (east) and heads up the ridge line. Two hundred fifty yards up the ridge there are lots of blowdowns that make detours off the trail necessary. The trail goes along the right (south) side of the ridgeline. There is a rock outcropping on the left side of the trail 0.5 mile up the ridge (El 6,540 ft.). Two hundred yards past the outcropping there are two more switchbacks. Two hundred yards farther and there is a large mud hole on the right side of the trail.

The trail heads north, then northeast, around another rock outcropping 0.5 mile past the mud hole. After passing the outcropping, the trail heads east. In a short distance there is a path taking off to the right. Bear left and head north for 250 yards to the junction with Mud Springs Cut-off Trail. At this unmarked junction the Cut-off Trail turns to the right (south). From the junction, the Ben Point Trail heads northeast 0.25 mile to another fork. This fork is in a semi-open area at 6,780 feet elevation. Take the right fork. The trail soon heads east, climbing gently through an open area. It goes through some timber for a few yards 0.4 mile past the fork. There are what appears to be a series of ditches on the hillside above the trail here. A quarter mile past the timber, the trail becomes badly eroded for 0.1 mile. The trail goes up steeply in the eroded area, then flattens out, and heads to the southeast. The old burn area of the Little Minam Fire can be seen several hundred yards below the trail, to the right here. The trail traverses the hillside for 0.25 mile, then turns uphill again. Mud Springs is up the hill 125 yards. The spring (El 7,280 ft.) is to the right of the trail. There is a campsite in some trees a few yards up the trail from the spring. Mud Springs is 4.8 miles from the junction with the Moss Springs/Horse Ranch Trail.

From the campsite, the trail heads southeast for 120 yards in the open, then enters a dense stand of timber for 200 yards. After going through the timber, it traverses an open hillside for 0.7 mile to the junction with the Jim White Ridge Trail 1918. This is an unmarked junction (El 7,590 ft.). See Hike 54 Jim White Ridge. At the junction the Ben Point Trail is more visible on the ground than is the Jim White Ridge Trail. In places the Ben Point Trail takes a lot of route finding ability to follow. There is generally no water available along this trail from the Little Minam River to Mud Springs.

A loop trip of 15.5 total miles can be made by returning on the Jim White Ridge Trail and the Upper Little Minam River Trail. To do this, turn right (south) at the junction. Take Jim White Ridge Trail to the Upper Little Minam River Trail and take it back to Moss Springs Trailhead. See Hikes 50 and 53.

A longer and more difficult loop of 19.1 miles total distance and nearly 1,000 feet more elevation gain can be done by turning left (north) on the Jim White Ridge Trail. Follow it down to the Moss Springs/Horse Ranch Trail and head left (southwest) on that trail to Moss Springs Trailhead. See Hike 51 Moss Springs/Horse Ranch.

53   MUD SPRINGS CUT-OFF

General description: A short but steep 1.75 mile trail connecting Ben Point Trail with Upper Little Minam River Trail.

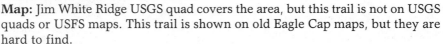

Difficulty: Strenuous.
Trail maintenance: None.
Best season: June through October.
Traffic: Light.
Elevation loss: 1,090 feet when going south.
Maximum elevation: 6,760 feet.
Map: Jim White Ridge USGS quad covers the area, but this trail is not on USGS quads or USFS maps. This trail is shown on old Eagle Cap maps, but they are hard to find.
For more information: U.S. Forest Service at Wallowa Mountain Visitors Center, Enterprise, Oregon. Further information will probably be very limited.
Finding the trail: The trail leaves the Ben Point Trail 1.4 miles northwest of Mud Springs. See Hike 52 Ben Point. The elevation at the unmarked junction is 6,760 feet. See map on p. 143.

0.0   Trail junction with Ben Point Trail.
0.3   Trail enters open hillside and starts downgrade.
1.7   Trail junction with Upper Little Minam River Trail.

The trail: The trail heads south southwest from the junction with Ben Point Trail. Two hundred yards from the junction is a path to the right. This path connects with the Ben Point Trail a short distance to the northwest.

One-fourth mile past the path is a small stream crossing (El 6,560 ft.). Next to this stream is about the only reasonable campsite along this trail. Three hundred fifty yards past the stream, the trail comes out of the timber onto an open hillside. The view from here looks down (south) into the Little Minam River Canyon. Once in the open, the trail makes four switchbacks, then heads straight down for 75 yards before turning to the left. It then becomes less steep, and begins to follow an old roadbed. Two hundred seventy-five yards after turning left on the roadbed, there is another switchback and the trail enters the trees again (El 6,150 ft.).

Seven hundred fifty yards farther, there is another set of four switchbacks. Just below the switchbacks, the trail gets back on the old roadbed (El 5,780 ft.).

After 250 yards of going down the roadbed the trail makes yet another set of three switchbacks. A short distance past these switchbacks is the junction with the Upper Little Minam River Trail 1942. The elevation at this junction is 5,670 feet. See Hike 50 Upper Little Minam River.

This junction is 1.75 miles from and 1.090 feet below the Ben Point Trail. This trail takes a little route finding, but it can be seen most of the way. In fact, it follows the old roadbed a good part of the way down. Return to Moss Springs Trailhead via Upper Little Minam River Trail.

54   JIM WHITE RIDGE

Trail 1918

General description: An 8.8 mile trail down Jim White Ridge, from Little Minam River Trail to Moss Springs/Horse Ranch Trail. This trail can be done as a day hike (by masochists) by going up the Upper Little Minam River Trail, down Jim White Ridge and back up the Moss Springs/Horse Ranch Trail.

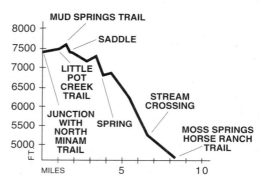

This makes a 21 mile round-trip, with 3,620 feet of elevation gain and loss.
Difficulty: Moderate to strenuous (heading down).
Trail maintenance: Infrequent.
Best season: Mid-June through October.
Traffic: Light, except during October and November hunting seasons, with light horse traffic.
Elevation gain: 200 feet Loss: 3,220 feet.
Maximum elevation: 7,600 feet.
Maps: Imus Geographics Wallowa Mountains Eagle Cap Wilderness or Jim White Ridge and Mount Fanny USGS quads.
For more information: U.S. Forest Service at Wallowa Mountain Visitors Center, Enterprise, Oregon.
Finding the trail: Jim White Ridge Trail begins at the junction with the Upper Little Minam River Trail 1942, Cartwheel Ridge Trail 1907 and Lackeys Hole Trail 1942. This junction (El 7,400 ft.) is in a saddle on the ridge that divides the Little Minam and Minam River drainages. This is a four way junction. See Hike 50 Upper Little Minam River.

0.0   Trail junction with Little Minam, Lackeys Hole and
       Cartwheel Ridge Trails.
1.2   Trail junction with Little Pot Creek Trail.
1.5   Trail junction with Ben Point Trail.

1.8	Saddle.
4.0	Spring.
5.2	Campsite next to trail.
7.2	Trail crosses larger stream twice.
8.8	Trail junction with Moss Springs/Horse Ranch Trail.

The trail: Jim White Ridge Trail heads north from the junction. At first the trail climbs a grassy slope, nearly reaching the top of the ridge. The view to the east is of the Minam River Canyon and the higher part of the Wallowa Mountains. A short distance more and the trail enters a burned area. Soon it comes to the

54 *Jim White Ridge*

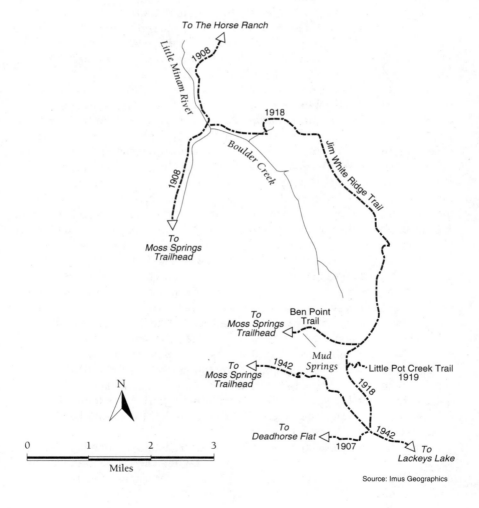

Source: Imus Geographics

junction with Little Pot Creek Trail 1919 (El 7,500 ft.). See Hike 55 Little Pot Creek. The unmarked junction with Little Pot Creek Trail is 1.2 miles from the junction with Upper Little Minam River Trail. Little Pot Creek Trail 1919 goes down to Big Burn on the Minam River 5.5 miles away. At the junction the Jim White Trail heads on to the north.

A quarter mile past the Little Pot Creek Trail junction is the unmarked junction with the Ben Point Trail. See Hike 52 Ben Point. The Ben Point Trail seems to get more use than the Jim White Ridge Trail, and it looks like the main trail here. At the junction take the less used trail to the right (northwest).

After passing Ben Point Trail junction, the trail traverses around the right side of Lackeys Point. It then drops to the saddle northeast of the point. Between Ben Point Trail junction and this saddle, watch for blazes and cairns marking the trail. The elevation at the saddle is 7,420 feet and it is 0.4 mile from the Ben Point Trail junction.

There is a faint path 0.1 mile past the saddle that drops off to the right to a campsite. The Jim White Ridge Trail goes back and forth across the ridge line a couple of times in the next 0.5 mile. Here the ridge becomes more rounded. The trail continues to descend through small timber. In another 0.3 mile it comes to a low point on the ridge (El 7,150 ft.).

From the low point, the trail climbs for 650 yards onto the now flat topped ridge. A couple hundred more yards and it starts to drop again for a short distance. Soon the trail becomes hard to see in a grassy area. The trail goes east a bit, then north on the fairly flat ridge top. Watch for blazes. The trail is hard to see in spots for the next 0.5 mile, then it drops off the right side of the ridge into the trees where it becomes easy to see again. In the next 0.2 mile the trail makes a switchback to the right, then a turn to the left. One-third mile after turning back to the left (north), there is a very large cairn on the right side of the trail. This cairn marks a spring, which is a few yards to the right of the trail. The spring is 4 miles from the Upper Little Minam River Trail at 6,800 feet elevation.

The trail climbs slightly after passing the spring. Soon it is back on top of the ridgeline. The trail becomes difficult to see again about 350 yards past the spring, as it goes slightly to the right of the ridgeline for 120 yards in an open area. The trail then goes back into the woods very near to the top of the ridge. Once in the woods, it is easy to see the trail again. Watch for cairns in the open area. There are many round rocks on the ridge in this area.

Another 0.75 mile and the trail begins to drop more steeply. After dropping for 0.25 mile, there is a campsite on the left side of the trail. There is a spring above the campsite. In September 1994, the water looked to be of poor quality. Elevation here is 6,200 feet. The trail stays fairly close to the ridge line for the next 0.25 mile. Then the trail bears to the left (west) and heads down more steeply.

After going down steeply for 700 yards, the trail flattens out a bit. The view to the left (southeast) is of Boulder Creek Canyon. The trail continues down 0.5 mile more to a small stream crossing. This is a very small stream. The trees have become much larger now than they were up above, and there are also lots of huckleberry bushes. These berries ripen in late August and September and can add pleasure and nourishment to the long hike down Jim White Ridge. As is usually the case in the Wallowa Mountains, watch for bears gorging themselves on the sweet purple fruit. After crossing the tiny stream, the trail wanders back and forth another 700 yards to a crossing (El 5,260 ft.) of a much larger stream.

After crossing the rushing stream, the trail turns right and crosses the same creek again. There is a campsite to the left between the crossings. A couple hundred yards after crossing the stream the second time, the trail makes a switchback to the left. A mile and one-half more and the trail meets the Moss Springs/Horse Ranch Trail 1908. This junction (El 4,580 ft.) is 8.8 miles from the Upper Little Minam River Trail. See Hike 51 Moss Springs/Horse Ranch. Check Hikes 51, 52, 53, 58, 59, 60, and 61 for possible loop hikes. The Jim White Ridge Trail takes considerable route finding skills.

55   LITTLE POT CREEK

Trail 1919

General description: A steep 5.5 mile backpacking and horse trail, connecting Jim White Ridge Trail and Upper Minam River Trail.
Difficulty: Strenuous.
Trail maintenance: Infrequent.
Best season: July through October.
Traffic: Light, except possibly moderate during October and November hunting seasons.
Elevation loss: 3,420 feet.
Maximum elevation: 7,500 feet.
Maps: Jim White Ridge USGS quad.
For more information: U.S. Forest Service at Wallowa Mountain Visitors Center, Enterprise, Oregon.

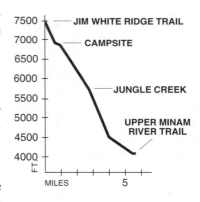

Finding the trail: This description of Little Pot Creek Trail begins at it's junction with Jim White Ridge Trail. This unmarked junction is 1.2 miles north of the junction of Upper Little Minam River and Jim White Ridge Trails in the second saddle reached when heading north on Jim White Ridge Trail. See Hike 54 Jim White Ridge and Hike 50 Upper Little Minam River. The location where Little Pot Creek Trail leaves Jim White Ridge Trail is 9 miles from Moss Springs Trailhead.

0.0   Trail junction with Jim White Ridge Trail.
0.8   Campsite next to meadow.
2.9   Trail crosses Jungle Creek.

5.4   Trail crosses Minam River.

5.5   Trail junction with Upper Minam River Trail.

The trail: From the junction with Jim White Ridge Trail 1918, Little Pot Creek Trail climbs a few feet to the east to the ridgeline (El 7,500 ft.). It then turns left and begins to descend on the open slope to the northeast. The trail comes to a spring and campsite 0.25 mile after leaving the Jim White Ridge Trail. The trail makes a switchback to the right in the grassy area just before crossing the small stream that comes out of the spring. This is an easy place to lose the trail. The trail makes three more switchbacks as it drops through open slopes and patches of alpine timber to a fork 0.5 mile past the spring. Little Pot Creek Trail bears left (northeast) at the fork. The right fork goes a short distance to a well used campsite next to a lush, and sometimes swampy, meadow. Part of this meadow (El 6,950 ft.) is shown as a lake on some maps.

After passing the fork, the trail heads northeast on flat ground for 100 yards, then descends steeply over nearly solid rock for a short distance. It makes a hard to see switchback to the left shortly after entering the rocky area, and a couple more that are easier to spot as it continues to descend through

55   *Little Pot Creek*

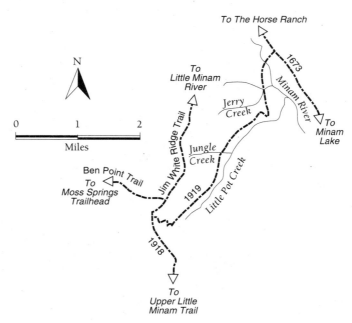

Source: Imus Geographics

the rocks. The trail makes eight more switchbacks as it continues on down to the less steep ground closer to Little Pot Creek.

Below the switchbacks the trail becomes harder to follow as it heads to the northeast down the valley. It is generally easy to find the trail in the timbered areas, but it can be difficult to spot in the open. The USGS map is quite accurate in this area and can be very helpful. Watch for blazes on the trees and cut logs as an indication of the exact route of the trail. About 0.75 mile after passing the last switchback, the trail becomes easier to follow again, as it descends gently through the forest of larger spruce and fir trees. Another 0.8 mile and the trail begins to drop steeply again.

The trail crosses Jungle Creek (El 5,730 ft.) 2.8 miles after leaving Jim White Ridge Trail. It is easy to see how this creek got it s name, as the creek bed is a jungle of slide alder. On the banks of Jungle Creek look for lavender to rose colored blooms of Lewis monkey face flowers, which are usually growing here. The trail rounds a steep finger ridge and crosses another stream 150 yards, after crossing Jungle Creek. Watch for sego lilies in the sunny openings in this area. Soon the trail begins another series of switchbacks on which it drops down to 4,500 feet elevation. Below the switchbacks it makes a 1.3 mile long descending traverse to the north, where it crosses the Minam River (El 4,080 ft.). The trail fords the river, as there is no bridge. This crossing may be difficult and dangerous during periods of high water. A couple hundred yards after crossing the river is the junction with the Upper Minam River Trail 1673. See Hike 42 Upper Minam River.

The area around this junction is called Big Burn, but the fire was long ago and the area is forested with large trees. There are many good campsites in this area and fairly good fishing in the Minam River. Check the Oregon Department of Fish and Wildlife Angling Synopsis for any special regulations before fishing here. There will probably be some special regulations on bull trout (Dolly Vardon) which are present here.

This trail is quite steep and requires good route finding skills to follow the trail in a few spots. A loop return trip can be made by going down (north) the Minam River Trail 6 miles to the Horse Ranch, then taking the Moss Springs/Horse Ranch Trail back up to Moss Springs Trailhead. See Hike 42 Upper Minam River and Hike 51 Moss Springs/Horse Ranch. Allow 2 or 3 days for this loop trip.

Trail 1905

General description: A 4.3 mile back-packing and horse trail connecting North Fork Catherine Creek Trail with Upper Minam River Trail, in a remote area of the western Wallowa Mountains.

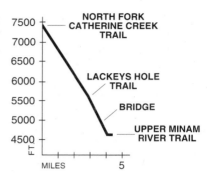

Difficulty: Moderate to strenuous.
Trail maintenance: Infrequent.
Best season: July through October.
Traffic: Light, except during October and November hunting seasons, when horse traffic can be moderate to heavy.
Elevation loss: 2,860 feet.
Maximum elevation: 7,430 feet.
Maps: China Cap USGS quad.
For more information: U.S. Forest Service at Wallowa Mountain Visitors Center, Enterprise, Oregon.
Finding the trail: This description of Rock Creek Trail begins at the junction of North Fork Catherine Creek Trail and Meadow Mountain Trail. See Hike 63 North Fork Catherine Creek and Hike 64 Meadow Mountain. There is no sign marking the junction, which is on the ridge, 0.3 mile northeast of the summit of Meadow Mountain.

0.0	Trail junction with North Fork Catherine Creek Trail.
3.0	Trail junction with Lackeys Hole Trail.
4.2	Trail crosses Minam River.
4.3	Trail junction with Upper Minam River Trail.

The trail: From the junction with North Fork Catherine Creek Trail 1905, and Meadow Mountain Trail 1927, Rock Creek Trail descends to the east on the right (south) side of the ridge on a slope covered with lupine, buckwheat and scattered timber. After descending for 0.25 mile, the trail enters an old burn area which it goes through for 0.2 mile. Upon leaving the burn, the trail continues down through spruce and fir forest, passing a meadow in another 0.25 mile. Just after passing the meadow, the trail crosses a small stream and soon begins to drop more steeply on an open slope covered with paintbrush, lupine and sego lilies. The trail makes six switchbacks as it descends the slope, then makes four more as it drops through the timber below. It crosses a small stream while descending the last few switchbacks. At the bottom of the switchbacks (El 6,000 ft.) the trail comes close to Rock Creek but does not cross it.

   The trail does not drop as steeply as the creek, so over the next mile it gradually gets farther away from the stream bed. On the right of the trail 0.6

mile past the last switchback there is a lodgepole pine with a large burl all the way around it.

The trail makes a switchback to the right 0.25 mile after passing the tree with the burl, then makes a switchback to the left a short distance farther along. The junction with Lackeys Hole Trail 1942 is reached 0.25 mile past this switchback. There is a sign at the junction with Lackeys Hole Trail (El 5,530 ft.). See Hike 57 Lackeys Hole. After passing the junction with Lackeys Hole Trail, Rock Creek Trail makes eighteen more switchbacks as it descends through the dense forest of fairly large fir, pine and tamarack trees, for the 0.8 mile to a bridge over Rock Creek. A quarter mile after crossing the bridge the trail crosses a small stream then heads south a short distance along a meadow. It soon turns left (east) and crosses the meadow to the Minam River. There is a campsite next to the river. The trail fords the Minam River and goes 0.1 mile more to the junction with Upper Minam River Trail. See Hike 50 Upper Minam River.

Crossing the Minam River may be dangerous during periods of high water. Be careful. Return is best done by going back on the same trail unless a very extended trip, possibly involving a car shuttle, is desired. Probably the most likely extended trip to take would be to head up the Minam River to Elk Creek Trail. See Hike 67 Elk Creek. Follow Elk Creek Trail back to either North Catherine Creek Trailhead or Buck Creek Trailhead.

56   Rock Creek
57   Lackeys Hole

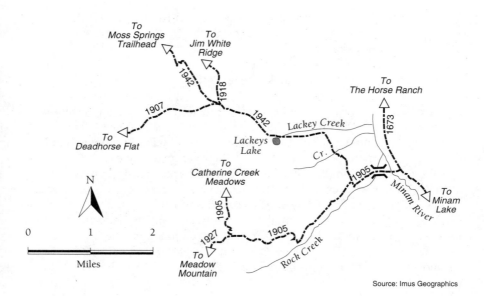

Source: Imus Geographics

Trail 1942

General description: A 5 mile long backpack and horse trail connecting Upper Little Minam River Trail, at its junction with Jim White Ridge Trail, with Rock Creek Trail.

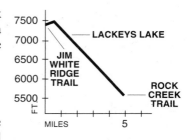

Difficulty: Moderate.
Trail maintenance: Infrequent.
Best season: July through October.
Traffic: Generally light, but there may be moderate horse traffic during October and November hunting seasons.
Elevation gain: 150 feet. Loss: 1,920 feet.
Maximum elevation: 7,510 feet.
Maps: Imus Geographics Wallowa Mountains Eagle Cap Wilderness. This trail is not shown on China Cap USGS quad, which covers this area.
For more information: U.S. Forest Service at Wallowa Mountain Visitors Center, Enterprise, Oregon.
Finding the trail: This trail is a continuation of Upper Little Minam River Trail 1942. See Hike 50 Upper Little Minam River. Lackeys Hole Trail, described below, begins at the four-way junction of Upper Little Minam River Trail, Cartwheel Ridge Trail 1907, and Jim White Ridge Trail 1918. See Hikes 61 and 54. The lower (southeast) end of Lackeys Hole Trail joins Rock Creek Trail 1905, 1.3 miles from the Minam River. See Hike 56 Rock Creek.

0.0	Trail junction with Upper Little Minam River, Jim White Ridge, and Cartwheel Ridge Trails.
1.5	Lackeys Lake.
3.2	Trail crosses unnamed creek.
5.0	Trail junction with Rock Creek Trail.

The trail: Lackeys Hole Trail begins at a junction in a high gentle saddle on the ridge dividing the Little Minam and Minam River drainages. The mostly open ridge top country around the junction abound with wild flowers in July, and elk are likely to be seen up here on their summer range.

From the junction (El 7,400 ft.) the trail heads southeast. It climbs slightly at first, through an area that was burned several years ago. This burn area is recovering from the fire nicely, as the ground is mostly covered with grass and flowers, and there are many small alpine trees growing up between the silver snags. A couple hundred yards after leaving the junction, the trail crosses a saddle and enters the North Fork Catherine Creek drainage. Catherine Creek Meadows can be seen from the saddle, far below to the southwest.

Campsite in the first saddle on Lackeys Hole Trail.

After crossing the saddle, the trail begins to traverse the steep open slope on the right side of the ridgeline. It crosses a small stream a short distance after beginning the traverse. There are some possible campsites in the saddle, and this stream is a source of water. Late in the summer and in the fall, this stream may be dry, however. The trail comes to another saddle 0.25 mile after crossing the stream. It follows the ridgeline for 100 yards in this saddle, then starts a slightly ascending traverse on the right side of the ridge again. This ascending traverse lasts 0.3 mile to where the trail reaches another saddle (El 7,510 ft.). As the trail crosses this saddle, it makes a switchback to the left and begins to descend on the the left side of the ridgeline. After descending 100 yards or so the trail makes another switchback to the right and continues to drop along a slope covered with subalpine fir and whitebark pine. The trail descends for 0.6 mile, makes a couple of switchbacks, then comes to yet another saddle on a sub-ridge (El 7,250 ft.). Soon after crossing the saddle, Lackeys Lake can be seen through the trees to the right. After crossing the saddle, the trail drops the last 0.25 mile to a stream crossing, making one more switchback along the way. This stream is the outlet of Lackeys Lake. The lake is a few yards to the right upstream from the trail. Lackeys Lake is more like a pond than a lake. The lake is shallow with marshy edges and lots of mosquitoes. There is a good camp-site along the east side of the lake, but there are no fish.

The trail continues to descend on a mostly open hillside after crossing the outlet stream. It makes a couple of switchbacks and crosses the stream two more times. The trail crosses a small stream which begins at a spring a few yards above the trail, 0.6 mile after leaving Lackeys Lake. It then winds its way down through the forest, making several switchbacks and crossing four tiny streams before rounding a ridge and leaving the Lackey Creek drainage 1.4 miles from the lake. The trail crosses an unnamed creek 0.3 mile after leaving Lackey Creek drainage. It may be wise to fill your water bottles here, as there may be no water available from here to Rock Creek. After crossing the creek, the trail passes a muddy spring, then traverses a steep hillside heading southeast. It soon makes a switchback to the left. The trail makes five more switchbacks, as it descends the remaining 1.3 miles to the junction with Rock Creek Trail 1905 (El 5,530 ft.). See Hike 56 Rock Creek.

Return can be made by the same trail, or an extended trip can be made by going 1.3 miles down Rock Creek Trail to the Minam River and the Minam River Trail. Head down (north) the Minam River Trail 6 miles to Little Pot Creek Trail, climb to the west on Little Pot Creek Trail to the junction with Jim White Ridge Trail, and go south on that trail to the junction with Upper Little Minam River and Lackeys Hole trails, the point of beginning. This makes a 19 mile loop. Add to that the 7.8 miles each way to reach the starting point from Moss Springs Trailhead for a 35.6 mile trip. See Hikes 56, 42, 54, and 50. Climbing Little Pot Creek Trail takes some route finding skills.

58   LODGEPOLE

Trail 1920

General description: A 6.7 mile hike along the southwestern boundary of Eagle Cap Wilderness, from Moss Springs Trailhead to the junction with Trail 1907. Parts of this trail follow old, mostly abandoned, roadbeds.

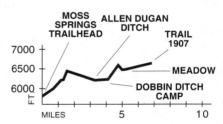

Difficulty: Easy, but requires some route finding and map reading skills.

Trail maintenance: Infrequent.

Best season: June through October.

Traffic: Light, except it can be moderate or even heavy during fall hunting seasons, with moderate horse traffic.

Elevation gain: 1,130 feet. Loss: 350 feet total.

Maximum elevation: 6,580 feet.

Maps: Imus Geographics Wallowa Mountains Eagle Cap Wilderness, or Mount Fanny and Little Catherine Creek USGS quads.

For more information: U.S. Forest Service at Wallowa Mountain Visitors Center, Enterprise, Oregon.

Finding the trail: Lodgepole Trail begins at Moss Springs Trailhead (El 5,800 ft.). See Hike 50 Upper Little Minam River for directions to Moss Springs Trailhead. There is a sign at the trailhead which points south along a closed dirt road, Forest Road 410.

0.0   Trail begins at Moss Springs Trailhead.
0.3   Trail junction with Trail 1920.
3.4   Allen Dungan Ditch.
4.1   Dobbin Ditch Camp.
5.0   Trail enters a meadow.
6.7   Trail junction with Trail 1907.

The trail: From Moss Springs Trailhead walk south on closed FR 410. Forty yards from the trailhead, continue past Forest Road 415 which turns off to the left. Another road goes off to the left 650 yards farther along. This one is unmarked. Forty yards past the unmarked road Forest Road 418 also heads to the left. Stay on FR 410. Three hundred fifty yards more is the junction with Forest Road 360. FR 360 turns to the right, Forest Road 420 goes straight ahead, and FR 410, our road, goes to the left. Head south southeast for 550 yards on FR

58   *Lodgepole*
59   *Dobbin Creek*
60   *Crib Point*

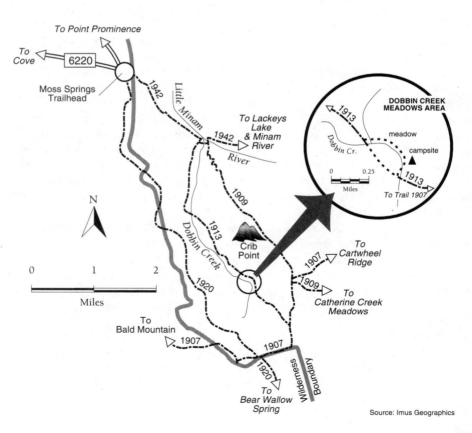

Source: Imus Geographics

410 to the junction with Trail 1920. This junction is 0.6 mile from Moss Springs Trailhead.

At the junction (El 5,950 ft.) FR 410 turns to the right, and the Lodgepole Trail goes straight ahead. There is a sign marking this junction. The forest to this point has been almost all lodgepole pine trees. Past the junction there are more spruce, fir and tamarack (western larch) trees.

One-half mile past the junction the trail appears to fork. This is a short section of trail realignment. Follow the main trail. The trail climbs over a small rise then drops again to a dirt road. Turn right on the road, go 20 yards, then bear left again on the trail. The elevation here is 6,170 feet. Two hundred yards after leaving the dirt road the trail makes a switchback to the right. Then it climbs for 0.25 mile to a point near the top of a ridge (El 6,440 ft.). The trail follows the ridge top for 0.25 miles to a rocky outcropping. The outcropping is a few yards to the left of the trail. There is a good viewpoint on the top of the outcropping. The Little Minam River Canyon is to the northeast, and the Elkhorn Mountains are to the south on the other side of the Powder Valley.

The trail goes around and under the southeast side of the outcropping. Then it bears slightly to the right and drops to the southeast. The trail is difficult to see in this area; watch for blazes. A half mile past the outcropping the trail becomes very difficult to see in a small opening. Head east southeast. Watch for blazes and cut logs. Three hundred yards past the opening the trail becomes wide like a jeep road, which it may have been at one time. Another 250 yards is a junction with another dirt road. Turn right on the road and head south southeast. Do not take the path that is across the opening at the junction. Soon the road becomes more of a trail again. The trail comes to the Allen Dungan Ditch 0.4 mile past the junction. Where the trail meets the ditch is 3.4 miles from Moss Springs Trailhead, and 6,190 feet elevation.

Turn left along the ditch bank and follow it for 0.5 mile. Here the trail crosses the ditch and heads east southeast. It climbs a small rise and comes to Dobbin Ditch Camp (El 6,260 ft.) 400 yards after crossing the ditch. In September 1994 when I walked this trail, there were two fires in this area. Fire fighters were picking up packages, that had been air dropped to them at Dobbin Ditch Camp. The camp is in a small meadow. There is a sign marking Dobbin Ditch Camp.

After leaving Dobbin Ditch Camp, the trail climbs gently. It crosses two stream beds, then heads up along a stream bed. These stream beds may have water at wetter times of the year. Two-thirds mile past the camp the trail bears left and climbs for 200 yards to the top of a small rise (El 6,560 ft.). There is an old 5 mile marker on the right side of the trail at the top of the rise. A quarter mile past the rise is another stream bed. Another 0.25 mile and the trail comes into a meadow. This meadow (El 6,460 ft.) is 5 miles from Moss Springs Trailhead.

The trail heads east through the meadow, but is hard to see. Watch for blazes and cut limbs on the small trees in the meadow. About 250 yards into the meadow the trail crosses a small stream. The trail becomes easy to see again at the east end of the meadow. Look for blazes on the trees at the east end of the meadow. There are some good campsites around the edges of this meadow.

There is a sign which says "Lodgepole Trail," on the right side of the trail 250 yards past the meadow. The junction with Trail 1907 is 0.5 mile past the sign. See Hike 61 Cartwheel Ridge for a description of this four-way trail junction. The junction with Trail 1907 is 6.7 miles from Moss Springs Trailhead. The elevation at the junction is 6,580 feet.

This trail requires route finding and map reading skills, but the hiking is easy. The Lodgepole Trail goes through forest for nearly its whole length. The views from the trail are generally not too spectacular, but it is a good place to check out the trees and flowers and to watch for wildlife.

From the junction with Trail 1907, a loop trip can be made by following Trail 1907 to either Dobbin Creek Trail or Crib Point Trail, then taking one of these trails down to Upper Little Minam River Trail and taking Upper Little Minam River Trail back to Moss Springs Trailhead. See Hike 61 Cartwheel Ridge, Hike 59 Dobbin Creek, Hike 60 Crib Point, and Hike 50 Upper Little Minam River. Both of these return trails have over 1,000 feet of elevation loss and the Upper Little Minam River Trail climbs 600 feet to get back to Moss Springs Trailhead from its junction with Crib Point or Dobbin Creek Trails. The distance back to Moss Springs Trailhead by either trail is 7.5 miles (including the distance to these trails on Trail 1907). Crib Point Trail is somewhat easier to find and follow. It is easier to do either of these loops in a counterclockwise direction.

59   DOBBIN CREEK

Trail 1913

General Description: A 4.4 mile trail connecting Cartwheel Ridge Trail 1907 with Little Minam River Trail. Do not confuse this with Hike 30 Dobbin Creek, which is in the Bear Creek drainage.

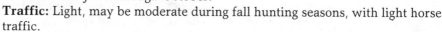

Difficulty: Moderate, but with route finding skills required.
Trail maintenance: Infrequent.
Best season: June through October.
Traffic: Light, may be moderate during fall hunting seasons, with light horse traffic.
Elevation gain: 100 feet. Loss: 1,170 feet (going northwest).
Maximum elevation: 6,420 feet.
Maps: Imus Geographics Wallowa Mountains Eagle Cap Wilderness shows this trail. This trail is not shown on newer USGS Little Catherine Creek and Mount Fanny quads, which cover this area.

For more information: U.S. Forest Service at Wallowa Mountain Visitor Center, Enterprise, Oregon.

Finding the trail: Dobbin Creek Trail leaves Trail 1907, 0.7 mile south of Deadhorse Flat. The place where Dobbin Creek Trail leaves Trail 1907 is difficult to see. It turns off to the northwest in a small clearing. There are two clearings close together on Trail 1907. Dobbin Creek trail turns off in the one closer to Deadhorse Flat. The elevation at this junction is 6,320 feet. See Hike 61 Cartwheel Ridge . There are old blazes marking Dobbin Creek Trail but no sign.

0.0	Trail junction with Cartwheel Ridge Trail.
0.6	Meadow.
3.0	Trail crosses Dobbin Creek.
4.4	Trail junction with Upper Little Minam River Trail.

The trail: After you find the place where Dobbin Creek Trail turns northwest off Trail 1907, Dobbin Creek Trail is easy to see in the woods, but soon becomes hard to see again in a small opening. A few yards from the start of the opening head northwest. Past the opening the trail climbs slightly for 0.3 miles to the top of a small rise (El 6,420 ft.). The trail then drops slightly and crosses Dobbin Creek in a meadow 0.6 mile past the rise.

After crossing the creek, turn right. Go downstream for 200 yards, then cross Dobbin Creek again. Turn left and follow it down through the meadow. Stay close to Dobbin Creek. Be careful not to go up a side stream which comes into the meadow from the other end (see map). Cross the side stream and continue down Dobbin Creek a few more yards. Soon you will pick up the trail again. This point can also be reached by going straight ahead through the trees after crossing Dobbin Creek the first time. This area can be very confusing. There is a nice campsite at the upper (southeast) end of this meadow.

After leaving the meadow area, the trail, which is now easy to see, climbs 50 yards to the right of Dobbin Creek. One-third mile past the meadow the trail becomes difficult to see in an open area. Stay level crossing the open area, then drop a few yards to the left at its far edge. Here the trail shows up again. The trail is quite wide at this point. It almost looks like an old roadbed.

The trail crosses a very small stream (El 6,090 ft.) 0.3 mile past the open area. Two hundred yards farther, the trail crosses another small stream. The trail is some distance above Dobbin Creek at this point. There is another stream crossing (El 5,990 ft.) 0.3 mile farther. Two hundred yards past this stream the trail starts to drop more steeply and crosses yet another small stream. There are lots of huckleberry bushes in this area among the lodgepole pine trees. Soon the trail makes a couple of semi-switchbacks. It then heads down towards Dobbin Creek. One-fourth mile past the switchbacks the trail crosses Dobbin Creek. The crossing is approximately 3 miles from the junction with Trail 1907. Elevation at the crossing is 5,520 feet.

One hundred seventy-five yards after crossing Dobbin Creek the trail crosses a small stream. Seventy-five yards past the stream is a fence line with a gate. The trail goes through the gate. It crosses two more small streams on the way down to the Upper Little Minam River Trail 1942, 1.4 miles past the last crossing of Dobbin Creek. The junction with the Upper Little Minam River Trail (El 5,250 ft.) is unmarked but very easy to see when coming down the Dobbin Creek Trail. See Hike 50 Upper Little Minam River .

Most of this trail is easy to see; however, a couple of spots are very difficult to find. Route finding skills are required. This trail can be very hard to find at the top which is at the junction with Trail 1907. The total mileage for this trail is 4.4 miles, and the elevation loss when heading northwest is 1,170 feet. Dobbin Creek Trail can be done as part of a loop hike with Hikes 58,61, and 50. See Hike 58 Lodgepole for loop hike description.

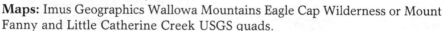

60   CRIB POINT

Trail 1909

General description: A 3.6 mile connecting trail from Upper Little Minam River Trail and Cartwheel Ridge Trail 1907 at Deadhorse Flat.
Difficulty: Strenuous.
Trail maintenance: Infrequent.
Best season: June through October.
Traffic: Light, with light horse traffic.

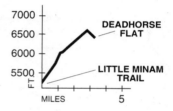

Elevation gain: 1,380 feet. Loss: 140 feet.
Maximum elevation: 6,600 feet.
Maps: Imus Geographics Wallowa Mountains Eagle Cap Wilderness or Mount Fanny and Little Catherine Creek USGS quads.
For more information: U.S. Forest Service at Wallowa Mountain Visitors Center, Enterprise, Oregon.
Finding the trail: Crib Point Trail leaves the Upper Little Minam River Trail 1942, 2.1 miles from Moss Springs Trailhead. The elevation at the junction is 5,220 feet. The trail turns right (southwest) off the Upper Little Minam River Trail. See Hike 50 Upper Little Minam River for directions. There are campsites at the junction, next to the Little Minam River.

0.0   Trail junction with Upper Little Minam River Trail.
1.3   Top of ridge.
3.6   Deadhorse Flat and trail junction with Cartwheel Ridge Trail 1907.

The trail: After leaving the Upper Little Minam River Trail, Crib Point Trail makes seven switchbacks as it climbs through thick timber 620 vertical feet in the first mile. After 1 mile there is an opening in the woods. The trail then makes a couple more switchbacks in and out of the trees as it climbs on up the ridge line. At 1.3 miles the trail gets on top of the ridge line at an elevation of 6,070 feet. Another 0.3 mile and the trail flattens out a bit and follows the semi-forested ridge line, through a mixed forest of lodgepole pine, sub-alpine fir, tamarack (western larch), and Engelmann spruce.

One more mile and the trail makes a couple of semi- switchbacks, then climbs to where the ridge broadens out at about 6,500 feet elevation. The trail climbs another 100 vertical feet, then drops a little. From here on the trail remains fairly flat, not gaining or losing more than about 100 feet in elevation. This area is mostly dense lodgepole pine forest. The trail is wide here and appears to have been an old jeep trail. As the trail gets closer to Deadhorse Flat, the forest contains more fir and hemlock.

The trail enters the meadow at Deadhorse Flat (El 6,460 ft.) 3.6 miles from the Upper Little Minam River Trail. The trail is hard to see in the large lush meadow that is Deadhorse Flat. However, there is a sign post in the middle of the meadow. This is the junction with Trail 1907. See Hike 61 Cartwheel Ridge. There are several good campsites and a spring at Deadhorse Flat.

Several loop trips are possible by connecting Crib Point Trail with others described in this book. See Hike 58 Lodgepole, Hike 59 Dobbin Creek, and Hike 61 Cartwheel Ridge.

61 CARTWHEEL RIDGE

Trail 1907

General description: A 4.3 mile long connecting trail from Lodgepole Trail 1920 to Upper Little Minam River Trail, via Deadhorse Flat. At Deadhorse Flat the trail connects with Crib Point Trail and Catherine Creek/Deadhorse Trail. After passing Deadhorse Flat, Trail 1907 becomes Cartwheel Ridge Trail and connects with the Upper Little Minam River Trail, Jim White Ridge Trail, and Lackeys Hole Trail.

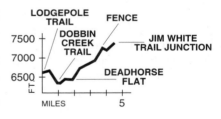

Difficulty: Easy to moderate.

Trail maintenance: Infrequent.

Best season: Mid-June through October.

Traffic: Light to moderate, heavier in the fall, with moderate horse traffic.

Elevation gain: 1,180 feet. Loss: 260 feet.

Maximum elevation: 7,400 feet.

Maps: Imus Geographics Wallowa Mountains Eagle Cap or Little Catherine Creek and China Cap USGS quads.

For more information: U.S. Forest Service at Wallowa Mountain Visitors Center, Enterprise, Oregon.

Finding the trail: Cartwheel Ridge Trail 1907 leaves the Lodgepole Trail at a four-way junction (El 6,580 ft.) 6.7 miles southeast of Moss Springs Trailhead. See Hike 58 Lodgepole. The other trails leaving this junction are Trail 1920

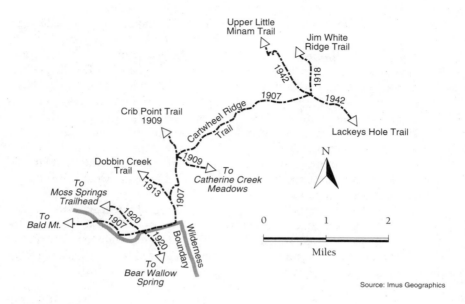

Upper Little
Minam Trail

Jim White
Ridge Trail

1942

1918

1907

1942

Crib Point Trail
1909

Cartwheel Ridge Trail

Lackeys Hole Trail

1909

N

Dobbin Creek
Trail

To
Catherine Creek
Meadows

To
Moss Springs
Trailhead

1913

1907

To
Bald Mt.

1920

1907

1920

Wilderness Boundary

0   1   2

Miles

To
Bear Wallow
Spring

Source: Imus Geographics

which heads to the southeast then to the south to Bear Wallow Springs, and Bald Mountain Trail which goes southwest then west, to Bald Mountain. The elevation at this junction is 6,580 feet.

0.0	Trail junction with Lodgepole Trail (four-way junction).
1.1	Trail junction with Dobbin Creek Trail.
1.8	Deadhorse Flat and trail junctions with Crib Point and Deadhorse Flat/Catherine Creek Trails.
4.3	Trail junction with Upper Little Minam River Trail, Jim White Ridge and Lackeys Hole Trails.

The trail: Trail 1907, which becomes Cartwheel Ridge Trail at Deadhorse Flat, heads east northeast from the junction. It climbs gently for 0.4 mile to the top of a rise (El 6,620 ft.). Past the rise the trail drops through mixed forest for 0.6 mile to the unmarked junction with Dobbin Creek Trail 1913. The elevation at this junction is 6,320 feet. See Hike 59 Dobbin Creek. This hard to spot junction is in the second of two small clearings. There is a path which turns left in the first clearing, but this path soon fades out. Dobbin Creek Trail turns left (northwest) in the second clearing. There are blazes marking Dobbin Creek Trail, but no sign.

After going 0.4 mile past Dobbin Creek Trail junction, the trail tops another rise (El 6,480 ft.). A quarter mile past this rise it crosses a small stream in a meadow. Another 50 yards is the junction with Crib Point Trail 1909. See Hike

60 Crib Point. The meadow is Deadhorse Flat. Deadhorse Flat (El 6,460 ft.) is 1.8 miles from the Lodgepole Trail.

At Deadhorse Flat there is another four-way junction. Crib Point Trail turns left and goes northwest. Catherine Creek/Deadhorse Flat Trail 1909 turns right and heads southeast down to Catherine Creek Meadows. See Hike 62 Catherine Creek/Deadhorse Flat. Here Trail 1907 becomes Cartwheel Ridge Trail and heads northeast. There are good campsites all around Deadhorse Flat. There is also a spring emerging from the green meadow near its east edge. Before leaving the meadow at Deadhorse Flat the trail crosses a stream. The crossing is just below the spring where the stream begins.

The trail is very wide where it leaves the meadow. It was a jeep road at one time. The trail climbs at a moderate grade through forest and open areas and reaches the top of a rise (El 6,770 ft.) 0.6 mile past Deadhorse Flat. The view to the right (southeast) is of the North Fork Catherine Creek Canyon and Catherine Creek Meadows.

Nine-tenths mile past the viewpoint at the top of the rise there are rock outcroppings on the right side of the trail. The trail steepens 700 yards past the outcroppings and climbs through thinning timber. There may be cattle in this area. Another 350 yards and the trail comes to a fence line. It crosses the fence through a gate. This is the end of the old jeep trail (El 7,240 ft.).

After going through the fence, the trail traverses around the right side of a high point on the ridge. After passing the high point, it drops slightly to a saddle (El 7,200 ft.). The trail enters an old burn area 150 yards beyond the saddle. After going 125 yards through the burn area, it begins a 300 yard long ascending traverse around the left side of the ridge. The junction with the Upper Little Minam River Trail 1942 is 130 yards past the end of the traverse. This junction (El 7,400 ft.) is 4.3 miles from the Lodgepole Trail and 2.5 miles from Deadhorse Flat. See Hike 50 Upper Little Minam River. This is also the junction with Jim White Ridge Trail and Lackeys Hole Trail. See Hikes 54 and 57. The timber here is still partly burned at the junction, but there are patches of green trees.

A return hike back to Moss Springs Trailhead can be made by taking the Upper Little Minam River Trail. This 18.2 mile loop including Lodgepole, Cartwheel Ridge and Upper Little Minam River Trails, is best done in two or more days. There is a much longer return alternative available for the hardy hiker, which is to take the Jim White Ridge Trail down to Moss Springs/Horse Ranch Trail and follow that trail back up to Moss Springs Trailhead. See Hike 54 Jim White Ridge and Hike 51 Moss Springs/Horse Ranch.

Trail 1909

General description: A short, 1.2 mile connecting trail between Catherine Creek Meadows and Deadhorse Flat.

Difficulty: Moderate.

Trail maintenance: Infrequent.

Best season: June through October.

Traffic: Light to moderate, with moderate horse traffic.

Elevation gain: 750 feet.

Maximum elevation: 6,420 feet.

Map: China Cap USGS quad.

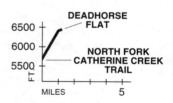

62 Catherine Creek/Deadhorse Flat

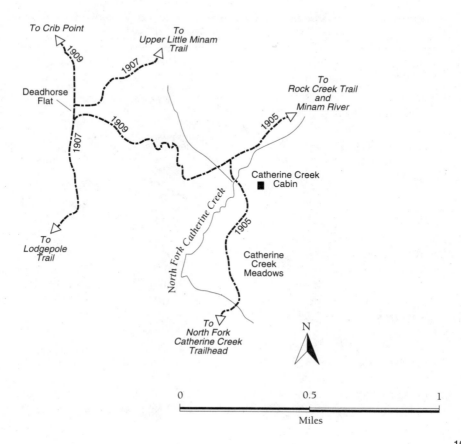

For more information: U.S. Forest Service at Wallowa Mountain Visitors Center, Enterprise, Oregon.

Finding the trail: This connecting trail starts at its junction with North Fork Catherine Creek Trail 1905, on the west side of Catherine Creek Meadows (El 5,670 ft.). See Hike 63 North Fork Catherine Creek.

0.0	Trail junction with North Fork Catherine Creek Trail in Catherine Creek Meadows.
1.0	Top of spur ridge.
1.2	Deadhorse Flat and trail junction with Cartwheel Ridge Trail 1907.

The trail: Catherine Creek/Deadhorse Trail 1909 heads west from the junction. After going 150 yards it makes a switchback and crosses a stream 200 yard farther along. The trail then climbs making eight switchbacks in the next 0.6 mile. Above the switchbacks the trail flattens out at the top of a spur ridge. It crosses a small stream 275 yards after topping out. Just after crossing the stream, the trail comes into a meadow. This meadow is Deadhorse Flat. The trail heads 125 yards out into the meadow to a signpost at the junction with Cartwheel Ridge Trail 1907 (El 6,460 ft.). See Hike 61 Cartwheel Ridge.

63   *NORTH FORK CATHERINE CREEK*

Trail 1905

General description: A 9 mile main backpacking and stock trail along the North Fork of Catherine Creek, from North Fork Catherine Creek Trailhead to the pass where Trail 1905 becomes Rock Creek Trail. The junction with Meadow Mountain Trail is also at this pass.

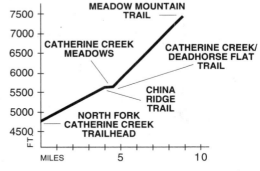

Difficulty: Easy to moderate.

Trail maintenance: Yearly.

Best season: June through October to Catherine Creek Meadows, Mid-June through October past there.

Traffic: Moderate to heavy, with moderate horse traffic.

Elevation gain: 3,230 feet.

Maximum elevation: 7,430 feet.

Map: China Cap USGS quad.

For more information: U.S. Forest Service at Wallowa Mountain Visitors Center, Enterprise, Oregon.

Finding the trail: The trail starts at the North Fork Catherine Creek Trailhead (El 4,200 ft.). To reach the trailhead take Oregon Highway 203 southeast from

63 *North Fork Catherine Creek*

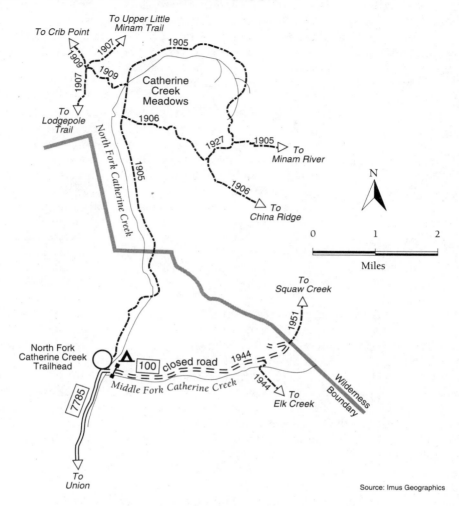

To Upper Little
Minam Trail

To Crib Point

1907
1905

1909
1907
1909

Catherine
Creek
Meadows

To
Lodgepole
Trail

1906

North Fork Catherine Creek

1905

1927
1905
To
Minam River

1906
To
China Ridge

N

0   1   2

Miles

To
Squaw Creek

1951

North Fork
Catherine Creek
Trailhead

100   closed road   1944

Middle Fork Catherine Creek

1944
To
Elk Creek

Wilderness
Boundary

7785

To
Union

Source: Imus Geographics

Union, pass Catherine Creek State Park 8 miles from town, and go 3.5 miles more to the junction with Forest Road 7785. Turn left on Forest Road 7785 and head east, then northeast for 6 miles to North Fork Catherine Creek Trailhead.

0.0	North Fork Catherine Creek Trailhead.
1.3	Trail crosses North Fork Catherine Creek.
2.0	Eagle Cap Wilderness Boundary.
4.5	Catherine Creek Meadows and trail junction with China Ridge Trail (to Meadow Mountain).
4.8	Trail junction with Catherine Creek Deadhorse Flat Trail.
7.1	Meadow.
9.0	Trail junction with Meadow Mountain Trail 1927, Trail 1905 becomes Rock Creek Trail.

The trail: From the trailhead the trail heads north northeast up the west side of the North Fork of Catherine Creek. It crosses six small to very small streams in the first 1.25 miles. At 1.25 miles (El 4,690 ft.) the trail crosses the North Fork of Catherine Creek. The forest along this creek bottom is a mixed stand of ponderosa pine, spruce, and cottonwood. There are also some open areas and some brush.

After crossing the North Fork of Catherine Creek, the trail crosses one more stream, Chop Creek, before reaching the Eagle Cap Wilderness Boundary (El 5,090 ft.) at 2 miles. Just past the wilderness boundary the trail crosses Jim Creek. Three hundred yards past the wilderness boundary there is a meadow between the trail and the North Fork of Catherine Creek. The meadow continues along the creek for about 350 yards. There are several campsites along the creek here, with paths leading down to them from the trail. At 3 miles the trail crosses Boot Hill Creek (El 5,320 ft.).

The trail widens into what looks like an old roadbed 500 yards past Boot Hill Creek. After going 300 more yards, there is a bridge over a small creek. A half mile past the bridge the trail has climbed above the North Fork of Catherine Creek, which is in a steep canyon at this point. There is a broken down old fence line and a gate that the trail goes through 0.8 mile past the bridge. Another 130 yards and the trail enters Catherine Creek Meadows (El 5,650 ft.).

After entering the meadow, the trail soon crosses a small stream. A short distance past the stream is a signpost. This is the junction with China Ridge Trail 1906, and the sign points to Meadow Mountain. China Ridge Trail turns to the right (east). See Hike 66 China Ridge. The trail continues up through the meadows, then goes through a strip of trees and crosses another stream on a wooden bridge. A little ways past the bridge the trail forks. Take the left fork, as the right forks goes a short distance to Catherine Creek Cabin. The trail crosses the North Fork of Catherine Creek 125 yards past the fork. Cross the creek, turn right, and go 125 yards to the junction with Catherine Creek/Deadhorse Flat Trail 1909 (El 5,670 ft.). This junction is 4.8 miles from the trailhead. Trail 1909 heads to the the left (west) to Deadhorse Flat. See Hike 62 Catherine Creek/Deadhorse Flat.

Past the junction the trail goes along the left side of the meadow through stands of trees for 400 yards. After leaving the meadow, the trail heads on up the left side of the North Fork Catherine Creek. It crosses several small side streams before reaching another meadow 2.3 miles after leaving Catherine Creek Meadows. There are campsites along the sides of this 200 yard long meadow. There is also a small stream at the far end of the meadow. At the southeast end of the meadow the trail enters the timber and crosses a larger stream. This larger stream is a fork of Catherine Creek. The elevation at the stream crossing is 6,550 feet.

After crossing the stream the trail heads generally south and up. The trail is braided here from use by cattle. Follow the blazes. There is a creek and campsite on the right side of the trail 0.3 mile after crossing the stream. One hundred twenty-five yards past the campsite is another stream crossing. Another 0.4 mile and there is a meadow on the left side of the trail. The trail enters a little open valley 0.4 mile past this meadow. This little valley is about 150 yards long. A small creek runs down through the valley. It was dry when I hiked this trail in September. There is a switchback to the right 300 yards after leaving the little valley, and 100 yards more is another switchback. A few yards past the switchback is a fence line and a gate. The trail goes through the gate then climbs 125 yards more to the top of a ridge. At the top of the ridge is the junction with Meadow Mountain Trail 1927 (El 7,430 ft.). This junction is 9 miles from the North Fork of Catherine Creek Trailhead.

This junction is the end of North Fork Catherine Creek Trail. From here on Trail 1905 is Rock Creek Trail and goes straight ahead down to Rock Creek and the Minam River. See Hike 56 Rock Creek. The river is 4.3 miles away and 2,860 vertical feet down. Meadow Mountain Trail turns right at the junction and heads up the ridge to the southwest. The North Fork Catherine Creek Trail is generally easy to see. It is a gentle grade except for the last couple of miles where the grade is moderate.

A loop hike is possible as a return to Catherine Creek Meadows. This loop is done by taking Meadow Mountain Trail for 0.4 mile over the top of Meadow Mountain to its junction with China Ridge Trail. Turn right (west) on China Ridge Trail and drop back down to Catherine Creek Meadows. See Hike 66 China Ridge and Hike 64 Meadow Mountain. The west end of China Ridge Trail takes tremendous route finding skill to follow.

64   MEADOW MOUNTAIN

Trail 1927

General description: A 0.4 mile long connecting trail from North Fork Catherine Creek Trail, over the summit of Meadow Mountain to China Ridge Trail.
Difficulty: Moderate.
Trail maintenance: Infrequent.
Best season: July through September.
Traffic: Light, with light horse traffic.
Elevation gain: 390 feet. Loss: 20 feet.
Maximum elevation: 7,820 feet.
Map: China Cap USGS quad.
For more information: U.S. Forest Service at Wallowa Mountain Visitors Center, Enterprise, Oregon.
Finding the trail: This trail starts at the junction with North Fork Catherine Creek and Rock Creek Trail 1905, 9 miles from North Fork Catherine Creek Trailhead. The junction (El 7,430 ft.) is on top of a ridge, northeast of Meadow Mountain. See Hike 63 North Fork Catherine Creek and Hike 56 Rock Creek.

64   *Meadow Mountain*

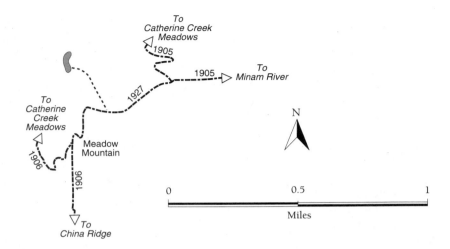

0.0   Trail junction with North Fork Catherine Creek Trail 1905.
0.1   Narrow meadow to the right of the trail, and path to pond.
0.4   Summit of Meadow Mountain and trail junction with China
       Ridge Trail 1906.

The trail: From the junction the trail heads southwest up the ridge. After a few yards it traverses around the left side of the ridge. The traverse ends a short distance farther in a saddle. At the saddle there is a fence a few feet to the right of the trail. A little farther along the fence crosses the trail (El 7,450 ft.).

At about 0.1 mile from Trail 1905 junction there is a long narrow meadow to the right of the trail at the base of Meadow Mountain. Along the right (east) side of the meadow is a path. The path goes northwest for 600 yards, dropping slightly to a pond. This is a fairly large pond with a meadow and campsites around it.

After passing the path and narrow meadow, Trail 1927 begins to climb Meadow Mountain. First there is an ascending traverse to the right. Up the traverse 200 yards is a switchback to the left. About the same distance farther is another switchback to the right. Past the second switchback, go 150 yards farther to the summit of Meadow Mountain (El 7,820 ft.). On the summit there is the remains of what appears to be an old lookout. There are also some mining prospect holes. From the summit Catherine Creek Meadows is far below to the west.

Past the summit the trail goes south along the ridge and drops slightly to the junction (El 7,800 ft.) with China Ridge Trail 1906. See Hike 66 China Ridge. The distance from Trail 1905 to Trail 1906 is only 0.4 mile.

SOUTHERN REGION

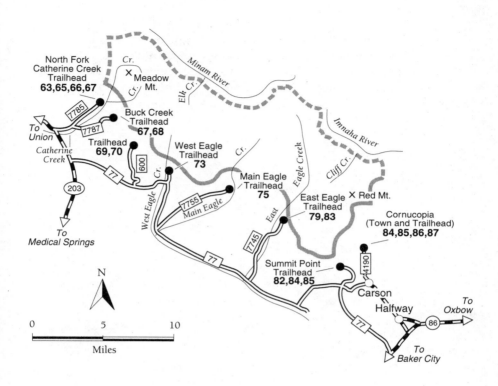

North Fork
Catherine Creek
Trailhead
63,65,66,67

× Meadow
Mt.

Cr.
Cr.

Minam River

Elk Cr.

Imnaha River

Buck Creek
Trailhead
67,68

Trailhead
69,70

West Eagle
Trailhead
73

Cr.

Eagle Creek

Cliff Cr.

To
Union

*Catherine
Creek*

To
Medical Springs

Main Eagle
Trailhead
75

East Eagle
Trailhead
79,83

× Red Mt.

Cornucopia
(Town and Trailhead)
84,85,86,87

West Eagle Cr.

Main Eagle

East

Summit Point
Trailhead
82,84,85

Carson

Halfway

To
Oxbow

To
Baker City

N

0   5   10

Miles

---

65   *SQUAW CREEK*

Trail 1951

General description: A 3.5 mile connecting
trail from Elk Creek Trail 1944 to China Ridge
Trail 1906.

Difficulty: Moderate to strenuous.
Trail maintenance: Infrequent.
Best season: Mid-June through October.
Traffic: Generally light, heavier in the fall,
with light horse traffic.
Elevation gain: 2,090 feet.
Maximum elevation: 7,430 feet.
Maps: Imus Geographics Wallowa Mountains

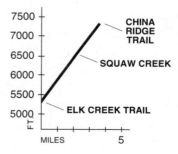

Eagle Cap Wilderness, or China Cap USGS quad. The Imus Geographics map
shows this trail more accurately.

For more information: U.S. Forest Service at Wallowa Mountain Visitors Center, Enterprise, Oregon, or U.S. Forest Service at Halfway Ranger Station, Halfway, Oregon.

Finding the trail: Squaw Creek Trail begins as closed Forest Road 100, 2.5 miles east of the North Fork Catherine Creek Campground at the junction (El 5,340 ft.) with Elk Creek Trail 1944, also a closed road at this point. See Hike 63 North Fork Catherine Creek for directions to the campground and trailhead. See Hike 67 Elk Creek for directions from the trailhead to the beginning of Squaw Creek Trail.

65 *Squaw Creek*
66 *China Ridge*

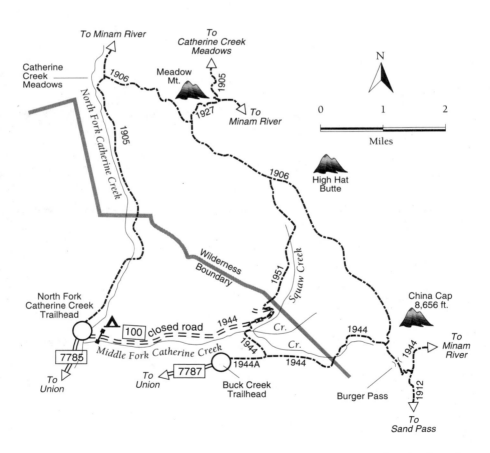

0.0	Trail junction with Elk Creek Trail.
2.3	Trail crosses Squaw Creek.
3.5	Trail junction with China Ridge Trail.

The trail: Squaw Creek Trail heads up the closed road (Forest Road 100) east northeast from the junction and makes a switchback to the left at 0.5 mile. One hundred fifty yards past the switchback, Squaw Creek Trail turns right off the closed road. There is a sign here that points up the trail and says Meadow Mountain 5 miles.

After leaving the road, the trail climbs through a partially logged area, makes a couple of switchbacks, then heads generally north. The trail here is well above and west of Squaw Creek. It crosses several very small streams as it climbs to the north. The trail enters a burn area 1.1 miles after leaving the road. It goes through this burn area for about 250 yards. The trail crosses Squaw Creek 0.5 mile after leaving the burn area. This crossing (El 6,600 ft.) is 2.25 miles from the junction with Elk Creek Trail.

After the crossing the trail heads up on the right (east) side of Squaw Creek, going through an open sloping meadow for some distance. In this open area watch for elk grazing on the grassy slopes above. There is a campsite 0.6 mile after the crossing on the left side of the trail near the creek. Beyond this point, there is no water in late summer and fall. Past the campsite the trail climbs fairly steeply for the last 0.75 mile to the junction with China Ridge Trail. See Hike 66 China Ridge. There is some burned area between the campsite and the junction. There is also some thick timber.

The junction with China Ridge Trail is in a saddle (El 7,430 ft.) on the ridge dividing Catherine Creek and Minam River drainages. The distance from the junction with Elk Creek Trail to the saddle and junction with China Ridge Trail is 3.5 miles. The trail at the junction may be hard to see because the saddle is covered with thick grass.

Squaw Creek Trail 1951 is fairly easy to follow. However, cattle use this area, so there are some "extra" trails. This trail may be done as part of a loop hike by going up Elk Creek Trail to China Ridge Trail, following China Ridge Trail to Squaw Creek Trail, then dropping down Squaw Creek Trail, the opposite direction on Squaw Creek from what is described above, to Elk Creek Trail and following it back to North Fork Catherine Creek Campground and Trailhead. See Hike 67 Elk Creek and Hike 66 China Ridge. This makes a 16 mile loop with about 4,000 feet of elevation gain and loss, making a very long day hike or better yet, a two day backpack.

Trail 1906

General description: An 8.5 mile connecting trail from Elk Creek Trail 1944 to North Fork Catherine Creek Trail 1905, at Catherine Creek Meadows. This trail also connects with Squaw Creek Trail 1951. This is a ridge top trail.

Difficulty: Strenuous.

Trail maintenance: Seldom.

Best season: July through mid-October.

Traffic: Light, with little or no horse traffic.

Elevation gain: 930 feet. Loss: 2,730 feet.

Maximum elevation: 8,010 feet.

Map: China Gap USGS quad.

For more information: U.S. Forest Service at Wallowa Mountain Visitors Center, Enterprise, Oregon, or U.S. Forest Service at Halfway Ranger Station, Halfway, Oregon.

Finding the trail: China Ridge Trail 1906 begins at a junction with Elk Creek Trail 1944, southwest of China Cap Mountain. See Hike 67 Elk Creek. See Hike 63 North Fork Catherine Creek for directions to North Fork Catherine Creek Trailhead. The elevation at the junction is 7,450 feet.

0.0	Trail junction with Elk Creek Trail.
0.7	Saddle below China Cap Mountain.
4.1	Trail junction with Squaw Creek Trail.
6.4	Trail junction with Meadow Mountain Trail.
8.5	Catherine Creek Meadows and trail junction with North Fork Catherine Creek Trail.

The trail: China Ridge Trail heads north from the junction with Elk Creek Trail. It climbs through open forest of lodgepole pine and subalpine fir, with China Cap Mountain to the right as it heads north. The trail crosses a very small stream 0.3 mile after leaving the junction. The first whitebark pines start showing up near this creek crossing. After the creek crossing the trail comes to a saddle in 0.3 mile. This saddle is on the ridge that divides the Minam River and Catherine Creek drainages. The saddle is 0.5 mile west northwest, of China Cap Mountain. From the saddle it is quite easy to climb to the peak. See Climb 16 China Cap Mountain in the climbing section of this book.

After crossing the saddle, the trail traverses northeast on the right side of the ridgeline offering a magnificent view of the Minam River Canyon to the northwest. The trail stays on the right side of the ridge for 0.6 mile, then crosses the ridge at 8,000 feet elevation. Another 150 yards and the trail crosses to the right side again, but now the trail stays close to the top of the ridgeline. The trail begins a traverse along the right side of the ridgeline about 700 yards farther along. This traverse lasts 0.5 mile before the trail regains the ridgeline again. After regaining the ridgeline, it goes off on the left side and passes some very old large whitebark pine trees. After being on the left side of the ridgeline for 0.6 mile, the trail traverses a steep rocky area. It then climbs nearly back to the ridgeline.

The trail stays close to the ridgeline while continuing to traverse the rocky steep sidehill. After traversing for 0.4 mile, the trail comes to a saddle in the ridge. There is another trail that turns off to the right. Be careful not to take it, as it drops off quickly the wrong way. This side trail is not marked and is not on Eagle Cap Wilderness Maps or USGS quads.

From the saddle our trial traverses on the left side of the ridge again. It crosses a grassy slope with stands of whitebark pine and subalpine fir. After traversing for 0.7 mile the trail gets back to the ridgeline. It then drops down the ridge 350 yards to the junction (El 7,430 ft.) with Squaw Creek Trail 1951. This unmarked junction is at a low spot in the ridge, 4.1 miles from Elk Creek Trail. The trails here are difficult to see because of the grass. Squaw Creek Trail turns off to the left (south southeast) at the junction. See Hike 65 Squaw Creek.

From the junction with Squaw Creek Trail, China Ridge Trail goes straight ahead up the ridge to the west. It stays generally left of the ridgeline but gets very near to it in a saddle 0.7 mile from the junction (El 7,580 ft.). Past the saddle, the trail climbs slightly. It stays on the left side of the ridge for just over 0.5 mile, then gets back on top. After getting back on top, the junction with Meadow Mountain Trail 1927 is 0.2 mile more. The elevation at this junction is 7,800 feet. See Hike 64 Meadow Mountain.

China Ridge Trail turns left at this junction and begins to drop off the west side of Meadow Mountain. This area is open hillside with groves of whitebark pine and subalpine fir. Cattle graze in this area, and in some places the trails may look more used than China Ridge Trail. Follow the blazes. Past the junction 700 yards the trail crosses two small muddy streams. Another 150 yards, is yet another small muddy stream.

The trail goes through a grove of whitebark pine 0.7 mile from the junction. Watch for blazes here. The trail continues 300 yards northwest past the grove and enters the timber. It then switchbacks to the left (a livestock trail goes straight ahead) and comes back in the open. We are now 0.9 mile from the junction with Trail 1927. The elevation here is 7,300 feet.

From here down, the trail is hard to find. Travel straight down along the edge of the open area for 250 yards to a path to the right. Take the path and head northwest and west. There may be many livestock paths here. Continue to traverse to the north, cross a couple of very small streams to reach a ridgeline. This ridgeline points straight down to Catherine Creek Meadows. It may be very difficult to find this ridge in weather with poor visibility. Head steeply straight down the ridgeline on a braided or nonexistent trail. After dropping 900 vertical feet on this ridge, the trail shows up again just to the left (south) of the ridgeline. From here the trail goes down a low rise between two small streams for 150 yards. It then crosses the stream to the right and heads northwest for 200 yards to the edge of Catherine Creek Meadows. In the meadows, is the junction with North Fork Catherine Creek Trail 1905. See Hike 63 North Fork Catherine Creek. There is a signpost at the junction. The junction (El 5,650 ft.) is 8.5 miles from Elk Creek Trail.

The first 6.4 miles of this trial is fairly easy to follow; however, the last 2.1 miles can be very difficult to find. The trail is there in places, but in other places it is not apparent on the ground, or worse yet, there are several cattle trails taking its place. If this description of the last 2.1 miles sounds vague, it is because the trail is vague. This part of Trail 1906 requires a lot of route finding skills to follow it safely. There are few good campsites and very little water along this trail, but the hike along a mostly open ridge with a great view makes it well worth hiking. See Hike 65 Squaw Creek for a possible loop trip that does not involve the last 3.3 miles of China Ridge Trail.

67   ELK CREEK

Trail 1944

General description: A backpack of 14.1 miles from North Fork Catherine Creek Campground and Trailhead to the Minam River. This trail also gives access to Squaw Creek, China Ridge, Sand Pass and Tombstone Lake Trails.

Difficulty: Moderate, but long.

Trail maintenance: Yearly.

Best season: Mid-June through October.

Traffic: Light to moderate, except may be heavy during fall hunting seasons, with moderate horse traffic.

Elevation gain: 3,740 feet. Loss: 3,030 feet.

Maximum elevation: 7,940 feet.

Maps: Imus Geographics Wallowa Mountains Eagle Cap Wilderness or China Cap and Steamboat Lake USGS quads.

For more information: U.S. Forest Service at Wallowa Mountain Visitors Center, Enterprise, Oregon, or U.S. Forest Service at Halfway Ranger Station, Halfway, Oregon.

Finding the trail: Elk Creek Trail starts a short distance south of North Fork Catherine Creek Campground (El 4,200 ft.). For directions to North Fork Catherine Creek Campground and Trailhead See Hike 63 North Fork Catherine Creek.

0.0	Trail begins at North Fork Catherine Creek Campground and Trailhead.
2.5	Trail junction with Squaw Creek Trail (road).
3.3	Trail junction with Elk Creek Alternate Trail 1944A.
6.3	Trail junction with China Ridge Trail 1906.
7.4	Trail crosses Burger Pass.
7.8	Trail junction with Sand Pass Trail 1912.
10.3	Trail junction with Tombstone Lake Trail 1943.
14.1	Trail crosses Minam River and trail junction with Minam River Trail 1673.

The trail: The trail is actually a closed road for the first 2.5 miles. Take Forest Road 100 heading east and cross the North Fork of Catherine Creek. A short distance past the creek is a gate. This gate blocks the road to vehicle traffic. Follow the road for 2.5 miles. Here Elk Creek Trail turns off to the right (south). Squaw Creek Trail 1951 goes straight ahead up the road. See Hike 65 Squaw Creek. There is a sign marking this turnoff (El 5,320 ft.).

The trail which is still another old roadbed drops slightly at first to cross Squaw Creek. There is no bridge, but there is a log to aid the crossing a few yards upstream. About 70 yards after crossing Squaw Creek the trail leaves the old roadbed. It crosses the Middle Fork of Catherine Creek 0.1 mile after crossing Squaw Creek. There is an old bridge here, but it's broken down too badly to be usable. A short distance after crossing the Middle Fork of Catherine Creek the trail makes some switchbacks. It then twists its way up a small ridge for 0.1 mile and flattens out a bit for 150 yards where it comes to a logged area. The logged area is on the right side of the trail. The trail goes along the logged area for 0.25 mile then climbs steeply for 300 yards. After climbing steeply, it flattens a bit for the last 125 yards to the junction with Trail 1944A. See Hike 68 Elk Creek Alternate. The elevation at the junction is 5,860 feet and it is 3.3 miles from North Fork Catherine Creek Campground.

At the junction, Elk Creek Trail 1944 turns left (east) and climbs along the left side of a logged area for 0.25 mile. Past the logged area the trail heads up the ridge for another 0.25 mile, then begins to traverse along the left side of the ridgeline. After traversing for 0.6 mile, it gets back on the ridgeline again (El 6,570 ft.). The trail goes up the ridgeline for 200 yards, then traverses up the right side for 600 yards where there is a switchback to the left. The Eagle Cap Wilderness Boundary is 0.25 mile past the switchback. The elevation at the wilderness boundary is 6,860 feet.

After crossing the wilderness boundary, the trail rounds a point overlooking Squaw Creek and the Middle Fork of Catherine Creek Canyons. It crosses a stream (El 7,060 ft.) 0.4 mile past the wilderness boundary. The trail crosses a rock slide area 0.4 mile after the stream crossing. From here one can see the flat topped peak of China Cap Mountain, to the northeast. A couple of hundred yards past the rock slide the trail crosses a small stream, which may not have water in late summer. There is a meadow below the trail here. After traveling 200 yards past the meadow, there is a trail going off to the right. Do not take this trail. Go 200 yards more to the junction with China Ridge Trail 1906. See Hike 66 China Ridge. This junction (El 7,440 ft.) is 6.3 miles from North Fork Catherine Creek Campground and is marked with a sign.

At the junction Elk Creek Trail 1944 turns to the right (south). It winds its way 0.75 mile to the top of Burger Pass (El 7,940 ft.). Then it makes a descending traverse for 0.3 mile to the south. After the traverse it makes several switchbacks down to the junction with Sand Pass Trail 1912 (El 7,620 ft.). See Hike 69 Sand Pass. This junction is 1.5 miles from the China Ridge Trail junction. The Sand Pass Trail junction is on the west side of Burger Meadows. From the junction the Sand Pass Trail can be seen as it climbs the light tan slope below Sand Pass, to the south.

Past the junction Elk Creek Trail heads north and northeast for 0.3 mile to the junction with the Old Elk Creek Trail. Bear left to stay on the main trail, heading northeast, for another 0.7 mile where the trail makes a switchback to the right. There is a spring above the trail 200 yards past the switchback. Watch for mule deer, which seem to be plentiful in this area. A very small stream runs down across the trail from the spring. The trail crosses three more very small streams in the next 600 yards to where it makes another switchback. There are two more small stream crossings in the 300 yards to the next switchback. After this switchback the trail descends, crossing two more small streams to another junction with the Old Elk Creek Trail. The old trail comes up from the left. Just past this junction the trail crosses a larger stream. There is a waterfall above the trail here. A few yards more is another junction with the old trail. It bears to the right here. The newer main trail heads to the left, and makes a couple of switchbacks. It then drops down across the meadow to the east and crosses Elk Creek as it goes the last few yards to the junction with Tombstone Lake Trail 1943. This junction (El 6,420 ft.) is 10.3 miles from North Fork Catherine Creek Campground. There is a good campsite just before crossing Elk Creek on the lower end of the lush, but sometimes wet meadow. See Hike 71 Tombstone Lake.

At the junction, Elk Creek Trail turns to the left (north). Between here and the next place the trail crosses Elk Creek some maps (Steamboat Lake USGS quad) show the trail on the wrong side of Elk Creek. Imus Geographics Wallowa Mountains Eagle Cap Wilderness map shows it correctly. The stream crossing 125 yards past the junction is the outlet of Tombstone Lake. There is a waterfall below the trail to the left, 175 yards past the creek crossing. After going 0.25 mile from the junction, there is a burn area. The trail goes through the burn for about 250 yards. Another 350 yards down the trail is a switchback to the left, and one to the right 250 yards farther along. Another 250 yards and the trail enters the burn area again. It stays in the burn area for about 350 yards this time, making two switchbacks and crossing a stream. The trail crosses

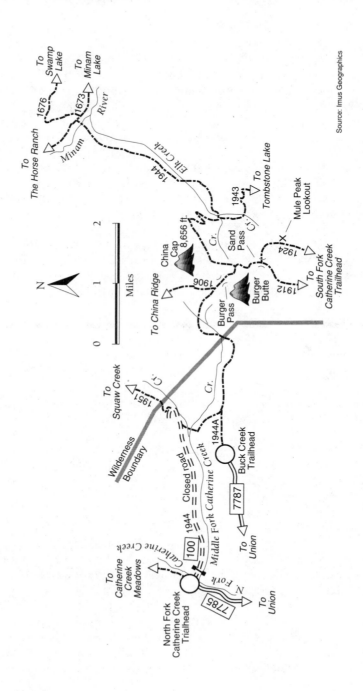

Source: Imus Geographics

another stream as it leaves the burn. Three hundred fifty yards after leaving the burn, the trail makes a switchback to the left and crosses a creek a short distance later. It then drops, making another switchback to where it crosses Elk Creek (El 5,870 ft.).

After crossing Elk Creek, the trail climbs a few feet and makes a switchback to the right. It crosses five small streams in the next 1.4 miles while it heads down the west side of Elk Creek, staying well above it most of the time. The forest here is thicker than it was up above, and the trees are larger. There are several log steps in the trail 3.3 miles below the Tombstone Lake Trail junction. The trail reaches the Minam River 0.5 mile past the steps.

The bridge over the Minam River was out when we hiked this trail in September 1994. A new bridge was supposed to be put in. There is a good campsite just before crossing the river. Until the new bridge is put in, the trail crosses the river a few yards below the old bridge site. This could be a dangerous crossing if the river is high. After crossing the river, the trail climbs for 100 yards to the junction with Minam River Trail 1673. This junction (El 4,910 ft.) is 14.1 miles from North Fork Catherine Creek Campground. See Hike 42 Upper Minam River.

An extended loop can be made by going down the Minam River Trail from the junction, and then taking Rock Creek Trail and North Fork Catherine Creek Trail back to North Fork Catherine Creek Trailhead. This loop totals 32.1 miles and would be best done in three or four days.

68   ELK CREEK ALTERNATE

Trail 1944A

General description: A short 0.7 mile connecting trail from Buck Creek Trailhead to Elk Creek Trail 1944.

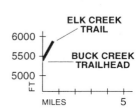

Difficulty: Easy.

Trail maintenance: Yearly.

Best season: June through October.

Traffic: Moderate, with moderate horse traffic.

Elevation gain: 470 feet.

Maximum elevation: 5,860 feet.

Maps: Imus Geographics Wallowa Mountains Eagle Cap Wilderness or China Gap USGS quad, either of which show part or all of this trail as a road.

For more information: U.S. Forest Service at Wallowa Mountain Visitors Center, Enterprise, Oregon, or U.S. Forest Service at Halfway Ranger Station, Halfway, Oregon.

Finding the trail: Buck Creek Trailhead can be a bit difficult to find. Both USFS and USGS maps show it vaguely, or incorrectly; however, the Imus Geographics map shows how to get to the trailhead correctly. From the town of Union, take State Highway 203, 11.5 mile southeast. Turn left on Forest

Road 7785, and follow it 4 miles to the junction with FR 7787. Turn right on FR 7787 and go approximately 3.5 miles to Buck Creek Trailhead.

0.0   Buck Creek Trailhead.
0.3   Trail enters timber.
0.7   Trail junction with Elk Creek Trail 1994.

The trail: Elk Creek Alternate Trail 1944A is an easier way to get on Elk Creek Trail than taking Elk Creek Trail from North Catherine Creek Trailhead. It shortens the distance by almost 3 miles and eliminates most of the road walking. Trail 1944A starts at Buck Creek Trailhead (El 5,390 ft.).

The trail begins as a road that is closed to motor vehicles. There are signs here marking the trail. It goes around the right (south) side of a logged area for 0.3 mile. It then cuts to the left through some timber to another logged area. The trail goes along the left (upper) side of this logged area. There is a road along the right side but do not take it. The trail climbs along the left side of the logged area for 0.1 mile to the junction with Trail 1944 (El 5,860 ft.). This junction is 0.7 mile from Buck Creek Trailhead. See Hike 67 Elk Creek.

69   SAND PASS

Trail 1912

General description: A steep, sometimes difficult to find, 6.3 mile trail connecting the obscure South Fork Catherine Creek Trailhead with Elk Creek Trail 1944. This trail also allows access to Mule Peak Trail.
Difficulty: Strenuous.
Trail maintenance: Seldom.
Best season: July through September.
Traffic: Light.
Elevation gain: 3,220 feet. Loss: 500 feet.
Maximum elevation: 8,120 feet.
Maps: Imus Geographics Wallowa

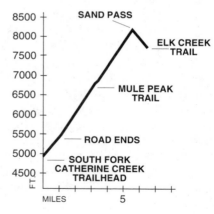

Mountains Eagle Cap Wilderness or Flagstaff Butte and China Cap USGS quads.
For more information: U.S. Forest Service at Wallowa Mountain Visitors Center, Enterprise, Oregon, or U.S. Forest Service at Halfway Ranger Station, Halfway, Oregon.
Finding the trail: To get to the South Fork Catherine Creek Trailhead, take Oregon Highway 203 for 13.5 miles southeast from the town of Union. Turn left on Forest Road 77, and follow it for approximately 9 miles to the junction

with Forest Road 600. Turn left on FR 600, and go approximately 3 miles to the junction with Forest Road 650. Turn right and find a parking spot. FR 650 is closed to vehicles and blocked off. This is the trailhead for Sand Pass and Mule Peak Trails (El 4,900 ft.). A good map is a big help in finding the trailhead.

0.0	South Fork Catherine Creek Trailhead.
0.2	Trail crosses Sand Creek.
0.4	Spring.
1.0	Roadbed ends.
1.3	Trail reaches ridgeline.
3.1	Trial junction with lower end of Mule Peak Trail.
5.3	Sand Pass and trail junction with upper end of Mud Peak Trail.
6.3	Trail junction with Elk Creek Trail.

The trail: The trail starts out as a continuation of FR 650. First the trail (road) crosses a creek and passes a trail sign. A quarter mile from the trailhead the trail crosses Sand Pass Creek. There is a spring above the trail (road), 0.2 mile past Sand Pass Creek. A tiny stream originates at the spring and crosses the trail. After going 0.3 mile past the spring, the trail turns left on spur FR 660. This is a much poorer road. There is a trail sign a few yards up FR 660. Elevation at the sign is 5,270 feet. After going 0.1 mile up FFR 660, the trail switchbacks to the left on yet another spur road which soon becomes a trail 1 mile from the trailhead.

After leaving the road, the trail climbs for 0.3 mile nearly to the top of a rounded ridgeline. It makes a couple of switchbacks while climbing to the ridgeline. Here it turns right (northeast) and heads up, just to the right of the ridgeline. After climbing along the ridge for 1.4 miles the trail comes to the top of a small open rounded hilltop (El 6,250 ft.). Here the trail drops a few feet then starts to climb again. After climbing for 300 yards, it makes a switchback to the left. A quarter mile past the switchback, the trail crosses a small stream and enters and open area. It makes a switchback to the left 300 yards after crossing the small stream. A path goes straight ahead at this switchback. Do not take it. At the switchback, the trail starts an ascending traverse to the northwest through an open area.

After climbing the ascending traverse for 500 yards, the trail comes to the junction with Mule Peak Trail 1924. This junction (El 6,760 ft.) is marked only with a pile of rocks. There was a post in the rock pile in September 1994 when I hiked this trail. The Mule Peak Trail, which turns off to the right (northeast), is difficult to see here as it has grown up to grass. To the northeast Mule Peak Lookout can be seen from this open area. It is quite a distance away and a bit hard to spot. See Hike 70 Mule Peak.

The trial leaves the open area 150 yards past the junction. It goes along a semi-open hillside for 0.25 mile then drops slightly to cross Sand Pass Creek. The elevation at the crossing is 6,670 feet. There is a campsite at the crossing. There is a trail that heads west southwest past the campsite. This trail can be taken for a short distance, then turn right up a semi-open ridge to regain Sand

Pass Trail, but Sand Pass Trail actually turns right just after the creek crossing. Up to this point the trail has been easy to follow, but from here on it is more of a challenge.

Turn right just after crossing Sand Pass Creek and head north. Watch for blazes marking the trail. There may be a lot of blown down trees in this area. Head north and up for 0.25 mile and enter an open area. The trail goes along the right (east) side of this open area. It crosses a small stream at 6,950 feet elevation, and 275 yards past the stream it bears to the left into the open area. Here it can be seen in most places. The trail, which is deeply eroded in places, twists its way up a small rib through country that is becoming more alpine. Continue to head up, to the north. After climbing the rib for 0.3 mile the trail turns off to the right. It soon heads steeply up to the north again for 400 yards. The trail then crosses a small stream and heads northeast for 150 yards. It then turns north again and heads up another 150 yards to another small stream. This stream comes out of the bottom of a rocky slope. Cross the stream and head northeast for 150 yards to another small stream. This stream also comes out of the rocky slope. After crossing this stream, the trail winds uphill, steeply, for 0.5 mile to Sand Pass.

69   *Sand Pass*
70   *Mule Peak*

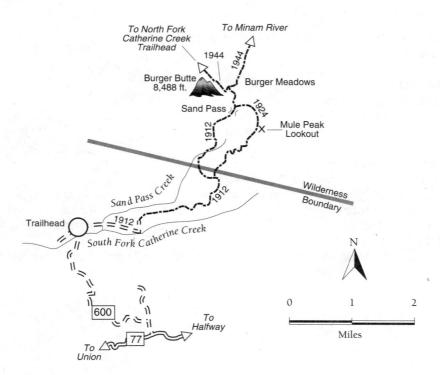

Sand Pass (El 8,120 ft.) is a light tan sandy notch between dark rock outcroppings on the ridgeline. There is a signpost at the pass pointing to Mule Peak, which is to the right (east). See Hike 70 Mule Peak. It also points straight ahead and down to the Minam River. At Sand Pass the view to the north opens up. Looking down to the north from this alpine notch is Burger Meadow and the nearly 3,000 foot deep Minam River Canyon. The high peaks of the North Central Wallowa Mountains are to the northeast in the distance, and China Cap Mountain is to the northwest.

After crossing Sand Pass, the trail makes six steep downhill switchbacks. It then bears left and winds its way down and goes along the west side of Burger Meadow to the junction with Elk Creek Trail 1944. The junction (El 7,620 ft.) is one mile from Sand Pass and 6.4 miles from the trailhead. See Hike 67 Elk Creek.

This trail is quite difficult to follow for two miles south of Sand Pass. Good route finding skills are required to follow this section. The rest of the trail is in good condition and is fairly easy to follow. Sand Pass Trail climbs 3,200 vertical feet and is a fairly strenuous hike. A loop hike can be made from Sand Pass by taking Mule Peak Trail to the right and rejoining Sand Pass Trail at the lower Mule Peak Trail junction. See Hike 70 Mule Peak.

70 MULE PEAK

Trail 1924

General description: A 3.1 mile trail along the ridge from Sand Pass to Mule Peak Lookout, and down to the Sand Pass Trail.
Difficulty: Strenuous.
Trail maintenance: Rare.
Best season: July through September.
Traffic: Light, with very little horse traffic.
Elevation gain: 460 feet. Loss: 1,810 feet.
Maximum elevation: 8,580 feet.

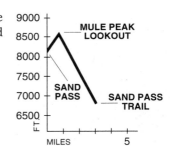

Maps: Imus Geographics Wallowa Mountains
Eagle Cap Wilderness, or Flagstaff Butte and China Cap USGS quads.
For more information: U.S. Forest Service at Wallowa Mountain Visitors Center, Enterprise, Oregon, or U.S. Forest Service at Halfway Ranger Station, Halfway, Oregon.
Finding the trail: Mule Peak Trail leaves Sand Pass Trail 1912 at Sand Pass (El 8,120 ft.). See Hike 69 Sand Pass.

0.0	Sand Pass and trail junction with Sand Pass Trail.
0.8	Mule Peak Lookout.
2.9	Eagle Cap Wilderness Boundary.
3.1	Trail junction with Sand Pass Trail.

The trail: From Sand Pass, Mule Peak Trail heads east up along the left side of the ridgeline. This is a fairly open alpine area with whitebark pine and subalpine fir trees. Burger Meadows can be seen below to the left. The trail is marked with cairns in this area.

After climbing for 0.2 mile, there is a switchback to the right. Follow the cairns and blazes. Past the switchback the trail winds uphill, first northeast, then east, then southeast for another 0.2 mile, to reach the ridgeline. After reaching the ridgeline, the trail heads up over light colored granite sand to the east northeast. It soon turns to the right and traverses on the right side of the ridgeline, heading southeast. The slope, along this traverse is covered with granite boulders and small alpine trees. The trail drops slightly and comes to a saddle (El 8,430 ft.) after traversing 0.2 mile.

After going across this saddle, the trail heads up the ridge to the east southeast for 0.1 mile to another saddle. It then climbs up the ridge 300 yards, passing an outhouse, to Mule Peak Lookout (El 8,580 ft.). The open area where Mule Peak Trail meets Sand Pass Trail, can be seen below, to the south southwest from here. Take a note of its location before descending.

A few yards past the lookout the trail turns down to the right (south). It makes six switchbacks in the next 600 yards, then turns down steeply for 150 yards. Watch for cairns and blazes. The trail makes six more switchbacks in the next 0.4 mile, then goes down steeply again for 50 yards. The trail is badly eroded here. It makes five more switchbacks in the next 0.1 mile to a stream crossing (El 7,790 ft.). This is a very small stream. In the next 0.5 mile the trail makes 6 more switchbacks. It then heads south on a grassy open hillside. The trail may be hard to see in this grassy area. After going 0.4 mile along and down this open hillside, it makes a switchback to the right. The Eagle Cap Wilderness boundary sign is 5 yards past the switchback on the left side of the trail. From the switchback to the junction with Sand Pass Trail, Mule Peak Trail heads southwest. It goes through a finger of timber and meets the Sand Pass Trail 350 yards from the last switchback. Elevation at the junction is 6,760 feet. There is no sign marking the junction. See Hike 69 Sand Pass. This trail takes some route finding skill to follow. It may be done as part of a loop hike with Sand Pass Trail.

Trail 1943

General description: An 8.1 mile backpack trail from Elk Creek Trail, over an 8,210 foot high pass to West Fork Eagle Creek Trail. Besides Tombstone Lake this trail is also the access to Diamond Lake.

Difficulty: Moderate to strenuous.

Trail maintenance: Yearly.

Best season: July through September.

Traffic: Moderate.

Elevation gain: 1,790 feet. Loss: 2,030 feet.

Maximum elevation: 8,210 feet.

Maps: Steamboat and Bennet Peak USGS quads.

For more information: U.S. Forest Service at Wallowa Mountain Visitors Center, Enterprise, Oregon, or U.S. Forest Service at Halfway Ranger Station, Halfway, Oregon.

Finding the trail: Tombstone Lake Trail begins at the junction with Elk Creek Trail 1944, 3.8 miles up Elk Creek Trail from the Minam River. See Hike 67 Elk Creek. See Hike 63 North Fork Catherine Creek for directions to the trailhead.

0.0	Trail junction with Elk Creek Trail
1.8	Trail junction with Diamond Lake Trail.
2.4	Tombstone Lake.
3.7	Pass.
4.9	Meadow.
8.1	Trail junction with West Fork Eagle Creek Trail.

The trail: From the junction with Elk Creek Trail (El 6,420 ft.) Tombstone Lake Trail heads southeast. It crosses a small stream 350 yards from the junction. It then makes a switchback to the left and crosses the same stream again. In the next 0.4 mile, the trail makes twelve more switchbacks to where it crosses another stream with a campsite by the crossing. Elevation at the campsite is 6,700 feet. A path goes to the left here, but the Tombstone Lake Trail goes straight ahead. In the next mile the trail makes thirteen switchbacks and climbs 600 feet. It goes over the top of a rise at 7,300 feet elevation then drops for 200 yards to the junction with Diamond Lake Trail (El 7,250 ft.). This junction is not marked with a sign, but a good path heads 0.1 mile to the left (north) to Diamond Lake. See Hike 72 Diamond Lake.

71 Tombstone Lake
72 Diamond Lake

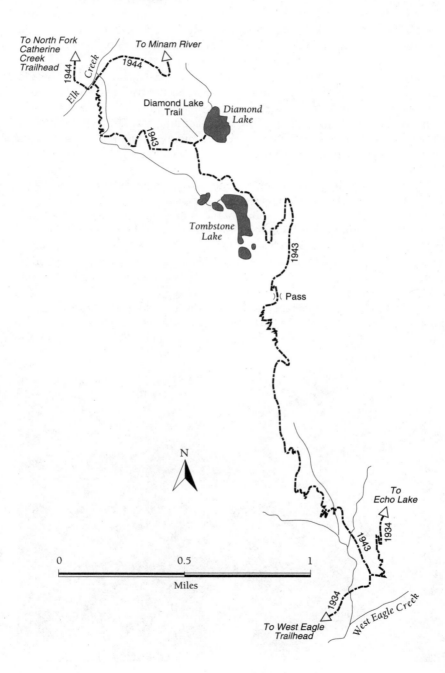

To North Fork
Catherine
Creek
Trailhead

1944

Elk Creek

To Minam River

1944

Diamond Lake
Trail

*Diamond
Lake*

1943

*Tombstone
Lake*

1943

)(Pass

N

To
Echo Lake

1934

1943

1934

To West Eagle
Trailhead

West Eagle Creek

0   0.5   1

Miles

Just past the Diamond Lake junction, the trail goes by a small meadow. It then makes an ascending traverse along a talus slope. The trail makes a switchback to the right 275 yards past the junction. It makes four more switchbacks in the next 400 yards as it climbs to the top of the rise. A few yards farther is Tombstone Lake. Tombstone Lake (El 7,421 ft.) is 2.4 miles from Elk Creek Trail. There are a few campsites at Tombstone Lake and like most of the lakes in the Wallowas, the fishing is good to excellent.

The trail goes along the left (northeast) side of the lake and soon begins to climb away from it. There is a campsite between the trail and the lake as it climbs away. The trail makes sixteen switchbacks in the first 0.8 mile after leaving Tombstone Lake. It then makes an ascending traverse to the south for another 0.5 mile. After the traverse, the trail makes three more switchbacks up to the pass (El 8,210 ft.). The ridge this pass is on divides Elk Creek and West Fork Eagle Creek drainages.

After crossing the pass, the trail heads down towards West Fork Eagle Creek. A few yards below the pass the trail makes a switchback. It then winds on down through granite outcroppings and scattered small trees. The trail makes another switchback 0.3 mile below the pass. In the next 0.9 mile, to a small meadow, the trail makes sixteen more switchbacks. The trail then makes a left turn as it comes into the meadow (El 7,520 ft.). There is a stream bed in the meadow, but it was dry in September when we hiked this trail. The trail crosses the meadow.

Two hundred seventy-five yards past the meadow, the trail makes a switchback to the left, then one to the right. Just past the switchbacks, the trail crosses a small stream which was also dry in September. The trail starts a set

Tombstone Lake. *Photo by Lowell Euhus.*

of thirty-three switchbacks, 250 yards past the stream. There is one small stream that goes through a culvert under the trail, and a small waterfall next to the trail on the twenty-ninth switchback. This set of switchbacks is 2.4 miles long, and drops 1,020 feet to a creek crossing. After the creek crossing the switchbacks begin again. There are thirteen more switchbacks on the way to another creek crossing. This set of thirteen is 0.4 mile long and drop 230 feet. This crossing is the West Fork Eagle Creek. The junction with West Fork Eagle Creek Trail 1934 (El 6,250 ft.) is 400 yards past the creek crossing. This junction is 8.1 miles from the junction with Elk Creek Trail. See Hike 73 West Fork Eagle Creek.

A one-way trip can be made from the West Fork Eagle Creek Trail junction by heading south on West Fork Eagle Creek Trail to West Eagle Trailhead, 2.6 miles away. This trip involves a car shuttle.

72   DIAMOND LAKE

General description: A short 0.1 mile long path, connecting Tombstone Lake Trail 1943 with Diamond Lake.
Difficulty: Easy.
Trail maintenance: None.
Best season: Mid-June through October.
Traffic: Light to moderate, with light horse traffic.
Elevation loss: 209 feet.
Maximum elevation: 7,250 feet.
Map: Steamboat Lake USGS quad.
For more information: U.S. Forest Service at Wallowa Mountain Visitors Center, Enterprise, Oregon, or U.S. Forest Service at Halfway Ranger Station, Halfway, Oregon.
Finding the trail: The path to Diamond Lake leaves the Tombstone Lake Trail 1943, 2 miles from its junction with Elk Creek Trail. See Hike 71 Tombstone Lake. The elevation where the path to Diamond Lake heads north northeast off the Tombstone Lake Trail is 7,250 feet.

0.0   Trail junction with Tombstone Lake Trail.
0.1   Diamond Lake.

The trail: From the Tombstone Lake Trail, the path to Diamond Lake drops slightly to the north northeast for 200 yards to a campsite overlooking the lake. There is a stream next to the campsite. The lake (El 7,041 ft.) is about 75 feet below the campsite. There are fish to be caught in the lake, but the campsites are very limited.

Trail 1934

General description: A 12.9 mile backpack from West Eagle Creek Trailhead to the junction with Trail Creek Trail, via Echo and Traverse Lakes.

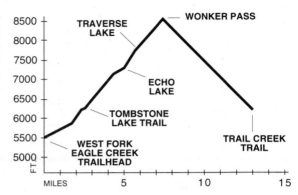

Difficulty: Strenuous.
Trail maintenance: Yearly.
Best season: Mid-July through September.
Traffic: Moderate.
Elevation gain: 3,040 feet.
Loss: 2,360 feet.
Maximum elevation: 8,500 feet.
Maps: Imus Geographics Wallowa Mountains Eagle Cap Wilderness, or Bennet Peak and Steamboat Lake USGS quads.
For more information: U.S. Forest Service at Wallowa Mountain Visitors Center, Enterprise, Oregon or U.S. Forest Service at Halfway Ranger Station, Halfway, Oregon.
Finding the trail: From Union take State Highway 203 southeast for 14.1 miles to the junction with Eagle Creek Road, Forest Road 77. Turn left (east) on FR 77 and follow it 15.2 miles to West Eagle Trailhead junction. Turn left (north) and go 0.4 mile to the trailhead and parking area. There are several campsites before reaching the trailhead.

0.0	West Eagle Creek Trailhead.
0.1	Trail junction with Fake Creek Trail.
0.8	Trail crosses West Fork Eagle Creek.
2.0	Trail crosses West Fork Eagle Creek again.
2.6	Trail junction with Tombstone Lake Trail.
5.0	Echo Lake.
6.0	Traverse Lake.
7.5	Pass.
12.9	Trail junction with Trail Creek Trail.

The trail: From the trailhead (El 5,460 ft.) the trail heads north, crossing a bridge over a small stream in a few yards. It then passes through the timber along the east side of West Eagle Meadows for 0.1 mile to the unmarked junction with Fake Creek Trail. Fake Creek Trail bears right and crosses the ridge to Main Eagle Road near Boulder Park 6 miles to the east.

Falls in the East Fork of the West Fork Eagle Creek.

At the junction West Eagle Creek Trail bears left (northwest). The trail crosses Fake Creek 0.2 mile past the junction. A few yards after crossing Fake Creek, the trail enters a lush meadow and crosses a small stream. It makes some small switchbacks 0.1 mile past the meadow, crosses a creek and soon comes to the slightly more than knee deep crossing of West Eagle Creek. This crossing may be much deeper and possibly dangerous during spring and early summer. After the crossing the trail crosses a small stream on a bridge and comes to the Eagle Cap Wilderness Boundary. Three-tenths mile after entering the wilderness, the trail enters an open sloping meadow covered with wildflowers. It crosses a couple of small streams, then climbs three small switchbacks to the top of a granite outcropping, overlooking the rushing waters of West Eagle Creek. Past the outcropping the trail makes several more switchbacks climbing through the woods, then comes out in another open slope that is partly covered with brush. The trail crosses West Eagle Creek (El 5,850 ft.) again, 1.1 miles past the wilderness boundary.

Shortly after the knee deep crossing, the trail begins to climb more steeply, as it heads up in switchbacks on lightly timbered slopes toward the junction with Tombstone Lake Trail. On the climb, the broad cascading waterfall of the East Fork of the West Fork Eagle Creek can be seen to the east. The waterfall drops over a granite ledge and tumbles into a jungle of boulders and slide

73   *West Fork Eagle Creek*

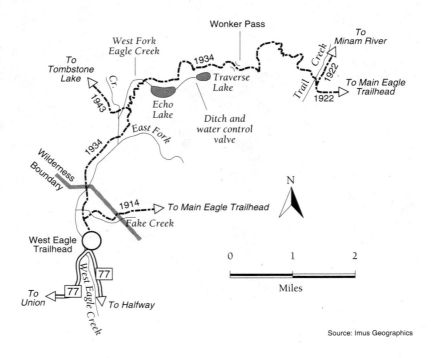

Source: Imus Geographics

alder. After climbing ten switchbacks, the trail junction with Tombstone Lake Trail 1943 is reached. See Hike 71 Tombstone Lake.

From the junction with Tombstone Lake Trail (El 6,250 ft.) the trail starts the switchbacks heading up to Echo Lake. In the next 2 miles the trail makes forty switchbacks and climbs 800 vertical feet. This climb is mostly on open slopes. After climbing the switchbacks, the trail crosses the West Fork of Eagle Creek, and gets off the side hill that it has been on for the last 2 miles. Here the trail heads to the east, up the high valley toward Echo Lake. There is a pond to the right of the trail, 200 yards past the stream crossing. Past the pond the trail turns to the left, then makes a switchback to the right. There are two very small stream crossings 0.25 mile past the pond. One hundred fifty yards past the last stream crossing there is a campsite on the right side of the trail. Near the campsite two more small streams go under the trail in culverts. Echo Lake is 200 yards farther on the right (south) side of the trail.

Echo Lake, like so many other lakes on the south side of the Wallowa Mountains, has been dammed. This damming allows the lakes to hold water for irrigation, but it makes them look a lot less beautiful than they once did. Because of the variation in water level, the lakes have areas of mud around their shorelines. The elevation at Echo Lake is 7,270 feet. The trail goes along the left (north) side of the lake. It crosses a couple more very small streams that flow through culverts. Past the lake 0.4 mile the trail makes four more switchbacks. The trail enters a talus slope 0.2 mile past the switchbacks. The talus slope is about 125 yards wide. Past the talus slope the trail traverses along a lightly wooded hillside, for 200 yards. Then it makes two more switchbacks as it climbs the last 200 yards to Traverse Lake.

Traverse Lake is also a reservoir. There is a notch cut through the rock at its outlet. This allows the water to be taken out below the lake's natural level. This notch is 5 or 6 feet deep, and maybe 3 feet wide. There is a little dam down in the notch with a gate valve in it. This allows the flow to be regulated. There are lots of possible campsites along the north side of Traverse Lake. When the water is low there is a sandy beach on the north side. Also, there are lots of brook trout in the lake. The elevation of Traverse Lake is 7,720 feet.

After going along the north side of Traverse Lake, the trail begins to climb again. It makes twelve switchbacks in the first 0.8 mile above the lake to where the trail comes very close to the ridgeline. To the left of the trail and up a few feet is a viewpoint that overlooks Lowery Creek. The trail makes a switchback to the left 300 yards past the viewpoint. This switchback is close to the base of a granite wall. The trail makes nine more switchbacks before reaching Wonker Pass. This pass (El 8,500 ft.) is on the ridge dividing the West Fork Eagle Creek drainage and Trail Creek in the Minam River drainage. The view to the east northeast is into Trail Creek Canyon. The slopes on the Trail Creek side are very alpine, having almost no trees for the first 1,000 feet down, unlike the Traverse Lake side which has scattered whitebark pines all the way up.

The trail heads down the Trail Creek side. It makes twenty-five switchbacks and then starts a long descending traverse. The trail crosses a very small stream 150 yards into the 0.75 mile long traverse. By the end of the traverse the trail is in a lightly forested area again. After the traverse the trail makes eleven switchbacks in the next 1.5 miles, then it crosses two very small streams in culverts, turns left, and goes 75 yards to a meadow. There is a finger of trees in the meadow with a campsite in it. The elevation at the meadow is 6,650 feet. The trail goes through the trees, and crosses a creek on the far (south) side of the meadow. The trail may be difficult to see in the grass of the meadow.

The trail soon begins to switchback down again through much larger timber than there was above. It makes six switchbacks in the 0.7 mile to Trail Creek. The trail crosses the creek and climbs a few feet to the junction with Trail Creek Trail 1922 (El 6,240 ft.). See Hike 76 Trail Creek. The distance from West Eagle Trailhead to the junction with Trail Creek Trail is 12.9 miles. This is a fairly strenuous hike, but the country you go through is well worth it.

The return trip may be made by the same route or by taking Trail Creek Trail and Main Eagle Creek Trail, back to Main Eagle Trailhead. See Hike 76 Trail Creek and Hike 75 Main Eagle Creek. A car shuttle can be done from Main Eagle Trailhead to West Eagle Trailhead. For the more ambitious and adventuresome hiker, the 6 mile long Fake Creek Trail, which is not described in this book, can be taken over the ridge from Main Eagle Trailhead back to West Eagle Trailhead. This eliminates the need for a car shuttle, but is quite strenuous and requires some route finding skills.

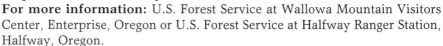

74   BENCH CANYON

Trail 1937

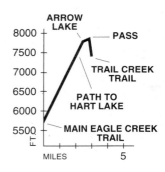

General description: A 3.1 mile trail climbing from Main Eagle Creek Trail to Trail Creek Trail. This trail is the access to Heart and Arrow (pond) Lakes.

Difficulty: Moderate to strenuous.

Trail maintenance: Infrequent.

Best season: July through October.

Traffic: Moderate, with light horse traffic.

Elevation gain: 2,090 feet. Loss: 430 feet.

Maximum elevation: 7,840 feet.

Map: Bennet Peak USGS quad.

For more information: U.S. Forest Service at Wallowa Mountain Visitors Center, Enterprise, Oregon or U.S. Forest Service at Halfway Ranger Station, Halfway, Oregon.

Finding the trail: Bench Canyon Trail leaves Main Eagle Creek Trail 1922, 2.6 miles north of Main Eagle Creek Trailhead. See Hike 75 Main Eagle Creek. The elevation at the junction with Main Eagle Trail is 5,750 feet.

0.0	Trail junction with Main Eagle Creek Trail.
1.5	Trail enters burn area.
2.1	Trail junction with path to Heart Lake.
2.6	Arrow Lake.
2.7	Trail crosses pass.
3.1	Trail junction with Trail Creek Trail.

74 *Bench Canyon*

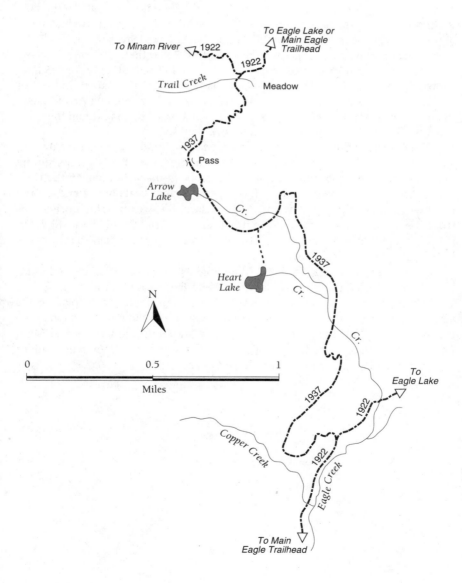

The trail: At the junction with Main Eagle Creek Trail, Bench Canyon Trail turns off to the left (northwest). At first the trail winds steeply uphill, then it makes a long ascending traverse to the north. The trail crosses a small stream 0.7 mile after leaving Main Eagle Creek Trail. This crossing is at approximately 6,300 feet elevation. The trail makes eight switchbacks in the next 0.5 mile, to where it crosses another small stream. Here the trail gets off the side hill and heads up Bench Canyon. It crosses another stream 500 yards farther and enters a small burn area. This area was burned in 1994. The burn area is only about 100 yards wide. The trail tops a rise 0.3 mile past the burn area.

There is a campsite on the right side of the trail 100 yards after topping the rise. The unmarked path to Heart Lake is about 300 yards past the campsite. Heart Lake is to the left (south) of the trail 0.25 mile. The path to the lake is hard to see, but the lake can be seen from the top of the small rise just south of the trail. The elevation, where the path to Heart Lake leaves the trail is 7,420 feet. The elevation of the lake is approximately 7,300 feet.

After passing the path to Heart Lake, the trail climbs steeply for 0.5 mile to Arrow Lake (El 7,800 ft.). Arrow Lake is the pond 100 yards to the left of the trail. There are probably no fish in Arrow Lake. After passing Arrow Lake, the trail climbs gently for 250 yards to the top of a pass (El 7,840 ft.) on the ridge dividing Eagle Creek and Minam River drainages.

After crossing the pass, the trail drops a couple hundred yards to two small steep, switchbacks, then 500 yards more to a meadow. The swampy alpine meadow with a gray granite cliff and talus slope at its east end is on the right side of the trail. The lush meadow has several springs in its upper end. At the northwest end of the meadow, the trail crosses the stream, which originates from the springs, and comes to the junction with Trail Creek Trail (El 7,410 ft.). This junction is 3.1 miles from the junction with Main Eagle Trail where Bench Canyon Trail started.

Note that Trail Creek Trail and Main Eagle Trail have the same trail number. Trail Creek Trail is a continuation of Main Eagle Creek Trail. See Hike 76 Trail Creek. Bench Canyon Trail is easy to follow, but it is fairly steep and gains almost 2,100 feet in the 2.75 miles up to the pass. From the junction a loop hike can be made by turning right on Trail Creek Trail and following it and Main Eagle Creek Trail back to Main Eagle Creek Trailhead, also known as Boulder Park Trailhead. See Hike 75 Main Eagle Creek.

Trail 1922 and 1931

General description: A 6.8 mile backpack, or long 13.6 mile day hike, from Main Eagle Creek Trailhead to Eagle Lake. This trail accesses Bench Canyon, Lookingglass Lake and Trail Creek Trails.
Difficulty: Moderate.
Trail maintenance: Yearly.
Best season: Mid-June through September.
Traffic: Heavy, with moderate to heavy horse traffic.
Elevation gain: 2.540 feet.
Maximum elevation: 7,450 feet.
Maps: Imus Geographics Wallowa Mountains Eagle Cap Wilderness or Bennet Peak, Krag Peak and Eagle Cap USGS maps.
For more information: U.S. Forest Service at Wallowa Mountain Visitors Center, Enterprise, Oregon, or U.S. Forest Service at Halfway Ranger Station, Halfway, Oregon.
Finding the trail: Main Eagle Creek Trail starts at Main Eagle Creek Trailhead. To reach the trailhead, take Big Creek Road, Forest Road 67, east from the town of Medical Springs. Follow FR 67 approximately 16 miles, to its

Eagle Lake. *Photo by Lowell Euhus.*

junction with Forest Road 77. Turn left on FR 77 and go 1 mile to the junction with Forest Road 7755. Turn right on FR 7755 and go 6 miles to Boulder Park and Main Eagle Creek Trailhead (El 4,910 ft.). This is the site of the old Boulder Park Resort which was wiped out by an avalanche some years ago.

0.0	Main Eagle Creek Trailhead and Boulder Park.
0.5	Trail crosses Eagle Creek.
1.7	Eagle Cap Wilderness Boundary.
2.2	Trail crosses Eagle Creek again.
2.6	Trail junction with Bench Canyon Trail.
4.0	Trail junction with Lookingglass Lake Trail.
5.7	Trail junction with Trail Creek Trail.
6.8	Eagle Lake.

The trail: The trail heads up the left (west) side of Eagle Creek and crosses Boulder Creek. It then climbs some distance away from Eagle Creek to get around the slide debris. The trail crosses another creek 0.5 mile after crossing Boulder Creek. Seventy-five yards after crossing this creek, it crosses Eagle Creek on a bridge (El 5,020 ft.).

The trail makes five switchbacks in the next 0.4 mile. After passing the switchbacks, the trail climbs 0.8 mile more to the Eagle Cap Wilderness Boundary (El 5,600 ft.). The trail crosses a side stream 0.1 mile past the wilderness boundary. There is a meadow between the trail and Eagle Creek 0.3 mile after crossing the stream. The trail goes along and through the meadow for 300 yards, then crosses back over Eagle Creek on another bridge (El 5,650 ft.). From here the trail heads up the left side of Eagle Creek again. There is another stream crossing 0.2 mile after crossing the bridge. The junction with Bench Canyon Trail (El 5,750 ft.) is another 0.2 mile past the stream crossing. This junction is 2.6 miles from Main Eagle Creek Trailhead. Bench Canyon Trail turns off to the left. See Hike 74 Bench Canyon.

The trail crosses a stream and traverses out onto an open hillside 0.3 mile past the junction with Bench Canyon Trail. It traverses this open hillside for just over 1 mile to the junction with Lookingglass Lake Trail 1921 (El 6,150 ft.). The trail is some distance above Eagle Creek in this area. At the Lookingglass Lake Trail junction there is a meadow between the trail and Eagle Creek. There are some good campsites along Eagle Creek next to this meadow. Lookingglass Lake Trail turns to the right, drops down, and crosses the meadow. See Hike 77 Lookingglass Lake.

Main Eagle Creek Trail goes by some campsites and crosses a couple of small streams in the next 0.5 mile, to where it makes a switchback. After making the switchback, the trail climbs, crossing two more very small streams, and then crosses Catched Creek. Catched Creek is 0.5 mile past the switchback. After crossing Catched Creek, the trail climbs on. It makes two more switchbacks, crosses a small stream, and makes two additional switchbacks to reach the junction with Trail Creek Trail (El 6,880 ft.). Trail Creek Trail junction is 5.7 miles from Main Eagle Creek Trailhead. See Hike 76 Trail Creek.

At Trail Creek Trail junction the trail number of Main Eagle Creek Trail changes to 1931, and trail number 1922 becomes Trail Creek Trail. Main Eagle Creek Trail turns right (northeast) at the junction. It crosses two small streams 0.2 mile past the junction and starts a series of six switchbacks 0.1 mile after crossing the streams. The trail comes to Eagle Lake 150 yards after the last switchback. Eagle Lake (El 7,448 ft.) is 1.1 miles from the Trail Creek Trail junction and 6.8 miles from Main Eagle Creek Trailhead.

Like so many other lakes on the south side of the Wallowas, Eagle Lake is dammed. This is good for storing water, but not so good for the looks of the lake. There is almost no timber around Eagle Lake and no really good campsites. The only area flat enough to camp on is just across the dam to the east. All the way around the lake the mountains drop steeply into the water. There are fish in Eagle Lake and the scenery is nice; however, it would be a good idea to camp somewhere else. Return trip is made by the same trail.

75   *Main Eagle Creek*

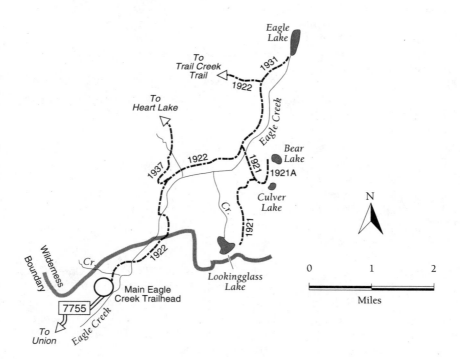

Source: Imus Geographics

Trail 1922

General description: A 10.3 mile backpack from Main Eagle Creek Trail to the Minam River. This trail connects with Bench Canyon and West Fork Eagle Creek Trails.

Difficulty: Moderate.

Trail maintenance: Yearly.

Best season: July through September.

Traffic: Moderate, with moderate horse traffic.

Elevation gain: 1,280 feet. Loss: 2,840 feet.

Maximum elevation: 8,160 feet.

Maps: Imus Geographics Wallowa Mountains Eagle Cap Wilderness or Krag Peak, Bennet Peak and Steamboat Lake USGS quads.

For more information: U.S. Forest Service at Wallowa Mountain Visitors Center, Enterprise, Oregon, or U.S. Forest Service at Halfway Ranger Station, Halfway, Oregon.

Finding the trail: Trail Creek Trail leaves Main Eagle Creek Trail 5.7 miles from Main Eagle Creek Trailhead. The elevation at this junction is 6,880 feet. See Hike 75 Main Eagle Creek.

0.0	Trail junction with Main Eagle Creek Trail.
1.5	Cached Lake.
3.1	Trail crosses pass.
4.6	Trail junction with Bench Canyon Trail.
7.3	Trail junction with West Fork Eagle Creek Trail.
10.3	Trail crosses Minam River and trail junction with Upper Minam River Trail.

The trail: From the junction with Main Eagle Creek Trail, Trail Creek Trail heads northeast and crosses three very small streams in the first 0.75 mile. It makes a switchback to the right 0.2 mile past the third stream crossing. The trail then makes two more switchbacks in the next 300 yards and crosses another very small stream 300 yards past the last switchback. Cached Lake comes into view 300 yards past the last stream crossing.

Cached lake (El 7,343 ft.) is 100 or so yards to the left (south) of the the trail. There is a meadow on the northeast side of the lake and several good campsites in the timber next to it. Cached Lake is a popular destination in July and August, so you may not be alone if you camp here. There are fish to be caught in the lake.

Cached Lakes. *Photo by Lowell Euhus*

Leaving Cached Lake, the trail crosses a stream and begins to climb again in switchbacks. It makes four switchbacks in the next 350 yards. The trail disappears in a grassy area 300 yards past the switchbacks. Head southwest for a short distance to pick it up again. After getting through the grassy area, the trail crosses another stream. It then makes thirteen switchbacks in the 1.2 miles to the top of a pass. The trail climbs 820 feet from Cached Lake to the top of the pass. The area near the pass (El 8,160 ft.) is mostly open alpine country. The pass area is definitely view property.

From the pass the trail heads north along the ridgeline. After 0.25 mile it switchbacks to the left. Here the trail begins a 0.5 mile long series of nine switchbacks as it drops down off the pass. There is a meadow with a wet weather pond on it to the right of the trail 0.9 mile after getting past the switchbacks. The junction with Bench Canyon Trail is 0.3 mile past the meadow. See Hike 74 Bench Canyon. This junction (El 7,410 ft.) is at the northwest end of a fairly large meadow with several springs in it. Bench Canyon Trail turns to the left (south).

A loop hike can be done from here back to Main Eagle Creek Trailhead. To hike this loop, turn left on Bench Canyon Trail and follow it 3.1 miles to the junction with Main Eagle Creek Trail. Then turn right on Main Eagle Creek Trail and head south the 2.6 miles to Main Eagle Creek Trailhead. See Hike 75 Main Eagle Creek.

After passing Bench Canyon Trail junction, Trail Creek Trail starts its descent into Trail Creek Canyon. It makes many switchbacks as it drops 1,170 feet in the 2.7 miles to the junction with West Eagle Creek Trail 1934

(El 6,240 ft.). See Hike 73 West Fork Eagle Creek. By the time the trail reaches the junction with West Fork Eagle Creek Trail the woods have changed from the open alpine setting near timberline at the top of the pass to dense transitional forest along lower Trail Creek.

Just below the junction the trail crosses a small stream in a culvert. It goes down along the right (east) side of Trail Creek for 2 miles, crossing five stream beds and going through several meadows. These stream beds may have water in them earlier in the summer, but were dry in September when we hiked this trail.

After going the 2 miles along Trail Creek the trail turns to the right and gets away from the creek. The trail turns and switchbacks down for the next 0.5 mile, then returns to and crosses Trail Creek. After crossing Trail Creek, the trail goes through a sloping meadow with a lot of avalanche debris in it. Soon it drops out of the meadow, switchbacks to the right, and crosses a bridge over the Minam River (El 5,320 ft.). After crossing the river, the trail winds its way up 300 yards to the Minam River Trail. This junction is 10.3 miles from the junction with Main Eagle Creek Trail. From this junction, Minam Lake is to the right (east) up river 6.1 miles. See Hike 42 Upper Minam River.

76   *Trail Creek*

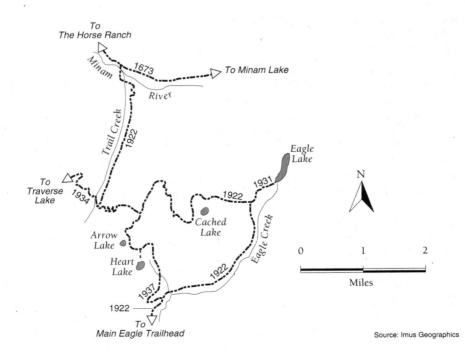

Source: Imus Geographics

77 LOOKINGGLASS LAKE

Trail 1921

General description: A 2.6 mile side trail connecting Main Eagle Creek Trail 1922 with Lookingglass Lake. This trail is also the access to Bear Lake Trail.

Difficulty: Moderate.

Trail maintenance: Infrequent.

Best season: Mid-June through October.

Traffic: Moderate.

Elevation gain: 1,380 feet. Loss: 228 feet.

Maximum elevation: 7,530 feet.

Map: Krag Peak USGS quad.

For more information: U.S. Forest Service at Wallowa Mountain Visitors Center, Enterprise, Oregon, or U.S. Forest Service at Halfway Ranger Station, Halfway, Oregon.

Finding the trail: Lookingglass Lake Trail leaves Main Eagle Creek Trail, 4 miles from Main Eagle Creek Trailhead. The elevation at the junction with Main Eagle Creek Trail is 6,150 feet. See Hike 75 Main Eagle Creek.

0.0   Trail junction with Main Fork Eagle Creek Trail.

1.0   Trail junction with Bear Lake Trail.

2.6   Lookingglass Lake.

Lookingglass Lake. *Photo by Lowell Euhus.*

77 Lookingglass Lake
78 Bear Lake

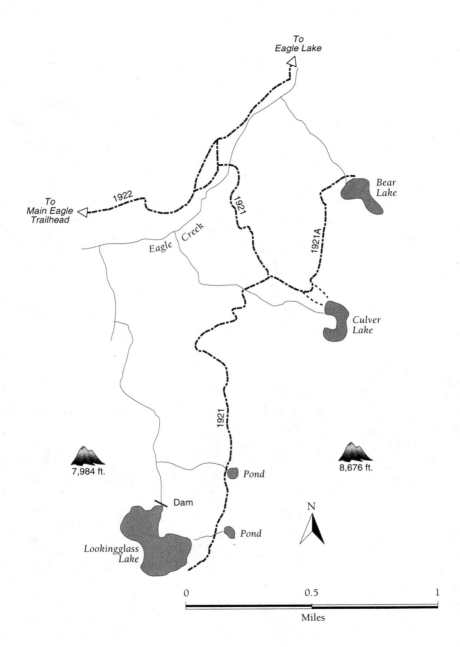

The trail: Lookingglass Lake Trail turns to the right (east) off Main Eagle Creek Trail. It drops slightly, crosses the meadow, then crosses Eagle Creek. After crossing Eagle Creek the trail starts to climb. It makes a switchback to the right 0.7 mile after crossing Eagle Creek. The junction with Bear Lake Trail (El 6,830 ft.) is 0.3 mile past the switchback. See Hike 78 Bear Lake. The 680 foot climb in this first mile makes the trail quite steep so far.

The trail crosses the outlet of Culver Lake, 175 yards past the Bear Lake Trail junction. Soon after crossing the stream, the trail starts to climb steeply. It makes two switchbacks while climbing the 0.4 mile to the top of the ridgeline. After reaching the ridgeline, the trail goes around to the other (southwest) side of the ridge and does an ascending traverse. From here the falls in the creek below Lookingglass Lake can be seen across the canyon to the south. After climbing for 0.1 mile, the trail flattens out a bit. It crosses three small streams, then climbs fairly steeply for another 100 yards and flattens out again. Soon Lookingglass Lake can be seen to the right (south), across the canyon. There is a pond on the left side of the trail 350 yards past the top of the last steep climb. The trail starts to drop and crosses a small stream 350 yards past the pond. Just before crossing the stream, this trail reached its highest point (El 7,530 ft.). After the stream crossing, the trail drops for 0.25 mile to Lookingglass Lake (El 7,302 ft.) 2.6 miles from Main Eagle Trail.

Lookingglass Lake is a reservoir, like most of the lakes on this side of the mountains. It is held up 15 feet or so by a dam. This makes the shoreline at low water mostly mud. The area around the lake is mostly timbered with subalpine fir and some whitebark pine. There are fish in the lake and a few campsites. Return is made via the same trail.

78   BEAR LAKE

Trail 1921A

General description: A short 1 mile trail from Lookingglass Lake Trail 1921 to Bear Lake.

Difficulty: Easy.
Trail maintenance: Infrequent.
Best season: Mid-June through October.
Traffic: Light to moderate, with light horse traffic.
Elevation gain: 400 feet. Loss: 100 feet.
Maximum elevation: 7,230 feet.
Map: Krag Peak USGS quad.
For more information: U.S. Forest Service at Wallowa Mountain Visitors Center, Enterprise, Oregon, or U.S. Forest Service at Halfway Ranger Station, Halfway, Oregon.

Finding the trail: Bear Lake Trail leaves Lookingglass Trail 1921, 1 mile from Main Eagle Creek Trail (El 6,830 ft.). See Hike 75 Main Eagle Creek and Hike 77 Lookingglass Lake.

0.0	Trail junction with Lookingglass Lake Trail.
0.3	Trail junctions with Culver Lake paths.
0.9	Trail crosses ridgeline.
1.0	Bear Lake.

The trail: Bear Lake Trail turns to the left (southeast) off the Lookingglass Lake Trail. After leaving the Lookingglass Lake Trail, it climbs for 0.3 mile to the unmarked junction with Culver Lake path.

There are actually two paths that lead to Culver Lake, which are about 125 yards apart. Both of the paths turn to the right (southeast) off Bear Lake Trail. The elevation at this junction is approximately 7,000 feet. Culver Lake (El 7,030 ft.) is about 200 yards off the Bear Creek Trail.

After passing the Culver Lake paths, Bear Lake Trail continues to climb 0.5 mile more to the top of a ridge. The elevation at the ridgeline is 7,230 feet. From the ridgeline the trail drops for 250 yards to Bear Lake. The trail goes on around to the north side of the lake, crossing the outlet stream.

Bear Lake (El 7,030 ft.) is 1 mile from Lookingglass Lake Trail. The lake area is heavily timbered with mostly subalpine fir and spruce, and some whitebark pine. There are campsites on the north side of the lake and trout to be caught in it. Unlike many lakes in this area, neither Culver Lake nor Bear Lake have dams. Return trip is via the same trail.

Bear Lake. *Photo by Lowell Euhus.*

Trail 1910

General description: A 13.6 mile backpack from East Eagle Trailhead to Mirror Lake. This trail also accesses Hidden Lake, Frazier Pass and Minam Lake/Mirror Lake Trails.

Difficulty: Moderate to strenuous, depending on snow cover over Horton Pass.

Trail maintenance: Yearly.

Best season: Mid-July through September.

Traffic: Moderate to heavy.

Elevation gain: 3,910 feet. Loss: 860 feet.

Maximum elevation: 8,470 feet.

Maps: Imus Geographics Wallowa Mountains Eagle Cap Wilderness or Krag Peak and Eagle Cap Mountain USGS quads.

For more information: U.S. Forest Service at Wallowa Mountain Visitors Center, Enterprise, Oregon, or U.S. Forest Service at Halfway Ranger Station, Halfway, Oregon.

Finding the trail: From Union, take Oregon Highway 203 and go 20 miles southeast to Medical Springs. At Medical Springs turn left southeast, on Big Creek Road, (County Road 71) and stay on Big Creek Road, which soon becomes Forest Road 67. FR 67 for 14.2 miles to the junction with Forest Road 77. Turn right, east, on FR 77 and go 6.6 miles to the junction with East Eagle Creek Road (FR 7745). Turn left (north) on FR 7745 and follow it 6.5 miles to East Eagle Creek Trailhead. There is a campsite and parking at the trailhead.

0.0	East Eagle Creek Trailhead.
1.8	Trail fords Curtis Creek.
6.5	Trail junction with Hidden Lake Trail.
7.5	Trail junction with Frazier Pass Trail.

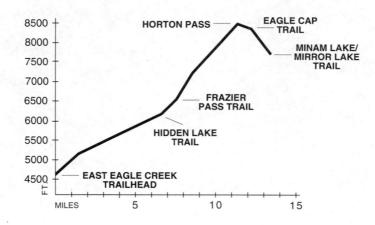

The trail: From the trailhead (El 4,580 ft.) East Eagle Creek Trail begins as a jeep road heading north. After going 0.25 mile, the trail bears to the right off the jeep road. There is a sign here marking the trail. The trail enters the Eagle Cap Wilderness after climbing a rocky grade for 300 yards. At the wilderness boundary there is a melt pond on the right side of the trail. The gray cliffs across East Eagle Creek to the west are called Granite Cliffs on the map. This is strange as they appear to be limestone. One half mile after entering the wilderness the trail crosses a creek and enters a brushy area. Like so many areas along East Eagle Creek, the lack of large trees is caused by the regular scouring done by avalanches. On the far side of the brushy area the trail crosses another creek. The trail fords Curtis Creek (El 5,150 ft.) 1.8 miles from the trailhead. Just after crossing Curtis Creek there is a falls in East Eagle Creek below the trail to the left. Soon the forest opens up for a view of the higher mountains ahead.

There is another falls in East Eagle Creek a short distance farther along. The trail crosses a side stream with a waterfall a few feet above the trail and soon goes back into large timber again. The big timber lasts only a couple hundred yards before the trail comes back out into another large opening and crosses a stream. The trail crosses the 300 yard wide opening, then climbs through a finger of timber to another opening. There are alternating open and

Upper Basin and Horton Pass.

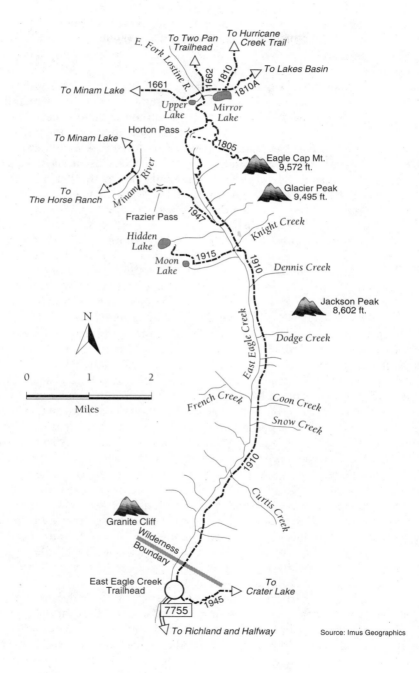

To Two Pan Trailhead

To Hurricane Creek Trail

E. Fork Lostine R.

1662

1810

To Lakes Basin

1661

1810A

To Minam Lake

Upper Lake

Mirror Lake

Horton Pass

To Minam Lake

1805

Eagle Cap Mt. 9,572 ft.

Minam River

Glacier Peak 9,495 ft.

To The Horse Ranch

Frazier Pass

1947

Knight Creek

Hidden Lake

Moon Lake

1915

1910

Dennis Creek

Jackson Peak 8,602 ft.

N

East Eagle Creek

Dodge Creek

0   1   2

French Creek

Coon Creek

Miles

Snow Creek

1910

Curtis Creek

Granite Cliff

Wilderness Boundary

East Eagle Creek Trailhead

To Crater Lake

7755

1945

To Richland and Halfway

Source: Imus Geographics

lightly timbered areas and a couple of small stream crossings in the next 0.7 mile to where the trail crosses Coon Creek (El 5,350 ft.). Just after crossing Coon Creek, the trail enters a flat park-like area with large cottonwood trees and a colony of red diggers (ground squirrels). The trail crosses the park-like area then crosses another stream as it begins to gently climb.

French Creek enters East Eagle Creek from the west 0.1 mile after leaving the park area. Another 0.4 mile ahead, after three small stream crossings, the trail comes to a finger of larger spruce and fir timber. A few feet into the trees, the trail makes a switchback to the right and climbs back into the open area. It then makes a switchback to the left and traverses the finger of timber. At the first switchback there is a campsite in the trees a few feet off the trail. The trail leaves the big timber and soon passes another waterfall in East Eagle Creek (El 5,570 ft,). The trail stays away from the creek and crosses several small streams in the next 0.5 mile, then comes back close to East Eagle Creek again. Here, East Eagle Creek foams and boils its way through a gorge below the trail. The trail crosses Dodge Creek (El 5,850 ft.), 0.1 mile, after passing the gorge. Watch for elk which abound in this area.

One mile and several small stream crossings after crossing Dodge Creek, the trail crosses Dennis Creek (El 5,970 ft.). Another 0.5 mile and a small stream crossing, the trail comes to the junction with Hidden Lake Trail 1915 (El 6,170 ft.). See Hike 80 Hidden Lake. The country is becoming much more open and alpine. After passing the Hidden Lake Trail junction, the trail climbs, crosses a small stream and makes a couple of switchbacks before crossing Knight Creek (El 6,310 ft.). The trail then climbs gently through this magnificent alpine valley and crosses several small streams in the mile to the junction with Frazier Pass Trail (El 6,520 ft.). See Hike 81 Frazier Pass. There is a good campsite between the trail and East Fork Eagle Creek next to the junction.

At the junction, East Fork Eagle Creek Trail turns to the right and heads east for a short distance before resuming its northerly course up the valley some distance away from East Eagle Creek. It crosses several small streams as it makes its way up the east side of the valley 1.3 miles to the first switchback (El 7,150 ft.) at the beginning of the climb up to Horton Pass. The trail makes 4 switchbacks as it climbs the mostly open slope strewn with granite boulders, crossing some of the same streams again. It then enters the lower of 2 small glacial basins 0.3 mile after making the last switchback. The trail crosses East Fork Eagle Creek as it enters the basin, then makes an ascending traverse along the west side of it to another stream crossing and the gully leading to the upper basin. The trail goes up the gully on the right side of the stream bed, into the upper basin which is the head of East Fork Eagle Creek Valley (El 8,000 ft.). Much of the granite in the upper basin was smoothed by glacial action, and some of it has a pink tinge.

In the upper basin the trail turns to the east and switchbacks its way up the last 450 vertical feet to Horton Pass (El 8,470 ft.). Parts of the trail in and above the upper basin may be snow covered until August. Horton Pass is the most easterly notch in the ridge above the upper basin, so even if snow covers most of the trail here it is not difficult to find. This is a fairly steep ascent, so an ice ax should be taken along for each person, and all members of the party should know how to use them if this trip is done when the trail is snow covered. Take some time to rest and take in the view at Horton Pass. The U-shaped valley to the north is the upper East Fork Lostine Canyon, to the north northeast is the limestone face of Matterhorn Mountain, and to the northeast is the Lakes Basin. As with all higher passes in the Wallowa Mountains, watch the weather when you are making the crossing.

At Horton Pass a rough path to the summit of Eagle Cap Mountain turns off to the right (southeast). After crossing the pass, East Fork Eagle Creek Trail 1910 descends, making several small switchbacks 0.9 mile to the junction with Eagle Cap Mountain Trail. See Hike 17 Eagle Cap Mountain. The area between Horton Pass and Eagle Cap Mountain Trail junction will likely be covered with snow until August, and it may be hard to find the junction, but this is open country and the route on down is not difficult to find. Ice axes may be needed on this descent when the trail is covered with snow. After passing the junction, the trail winds its way down the 1.1 miles to Upper Lake at the west end of the lakes basin. The junction with Minam Lake/Mirror Lake Trail is reached 0.2 mile after passing Upper Lake. Mirror Lake (El 7,595 ft.) is 0.2 mile to the right (east) on the Minam Lake/Mirror Lake Trail. See Hike 19 Minam Lake/Mirror Lake. There are lots of campsites around Mirror Lake. Be sure to camp at least 200 feet from the lake as Forest Service regulations require. Fishing for brook trout is usually excellent in the lake.

One of the best trips in the Wallowa Mountains can be made by combining East Fork Eagle Creek Trail and Hurricane Creek Trail. See Hike 14 Hurricane Creek. This 25.6 mile trip goes through what are unquestionably two of the most spectacular canyons in the range. A car shuttle of about 120 miles is required to make this one-way trip.

80   HIDDEN LAKE

Trail 1915

General description: A 1.8 mile side trail from East Fork Eagle Creek Trail to Hidden Lake.
Difficulty: Moderate.
Trail maintenance: Infrequent.
Best season: July through October.
Traffic: Moderate.
Elevation gain: 1,110 feet. Loss: 117 feet.
Maximum elevation: 7,280 feet.
Map: Eagle Cap Mountain USGS quad. See map on p. 214.
For more information: U.S. Forest Service at Wallowa Mountain Visitors Center, Enterprise, Oregon, or U.S. Forest Service at Halfway Ranger Station, Halfway, Oregon.
Finding the trail: The trail begins at the junction with East Fork Eagle Creek Trail 1910, 6.5 miles north of East Eagle Creek Trailhead. See Hike 79 East Fork Eagle Creek.

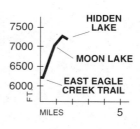

Hidden Lake in early June.

0.0	Trail junction with East Fork Eagle Creek Trail.
1.1	Moon Lake.
1.4	Trail crosses pass.
1.8	Hidden Lake.

The trail: The Hidden Lake Trail turns left (west) off the East Fork Eagle Creek Trail (El 6,170 ft.). It drops slightly for 50 yards then crosses East Eagle Creek. After crossing the creek it heads northwest for 0.2 mile, then makes a switchback to the left at the edge of the timber. There is a campsite in the timber, next to the switchback. After making the switchback, the trail works its way up, staying on the north side of the outlet stream of Moon Lake. At first it goes through some timber, then it climbs on mostly open slopes and crosses several small streams to reach Moon Lake (El 7,060 ft.). There are several spots to camp in the trees around Moon Lake.

The trail goes around Moon Lake on the east and north sides, then climbs to a pass (El 7,280 ft.) northwest of the lake. A very large bear crossed this pass, just ahead of me when I hiked this trail. After crossing the pass, the trail passes a pond which is on the left side of the trail. The trail continues northwest a short distance, then turns northeast, crosses a stream and comes to the east end of Hidden Lake (El 7,173 ft.). There is a pond just to the east of Hidden Lake to the right of the trail.

There are nice campsites at Hidden Lake and fish to be caught. There is a good view of Eagle Cap Mountain when looking northeast from Hidden Lake; however, Eagle Cap is not as spectacular from this side as it is from the Mirror Lake side. The return trip is made by the same trail.

81   FRAZIER PASS

Trail 1947

General description: A 2.7 mile connecting trail from Upper Minam River Trail to East Fork Eagle Creek Trail.
Difficulty: Moderate.
Trail maintenance: Infrequent.
Best season: Mid-June through October.
Traffic: Moderate, with moderate horse traffic.
Elevation gain: 810 feet. Loss: 1,030 feet.
Maximum elevation: 7,560 feet.
Map: Eagle Cap Mountain USGS quad.

For more information: U.S. Forest Service at Wallowa Mountain Visitors Center, Enterprise, Oregon, or U.S. Forest Service at Halfway Ranger Station, Halfway, Oregon.
Finding the trail: Frazier Pass Trail leaves Upper Minam River Trail 2 miles south of Minam Lake. See Hike 42 Upper Minam River. The elevation at the

junction with Upper Minam River Trail is 6,750 feet. Many good campsites are available along the Minam River close to this junction.

0.0   Trail junction with Upper Minam River Trail.
1.3   Trail crosses Frazier Pass.
2.6   Trail crosses East Fork Eagle Creek.
2.7   Trail junction with East Fork Eagle Creek Trail.

The trail: Frazier Pass Trail heads east off the Minam River Trail. It drops slightly, crosses a meadow, then crosses the Minam River. Watch for blazes on the trees near the river. The trail becomes easier to see on the east side of the river. The trail crosses a stream 125 yards after crossing the river. A short distance after crossing the stream, the trail becomes difficult to see in a swampy area. Watch for the blazes on the far side of the swampy area. The trail crosses a small stream after leaving the swampy area. Past the stream, the trail starts to climb. It makes a switchback to the left 0.2 mile after crossing the small

East Eagle Creek Canyon from Frazier Pass Trail. *Photo by Gary Fletcher.*

80 *Hidden Lake*
81 *Frazier Pass*

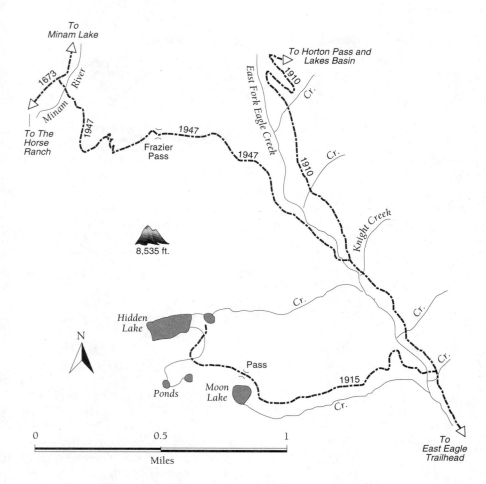

To
Minam Lake

1673

Minam River

To The
Horse
Ranch

1947

1947

Frazier
Pass

1947

1947

East Fork Eagle Creek

To Horton Pass and
Lakes Basin

1910

Cr.

1910

Cr.

Knight Creek

8,535 ft.

Cr.

Cr.

Hidden
Lake

N

Pass

Cr.

Cr.

Ponds

Moon
Lake

1915

Cr.

0   0.5   1

Miles

To
East Eagle
Trailhead

stream. In the next 0.4 mile the trail makes four more switchbacks. Above the switchbacks the trail climbs for 0.5 mile to Frazier Pass (El 7,560 ft.). Frazier Pass is 1.3 miles from the Upper Minam River Trail.

After crossing Frazier Pass, the trail starts to drop fairly steeply. It makes four small switchbacks 125 yards below the pass. Past the switchbacks the trail twists its way down a couple hundred yards, then flattens out for 50 yards or so. The trail starts to drop again, making five more switchbacks in the next 0.3 mile, then crossing three small streams. There is a large spring on the left side of the trail 0.4 mile after crossing the small streams. The trail crosses the East Fork of Eagle Creek 0.25 mile past the spring. The elevation at the crossing is 6,530 feet. A short distance past the crossing the Frazier Pass Trail meets East Fork Eagle Creek Trail 1910. See Hike 79 East Fork Eagle Creek. This junction is 2.7 miles from the Upper Minam River Trail.

Trail 1885

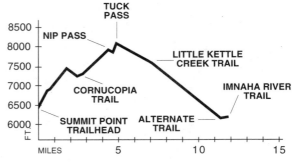

General description: An 11.8 mile backpack from Summit Point Trailhead to the Imnaha River. This trail also accesses Cornucopia Trail, Pine Lakes Trail, Little Kettle Creek Trail, and Crater Lake.

Difficulty: Moderate.

Trail maintenance: Infrequent.

Best season: Mid-July through September.

Traffic: Moderate to heavy to Little Kettle Creek Trail junction near Crater Lake; light past there with light to moderate horse traffic.

Elevation gain: 1,850 feet. Loss: 2,160 feet.

Maximum elevation: 8,040 feet.

Maps: Imus Geographics Wallowa Mountains Eagle Cap Wilderness, or Cornucopia and Krag Peak USGS quads.

For more information: U.S. Forest Service at Wallowa Mountain Visitors Center, Enterprise, Oregon or U.S. Forest Service at Halfway Ranger Station, Halfway, Oregon.

Finding the trail: From Halfway, take Cornucopia Road, Oregon Highway 413, and go 5.4 miles northwest to the poorly marked Carson Grade junction. The junction is marked with a sign pointing to Eagle Creek. Turn left (west) at the junction and head up Carson Grade, which soon becomes Forest Road 7710. Follow FR 7710 for 3.3 miles to the junction with Forest Road 77. Turn right on FR 77 and go 8.0 mile to the junction with Forest Road 7715. This junction is directly across the road from McBride Campground. Turn right (north) on FR 7715 and follow it 4.8 miles to Summit Point Trailhead. There is a parking area at the trailhead. The Imus Geographics map shows this trailhead correctly, but Forest Service maps do not.

0.0	Summit Point Trailhead.
0.6	Trail junction with trail to Summit Point Lookout (road).
2.3	Eagle Cap Wilderness Boundary.
2.8	Trail junction with Cornucopia Trail.
4.4	Nip Pass and trail junction with unmarked Trail 1946.
4.9	Tuck Pass and trail junction with Pine Lakes Trail.
7.0	Trail junction with Little Kettle Creek Trail.
11.2	Trail junction with Alternate Trail 1885A.
11.8	Imnaha River and trail junction with South Fork Imnaha River Trail.

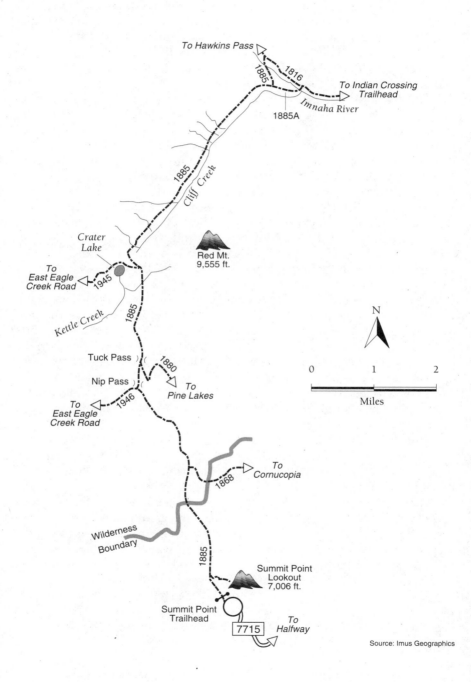

To Hawkins Pass

1816

1885

To Indian Crossing
Trailhead

Imnaha River

1885A

1885

Cliff Creek

*Crater
Lake*

Red Mt.
9,555 ft.

*To
East Eagle
Creek Road*

1945

Kettle Creek

1885

N

Tuck Pass

1880

Nip Pass

*To
Pine Lakes*

*To
East Eagle
Creek Road*

1946

0   1   2

Miles

*To
Cornucopia*

1868

Wilderness
Boundary

1885

Summit Point
Lookout
7,006 ft.

Summit Point
Trailhead

7715

*To
Halfway*

Source: Imus Geographics

The trail: The trail begins as the old road to Summit Point Lookout. From the trailhead (El 6,450 ft.) it heads up to the north northwest, climbing fairly steeply. A short distance from the trailhead the trail passes an iron gate which blocks it to motor vehicle use. After climbing for 0.6 mile, the trail leaves the road which makes a switchback to the right and climbs a short distance more to Summit Point Lookout. There is a sign marking the trail which goes straight ahead to the north northwest from the junction. The trail still follows the remains of an old road for some distance.

After leaving the Summit Point Road, the trail traverses along the left (west) side of the ridgeline for 0.4 mile to a saddle. A few feet before reaching the saddle the trail bears to the left and leaves the old road. The old road goes through the saddle. The trail continues to traverse on the left side of the ridge through sage covered slopes and groves of alpine trees. It reaches the now rounded ridgeline 0.4 mile from the saddle. Here on the grass and flower covered ridge top the view of the mountains to the north opens up.

Along the ridge top the trail drops gently to the Eagle Cap Wilderness Boundary and a small pond (El 7,200 ft.). The trail reaches the junction with Cornucopia Trail 0.5 mile after entering the wilderness. See Hike 84 Cornucopia. There are many possible campsites in this area around the fingers of timber, some distance away from the trail. Upon entering the scattered timber just past the junction the trail may become difficult to see for a few yards. It climbs slightly to the north through a small opening and soon becomes obvious again. From here to the junction with unmarked Trail 1946 at Nip Pass, the trail traverses the steep, lightly-timbered west side of Cornucopia Peak. Nip Pass and the junction are 1.6 miles from the junction with Cornucopia Trail. At the pass, Cliff Creek Trail turns to the right (northeast) and continues to traverse another 0.5 mile to the junction with Pine Lakes Trail 1880, which is in the small notch called Tuck Pass. See Hike 85 Pine Lakes. Tuck Pass (El 8,040 ft.) is the highest point on Cliff Creek Trail. From the pass, Crater Lake can be seen in the distance to the north.

From Tuck Pass, Cliff Creek Trail continues its traverse on a steep granite boulder-strewn slope dotted with subalpine fir and whitebark pine. The trail rounds a point 0.6 mile into the traverse, then continues to traverse 0.3 mile farther. After the traverse the trail makes a turn to the right, then one to the left, climbs slightly and rounds another point. It then heads east for 150 yards and crosses a small lush meadow surrounded by granite boulders. The trail soon enters thicker timber and drops slightly. Half a mile after crossing the meadow, the trail crosses a stream as it makes its way through the alpine timber and granite outcroppings. This stream crosses the trail in two channels. There is a waterfall in the stream a short distance above the trail, but it cannot be seen from the crossing. After crossing the stream, the trail climbs gently for 0.4 mile to the junction with Little Kettle Creek Trail 1945 (El 7,550 ft.). See Hike 83 Little Kettle Creek. Crater Lake is 0.2 mile to the left (west) from the junction.

At the junction Cliff Creek Trail turns to the right (north), crosses 75 yards of flat ground, then begins its descent through a forest of small subalpine fir.

As the trail starts down, the ground is covered with mountain heather which may be covered with pink blooms. The trail descends gently but steadily, through the woods which quickly get larger with the loss of altitude. The trail crosses a stream and enters an open slope 0.4 mile after leaving the Crater Lake junction. From here, the 9,555 foot high summit of Red Mountain dominates the view to the right (east). The open slope is covered with grass and lupine; there are also a few sego lilies. The trail heads on down the left side of Cliff Creek Valley crossing mostly open slopes that are occasionally dissected with fingers of timber, for 0.9 mile to another stream crossing. It crosses several very small streams on the way as it goes across the slopes covered with paintbrush, sego lilies and many other flowers. At the stream crossings, look for the lewis monkey face flowers which grow there. The trail crosses another stream 0.5 mile farther along, then another 0.7 miles after that. One tenth mile after the second stream crossing, the trail makes a couple of switchbacks, before crossing another small stream. It crosses several more small streams in the next 1.4 miles to the junction with Cliff Creek Alternate Trail 1885A. There are very few good campsites along this trail between Little Kettle Creek Trail junction and the Imnaha River. However, there are some possible sites in the openings next to Cliff Creek a few hundred yards east of the trail.

At the junction (El 6,090 ft.), Cliff Creek Trail turns to the left (northwest). The trail climbs slightly over a small rise, then descends gently through the timber to the Imnaha River 0.6 mile from the junction with trail 1885A. The trail fords the river and meets the South Fork Imnaha River Trail a few yards after the crossing. The elevation at the junction with the South Fork Imnaha River Trail is 6,100 feet. See Hike 92 South Fork Imnaha River.

If you intend to go down river to the east on the South Fork Imnaha River Trail, bear right at the junction with Trail 1885A and take it 0.6 mile to a crossing of the Imnaha River and junction with the South Fork Imnaha River Trail. This junction (El 5,910 ft.) is 0.8 mile below the junction with Cliff Creek Trail. The return trip can be made by the same trail or one can hike on down the Imnaha River to Indian Crossing Trailhead. See Hike 100 Imnaha River along with Hike 92 for trail description of this trail and directions to Indian Crossing Trailhead. There are many campsites along the Imnaha River. A car shuttle is required if you end your hike at Indian Crossing Trailhead.

83   LITTLE KETTLE CREEK

Trail 1945

General description: A 6.5 mile backpack or day hike from East Eagle Creek Trailhead to Crater Lake and the junction with Cliff Creek Trail.
Difficulty: Moderate.
Trail maintenance: Infrequent, but this trail only passes short distances through woods, so downed logs are not much of a problem.
Best season: Mid-July through September.

Traffic: Moderate.
Elevation gain: 3,040 feet. Loss: 70 feet.
Maximum elevation: 7,620 feet.
Maps: Krag Peak USGS quad.
For more information: U.S. Forest Service at Wallowa Mountain Visitors Center, Enterprise, Oregon, or U.S. Forest Service at Halfway Ranger Station, Halfway, Oregon.
Finding the trail: Little Kettle Creek Trail begins at East Eagle Creek Trailhead. For directions to the trailhead, See Hike 79 East Fork Eagle Creek.

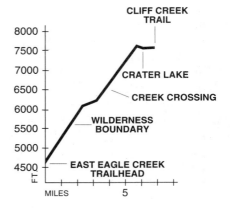

0.0	East Eagle Creek Trailhead.
1.6	Eagle Cap Wilderness Boundary.
3.7	Creek crossing.
6.0	Trail reaches Crater Lake.
6.5	Trail junction with Cliff Creek Trail.

The trail: Little Kettle Creek Trail starts on the east side of the turnaround parking area at East Eagle Creek Trailhead (El 4,580 ft.). At first the trail climbs gently through a forest of large spruce and fir on the remains of an old road-bed. After 150 yards the trail bears to the right off the roadbed. The trail makes a switchback to the right 0.1 mile after leaving the roadbed. It soon makes another switchback and climbs out of the dense forest, entering a semi-open, brush-covered slope. After getting on the brush-covered slope, the trail continues to climb, making twenty-six more switchbacks in the next 2.3 miles. The trail passes the Eagle Cap Wilderness Boundary which is 1.6 miles from the trailhead as it climbs these switchbacks.

At the top of the switchbacks the trail begins an ascending traverse to the east along the mostly open but brushy mountain side. About 0.25 mile into the traverse, the trail crosses a shallow gully filled with paintbrush, fireweed, asters, and many other wildflowers. After crossing the flower-filled gully, the trail goes up steeply for 50 yards and soon crosses another gully. This one is strewn with boulders but still has room for lots of flowers. The trail enters a stand of fairly large fir trees a short distance after crossing the boulder-strewn gully. It goes through the timber for 150 yards before coming out into the open again. In the open, the trail makes a couple of switchbacks, then climbs steeply for 100 yards to a creek crossing. After crossing the creek, the trail climbs steeply again for 200 more yards on a slope covered with sage and flowers. It soon bears to the right and crosses the slope, then begins a series of switchbacks. Watch the ground for sego lilies in this area. The trail climbs the series of four switchbacks then enters some timber. In the timber there is a very small stream along the right side of the trail for a few yards. The trail comes out of the timber after a short distance and climbs a semi-open slope,

Crater Lake and Red Mountain.

83   *Little Kettle Creek*

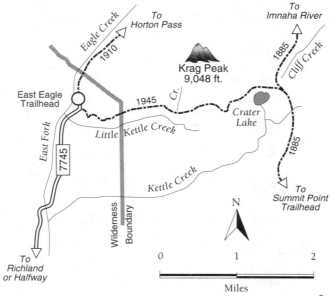

Source: Imus Geographics

making several more switchbacks. It then enters a talus slope dotted with small groves of scrubby subalpine fir. The trail makes eight switchbacks as it climbs the talus slope. Above the talus slope the trail crosses a small stream which flows through a culvert under the trail, then passes a pond. The pond, which is to the right of the trail, has a lush meadow around it. There is another smaller pond just to the east of the first one. The trail makes a couple more switchbacks in the next 0.25 mile through scattered small alpine trees, granite outcroppings, and mountain heather, to the top of a rise. The top of this rise is the highest elevation reached on this trail, 7,620 feet. From the top of the rise the trail drops slightly for the 0.1 mile to Crater Lake (El 7,560 ft.) making a switchback to the left just before reaching it. The trail works its way for 0.25 mile around the north shore of the lake to the dam on its northeast corner. It crosses the dam and heads east for 300 yards over the top of a couple of small rises to the junction with Cliff Creek Trail (El 7,550 ft.). See Hike 82 Cliff Creek.

From the dam to the the junction is the roughest part of the entire trail. This section is easy to follow but it is not graded. There are few reasonably good campsites around Crater Lake, but with a little looking a place to pitch a tent can be found. Lots of fish are available for the catching in the lake. The lake level fluctuates because of the dam, but the muddy shorelines, present at some of the lakes on this side of the mountains, are not a problem here. From Crater Lake the return trip is best made by the same trail, unless an extended trip involving a car shuttle is desired. If you want to make an extended trip See Hike 82 Cliff Creek section in this book for the possibilities.

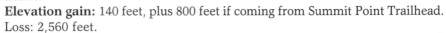

84 *CORNUCOPIA*

Trail 1868

General description: A 4 mile downhill day hike from Cliff Creek Trail to Cornucopia. This trail is mostly on old mine trails and roads. To hike this one way as described here, a car shuttle is required. It is a 6.5 mile hike if starting from Summit Point Trailhead.

Difficulty: Moderate as described, or strenuous if going the other direction. Much of this trail is rough and rocky.

Trail maintenance: Rare.

Best season: Mid-June through October.

Traffic: Moderate, with light to moderate horse traffic.

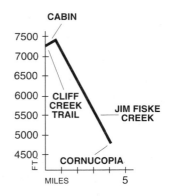

Elevation gain: 140 feet, plus 800 feet if coming from Summit Point Trailhead. Loss: 2,560 feet.

Maximum elevation: 7,420 feet.

Maps: Imus Geographics Wallowa Mountain Eagle Cap Wilderness, or Jim Town, Sparta Butte, Krag Peak and Cornucopia USGS quads. This trail is in the corner of four quad maps. Cornucopia quad covers most of it.

For more information: U.S. Forest Service at Wallowa Mountain Visitors Center, Enterprise, Oregon, or U.S. Forest Service at Halfway Ranger Station, Halfway, Oregon.

Finding the trail: The Cornucopia Trail begins at the junction with Cliff Creek Trail 1885, 2.5 miles north of Summit Point Trailhead. See Hike 82 Cliff Creek. The altitude at the junction with Trail 1885 is 7,280 feet. The area around the junction is mostly ridge top meadows. It is a likely place to see mule deer, especially big bucks. There are ponds and streams here which makes it a good place to camp.

0.0   Trail junction with Cliff Creek Trail.
0.5   Schneider Cabin.
3.2   Trail crosses Jim Fiske Creek.
4.0   Cornucopia.

The trail: Cornucopia Trail heads southeast from the junction. At first it follows old road ruts. After going 250 yards, there is a post marking the place where the trail turns to the left (east). There is no trail on the ground here. Follow the line of posts a short distance. From the third post walk 20 yards east southeast to where the trail shows up again. The trail soon bends around to the east northeast. Seventy-five yards after passing the fourth post, it crosses two small streams. The trail comes to Schneider Cabin 0.1 mile after crossing the streams. This cabin, with its pole fence around it, is well kept up and is being used. The elevation at the cabin is 7,320 feet. Please do not bother the cabin.

84   *Cornucopia*

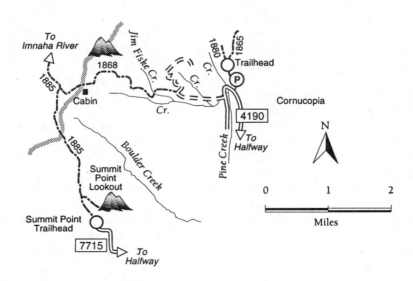

223

Schneider Cabin. *Photo by Lowell Euhus.*

The trail heads slightly uphill to the east and a little north from the cabin. It crosses a small gully. After about 250 yards it begins a traverse on an open slope. The trail traverses for 0.25 mile before turning to the right and heading down. The elevation at the end of the traverse is 7,420 feet.

From the end of the traverse the trail drops 700 feet in the next 0.9 mile, making eight switchbacks. Below the switchbacks, the trail follows a steep rough old road bed down a ridge. There is a saddle in the ridgeline, 0.5 mile and 600 vertical feet below the last switchback.

The trail makes a switchback to the right 250 yards past the saddle. Another 250 yards down and the trial turns nearly straight uphill for a couple of hundred yards. It soon heads down again and becomes a much wider roadbed. Soon there is a fork in the road, head down. There are many signs of old mining operations in this area.

The trail (road) crosses Jim Fiske Creek 500 yards below the fork. This crossing (El 5,430 ft.) is 3.25 miles from the junction with Trail 1885 where we started. The trail comes to a road that is in use 200 yards past the crossing. Follow this road down 0.7 mile to the old mining town of Cornucopia. There is a sign marking this trail in Cornucopia. The total distance from Trail 1885 to Cornucopia is four miles. In Cornucopia this trailhead is some distance south and across Pine Creek from the main Cornucopia Trailhead.

This trail is best hiked one way from the Summit Point Trailhead. It is not only mostly downhill in this direction, but it is also easier to follow. There is some private land in Cornucopia, but if you stay on the road, which is also the trail, no special permission is necessary.

Trail 1880

General description: A 10.3 mile day hike, or a two day backpack. It will be 13.1 miles if done from Summit Point Trailhead. In this book I am describing Pine Lakes Trail from its junction with Cliff Creek Trail 1885 to Cornucopia. This may seem backwards, but it is a much easier hike in this direction. Even including the 3.7 mile hike from Summit Point Trailhead to the beginning of Pine Lakes Trail at the junction with Cliff

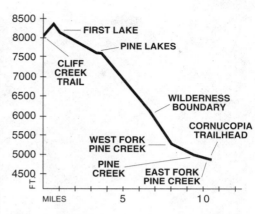

Creek Trail, it is no farther than the round trip to Pine Lakes from Cornucopia. The elevation gain going the direction I describe is much less, and you do not have to cover the same ground twice. However, it does require a car shuttle.

Difficulty: Moderate in the direction described, strenuous if coming up from Cornucopia.

Trail maintenance: Yearly.

Best season: July through September.

Traffic: Moderate to heavy, with moderate horse traffic.

Elevation gain: 360 feet from Cliff Creek Trail, approximately 1,900 feet if hiking from Summit Point Trailhead. Loss: 3,550 feet.

Maximum elevation: 8,380 feet.

Maps: Krag Peak and Cornucopia USGS quads, also Jim Town USGS quad, if coming from Summit Point Trailhead. Imus Geographics Wallowa Mountains Eagle Cap Wilderness covers the entire trip.

For more information: U.S. Forest Service at Wallowa Mountain Visitors Center, Enterprise, Oregon, or U.S. Forest Service at Halfway Ranger Station, Halfway, Oregon.

Finding the trail: Pine Lakes Trail starts at the junction with Cliff Creek Trail (El 8,020 ft.), 3.7 miles south of Summit Point Trailhead. See Hike 83 Cliff Creek. The Cornucopia Trailhead can be reached by following Cornucopia Road north from the town of Halfway, 10 miles to Cornucopia. The trailhead is at the north end of town.

0.0	Trail junction with Cliff Creek Trail.
0.7	Trail crosses pass.
1.0	Trail passes first lake (pond).
3.7	Pine Lakes.
6.5	Eagle Cap Wilderness Boundary.

Pine Lakes. *Photo by Lowell Euhus.*

8.0	Trail crosses West Fork Pine Creek.
9.2	Trail crosses Pine Creek.
10.0	Trail crosses East Fork Pine Creek.
10.3	Cornucopia Trailhead.

The trail: From the junction with Cliff Creek Trail, Pine Lakes Trail climbs to the south southeast for 0.5 mile. It then makes a switchback to the left. The trail reaches a pass (El 8,380 ft.), 0.25 mile past the switchback. Pine Lakes can be seen from the pass.

The trail makes ten switchbacks in the next 0.5 mile down the steep open slope to the first lake. This lake is little more than a pond. It is to the right (south) of the trail 50 or so yards. The elevation at this first lake is approximately 8,100 feet. After passing the first lake, the trail makes a couple more switchbacks, then it winds its way down through granite outcroppings to a stream crossing. There is a small rock bridge over this stream. The elevation here is 7,840 feet.

After crossing the stream, the trail goes along the right side of a meadow. A little less than 0.5 mile past the stream crossing the trail starts down another series of switchbacks. There are eight switchbacks in the next 0.5 mile. Upper Pine Lake (El 7,540 ft.) is at the bottom of the switchbacks. A short distance farther is Lower Pine Lake. Pine Lakes are 3.5 miles from the junction with Cliff Creek Trail, and there are 7.1 miles more to go to Cornucopia. A few good campsites can be had at Pine Lakes, and there seem to be plenty of fish. There is a short steep stream between the lakes. The trail goes around the left side of Lower Pine Lake, then crosses the outlet stream just below the dam.

Below Pine Lakes, the trail makes eighteen switchbacks, and crosses several small streams while descending into a lush alpine valley. This valley faces northeast which is probably why it has so much lusher vegetation than the country just over the ridge to the west. The trail heads down the valley for a short distance. It then makes four more little switchbacks and crosses a meadow on an elevated trail. After crossing the meadow, the trail crosses the outlet stream of Pine Lakes. Here there is a waterfall to the left of the trail.

The trail begins to descend more steeply again 0.25 mile after the creek crossing. It makes four switchbacks, crosses a couple of small streams, then makes another switchback. This area was burned many years ago. There are many silver snags. The burned area is about 600 yards across. Past the burn is a set of four more switchbacks. These switchbacks take the trail down a granite talus slope. There is a small stream crossing 0.3 mile past the last switchback. The Eagle Cap Wilderness Boundary (El 6,070 ft.) is just under 0.5 mile past the small stream crossing.

The trail crosses a ridgeline 0.25 mile past the wilderness boundary. It soon starts another series of nine switchbacks that bring it down to the bridge over the West Fork of Pine Creek (El 5,260 ft.). The trail becomes an old roadbed after crossing the bridge.

The trail crosses a small stream 0.7 mile after crossing the West Fork of Pine Creek. A couple hundred yards after crossing the stream, the trail crosses Pine Creek on a bridge. This bridge was in very poor condition in 1994. The elevation here is 4,980 feet. After crossing Pine Creek, the trail goes 0.25 mile to the crossing of another very small stream. There is a foot bridge over an-

85   Pine Lakes

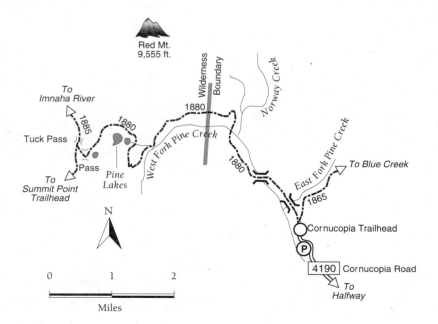

other stream 300 yards past the small stream crossing. In another 150 yards is the foot bridge over the East Fork of Pine Creek. Just after crossing the East Fork, the trail crosses another small stream. Five hundred yards more down the trail is the pack station and the Cornucopia Trailhead sign. The elevation at the trailhead is 4,830 feet.

The Cornucopia Trailhead is 10.3 miles from the junction with Cliff Creek Trail. Cornucopia is an interesting old mining town. There is a fairly large parking area 0.25 mile south of the trailhead on the main road.

86   NORWAY BASIN

Trail 1896

General description: An alternate route for a section of East Pine Creek/Blue Creek Trail 1865. This 4.8 mile trail is generally more scenic than East Pine Creek Trail, but is somewhat steeper and rougher. It follows old mine roads part of the way.

Difficulty: Moderate to strenuous.

Trail maintenance: Frequent on road section, and infrequent past there.

Best season: July through October.

Traffic: Light, with light horse traffic.

Elevation gain: 1,990 feet, not including East Fork Pine Creek Trail. Loss: 830 feet.

Maximum elevation: 7,630 feet.

Map: Cornucopia USGS quad.

For more information: U.S. Forest Service at Wallowa Mountain Visitors Center, Enterprise, Oregon, or U.S. Forest Service at Halfway Ranger Station, Halfway, Oregon.

Finding the trail: The Norway Basin Trail begins at its junction with the East Pine Creek Trail 1865. This junction is 1.2 miles north of the Cornucopia Trailhead. See Hike 87 East Pine Creek/Blue Creek. The elevation at the junction is 5,640 feet. The trail is actually an old road here, as are many trails, or parts of trails, in the Cornucopia area. See map on p. 231.

0.0	Trail junction with East Pine Creek Trail.
1.6	Cabin.
3.6	Trail junction with Sugarloaf Trail.
4.8	Trail junction with Blue Creek Trail.

The trail: Norway Basin Trail leaves East Fork Pine Creek Trail just after that trail crosses the East Fork of Pine Creek, 1.2 miles from Cornucopia Trailhead. Norway Basin Trail turns to the left. There is a sign marking this junction. The trail heads southwest, crosses a creek, and soon climbs around the end of a ridge. After rounding the ridge, it heads to the north and climbs steeply.

The trail flattens out some 0.5 mile after leaving East Pine Creek Trail. After climbing at a gentler grade for 275 yards, it crosses one of the forks of Simmons Creek. This crossing (El 6,000 ft.) is just above a fork in the creek. After crossing the creek, the trail steepens again and heads up a ridgeline to the northwest. The forest opens up along this ridge which makes it a good area to see elk, as I did when I hiked this trail.

The trail climbs up the ridgeline for 0.7 mile, then turns off to the left. There is an old roadbed going straight up the ridge here, but the trail sign points us to the left. There is a fallen down cabin on the left side of the trail 200 yards after turning off the ridge. Another old roadbed crosses the trail 350 yards past the cabin. The trail sign here points us straight ahead. After going 350 yards past the roadbed crossing, Norway Basin Trail finally bears right off the roadbed it has been on all the way from the East Pine Creek Trail. There is a trail sign here pointing to the right (north).

An old mine can be seen far below the trail 0.25 mile after leaving the roadbed. This mine is across Norway Creek on the other side of the canyon. The roadbed we turned off of leads to the mine. The Eagle Cap Wilderness Boundary is another 0.3 mile up the trail. The elevation at the boundary is 7,120 feet.

The trail crosses Norway Creek 1.1 miles past the wilderness boundary. Three hundred fifty yards after crossing Norway Creek the trail comes to the junction with Sugarloaf Trail 1887. See Hike 89 Sugarloaf. This junction is in a saddle on the ridge dividing Pine Creek and the Imnaha River drainages. The elevation at the junction is 7,630 feet. There is a ditch coming through the saddle which takes water from the Imnaha side and puts it on the Pine Creek side. A fairly good campsite is located to the right (east) of the trail at the saddle.

Cabin along Norway Basin Trail.

Norway Basin Trail goes across the saddle and starts to drop down the Imnaha River and Blue Creek side of the ridge. Just below the saddle it goes through an area of springs. After crossing the wet area the trail continues to drop, crossing four small streams in the mile to the junction with East Pine Creek/Blue Creek Trail 2.8 miles above the Imnaha River. This is the end of Norway Basin Trail (El 6,800 ft.). Return trip can be made on East Pine Creek/Blue Creek Trail back to Cornucopia Trailhead. See Hike 87 East Pine Creek/Blue Creek.

87   EAST PINE CREEK/BLUE CREEK

Trail 1865

General description: A 9.7 mile day hike or backpack, from Cornucopia Trailhead to the Imnaha River. This trail provides access to Norway Basin and Sugarloaf Trails.

Difficulty: Moderate to strenuous.
Trail maintenance: Infrequent.
Best season: July through October.
Traffic: Moderate to Norway Basin Trail, light from there to the Imnaha River, with light horse traffic. There may be occasional motor vehicle traffic up to Norway Basin Trail junction.
Elevation gain: 2,710 feet. Loss: 1,710 feet.
Maximum elevation: 7,540 feet.
Maps: Cornucopia USGS quad.

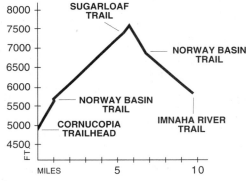

For more information: U.S. Forest Service at Wallowa Mountain Visitors Center, Enterprise, Oregon, or U.S. Forest Service at Halfway Ranger Station, Halfway, Oregon.

Finding the trail: The trail begins at Cornucopia Trailhead. To reach the trailhead go 10 miles north from Halfway to Cornucopia. The trailhead is at the north end of the old town next to the pack station. There is a large open area for parking 0.25 mile before reaching the trailhead. A signboard at the trailhead points out the trails, which begin from here on old mining roads.

0.0	Cornucopia Trailhead.
1.2	Trail junction with Norway Basin Trail.
5.4	Trail junction with Sugarloaf Trail.
5.8	Pass.
6.9	Trail junction with Norway Basin Trail.
9.7	Imnaha River and trail junction with Imnaha River Trail.

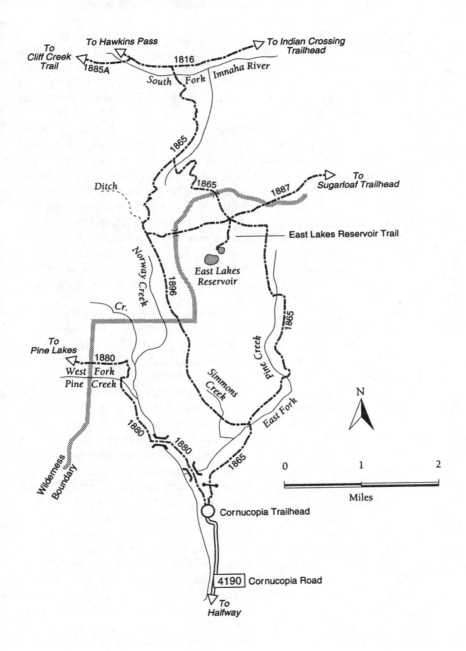

The trail: Trail 1865 begins at Cornucopia Trailhead (El 4,830 ft.). Like several other trails in the Cornucopia area, this trail starts out as an old roadbed. The trail, or road, heads north from the trailhead. After going 200 yards there is a stream crossing and a junction. Bear to the right (north northeast). There is another junction 200 yards farther up the trail. Bear right (north northeast) again. A few yards past this junction is an iron gate blocking the road to vehicles. The elevation at the gate is 4,950 feet. The trail continues to climb and crosses a small stream 0.7 mile past the gate. It crosses the East Fork of Pine Creek 0.3 mile after crossing the small stream. The junction with Norway Basin Trail is reached a few yards after crossing the East Fork of Pine Creek. The elevation at the junction is 5,640 feet. Norway Basin Trail turns to the left (southwest). See Hike 86 Norway Basin.

In the next 0.9 mile there are three cattle trails which turn off the main trail. Stay on the main trail heading up the left side of the creek. After going 0.9 mile up the left side of the creek, the trail turns to the right and crosses the East Fork of Pine Creek again. There is a waterfall just above the crossing. After the crossing the trail climbs, making some switch backs, then heads up through mostly open meadows to another creek crossing 0.9 mile after crossing the East Fork. The trail crosses three more streams as it climbs through alternating timber and sloping meadows, in the 1.7 more miles, to the junction with Sugarloaf Trail and East Lakes Reservoir Trail. See Hike 87 Sugarloaf and Trial 88 East Lakes Reservoir. This junction (El 7,320 ft.) is 5.4 miles from Cornucopia Trailhead. Follow the signs at the junction. This is where East Fork Pine Creek Trail becomes Blue Creek Trail.

From the junction, Blue Creek Trail heads up and to the northwest. It climbs for 0.4 mile to a saddle (El 7,540 ft.). In the saddle the trail enters Eagle Cap Wilderness. There is a sign at the boundary. After going through the meadow in the saddle, the trail makes five switchbacks as it drops the first mile towards the Imnaha River. In the 0.5 mile more to the junction with Norway Basin Trail the trail crosses two small streams on bridges as it descends through the forest. It then crosses Blue Creek and comes to the junction (El 6,800 ft.).

Bear right (northeast) at the junction, cross a small muddy stream and head on down Blue Creek. The trail crosses a wooden bridge over a small stream 150 yards from the junction, and soon enters an area of sloping meadows dissected by strips of timber. A bit over a mile after passing the junction the trail begins to descend more steeply. It makes eight switch backs as it drops through thick forest for 1.6 miles to a wooden bridge over a small stream. On the way down much of the forest floor is covered with huckleberry bushes. After crossing the bridge, the trail heads northwest through the woods on nearly flat ground for 0.2 mile to the Imnaha River. The trail fords the Imnaha River, angling upstream, then goes the last few yards to the junction with Imnaha River Trail (El 5,832 ft.). See Hike 92 South Fork Imnaha River. This crossing could be dangerous during periods of high water.

There are no really good campsites along this trail, but several can be found near the junction with the Imnaha River Trail on the north side of the Imnaha River. An excellent one way trip can be made by combining this trail with part of the Imnaha River Trail. To do this trip, head down the Imnaha River to Indian Crossing Trailhead. This combination trip requires a car shuttle. See Hike 100 Imnaha River for directions to Indian Crossing Trailhead.

88   EAST LAKES RESERVOIR

General description: A short 0.5 mile side trip from the junction of Sugarloaf and East Pine Creek Trails to East Lakes Reservoir.

Difficulty: Easy.
Trail maintenance: None.
Best season: Mid-June through October.
Traffic: Light except for cows.
Elevation loss: 60 feet.
Maximum elevation: 7,320 feet.
Map: Cornucopia USGS quad covers the area, but this trail is not shown on the map.
For more information: U.S. Forest Service at Wallowa Mountain Visitors Center, Enterprise, Oregon, or U.S. Forest Service at Halfway Ranger Station, Halfway, Oregon.
Finding the trail: The path to East Lakes Reservoir begins at the junction of Sugarloaf, East Pine Creek and Blue Creek Trails. See Hike 87 East Pine Creek/ Blue Creek and Hike 89 Sugarloaf. See map on p. 231.

0.0   Trail junction with Sugarloaf Trail.
0.5   East Lakes Reservoir.

The trail: From the junction with Sugarloaf Trail, East Lakes Reservoir Trail heads southwest. After going about 500 yards the trail becomes difficult to see in some woods. Keep going southwest. Stay nearly level, then go over a small rise to where the trail shows up again and the lakes come into view. The trail then drops down slightly to the lakes (El 7,272 feet.)

East Lakes Reservoir is two lakes that have been dammed in order to hold more water for irrigation. This damming was a common practice with the lakes on the south side of the Wallowa Mountains, in past years. It does hold water for summer use, but it makes a real mess out of lake shores. To compound the mess at East Lakes Reservoir, the muddy shore lines are further degraded by cattle tromping in the mud. The area around the reservoir is a high ridge top plateau. There is much open grassland and groves of subalpine trees. This is prime summer range for elk. Return to the junction via the same trail.

Russell Mountain Lookout.

EASTERN REGION

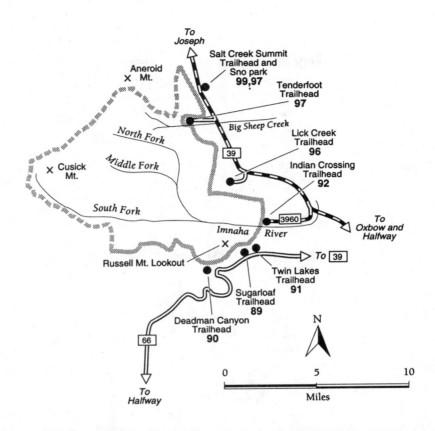

---

89   SUGARLOAF

Trail 1887

General description: A 9.9 mile backpack from Twin Lakes to Norway Basin Trail, along the south rim of the Imnaha Canyon.

Difficulty: Easy

Trail maintenance: Infrequent

Best season: July through October.

Traffic: Moderate.

Elevation gain: 2,300 feet. Loss: 1,160 feet.

Maximum elevation: 7,930 feet.

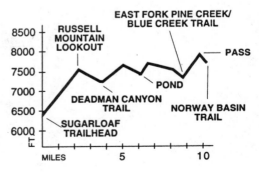

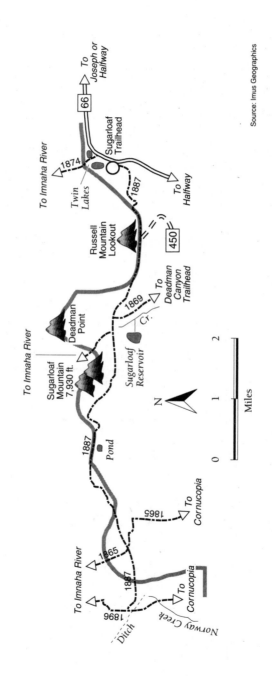

Source: Imus Geographics

Maps: Imus Geographics Wallowa Mountains Eagle Cap Wilderness, or Deadman Point and Cornucopia USGS quads.

For more information: U.S. Forest Service at Wallowa Mountain Visitors Center, Enterprise, Oregon, or U.S. Forest Service at Halfway Ranger Station, Halfway, Oregon.

Finding the trail: Sugarloaf Trailhead is 0.2 miles west of Twin Lakes Campground, on Forest Road 66. The trailhead is marked with a small sign, and is on the right (west) side of the road. For directions to Twin Lakes see Hike 91 Twin Lakes section in this book.

0.0	Sugarloaf Trailhead.
2.2	Russell Mountain Lookout.
3.8	Trail junction with Deadman Canyon Trail (to trailhead).
4.0	Trail junction with Deadman Canyon Trail (to Imnaha River).
6.2	Pond.
8.7	Trail junction with East Pine Creek/Blue Creek Trail and East Lakes Reservoir Trail.
9.9	Trail junction with Norway Basin Trail.

The trail: The Sugarloaf Trail heads west southwest from the rough parking lot at the trailhead (El 6,490 ft.). The trail, which is an abandoned roadbed for the first mile, climbs through the burned timber of the 1994 Twin Lakes Forest Fire. The trail heads southwest and climbs in a narrow sloping meadow, 0.3 mile after leaving the parking lot. At the top of the meadow the trail turns to the right. Watch for blazes and sawed logs marking the trail. It soon turns left again and goes up another meadow.

About 1 mile from the parking lot the trail climbs up through an open area. It is difficult to see the trail here. The trail goes back into the woods at the north northwest corner of the open area. The trail soon enters another open area. After going 300 more yards there will be a creek a few yards to the left of the trail. The trail soon enters yet another open area. There is a large lodgepole pine in the middle of this open area, with a blaze on it. Head west southwest past the lodgepole pine. Turn left slightly at the upper end of the opening, and then climb to the top of a low rounded ridge. At the top of the ridge the trail turns left and heads south southwest.

The trail soon enters another meadow. Go up the middle of this meadow, then left, slightly, at the top. The trail hits another meadow 0.25 mile farther along. Head west northwest and look for the cut logs that make an opening for the trail on the other side. Go through a line of trees and head west southwest across a wet meadow for 200 yards. At the upper end of the wet area there is another cut log, marking an opening for the trail. The trail comes to the Russell Lookout Road, Forest Road 450, 0.25 mile past the wet area. The trail from Twin Lakes to Russell Mountain Lookout Road takes some route finding skills. Most of this section was at least partly burned in the fire, so some of the best trail markers are the logs that were sawed off to reopen the trail.

The trail turns right (northwest) on the Russell Mountain Lookout Road and climbs 250 yards to Russell Mountain Lookout. This is also a trailhead, but the road to it is very rough. The elevation here is 7,508 feet. From the lookout the trail begins to drop slightly to the west. The trail enters a meadow 0.7 mile past the lookout. The trail goes along the left side of this long meadow. It stays on the edge of the trees and heads to the west. There are posts marking the trail near the west end of the meadow. This meadow is nearly 0.5 mile long. The junction with Deadman Canyon Trail 1869 is 0.3 mile through another patch of burnt forest past the end of the meadow. The elevation at this junction is 7,230 feet. The Deadman Canyon Trail junction is 1.8 miles from Russell Mountain Lookout. See Hike 90 Deadman Canyon. This is where the trail leaves the burned area.

Deadman Canyon Trailhead is to the left (south) at the junction. The trail that goes to the right dead ends. The Sugarloaf Trail, which is marked with posts, goes straight ahead to the west southwest. The Sugarloaf Trail is very difficult to see here. Head west southwest and follow the posts. The first post is 200 yards from the junction, across two streams. Deadman Canyon Trail and Sugarloaf Trail follow the same route for about 500 yards here. At the third post Deadman Canyon Trail turns off to the right (northwest) and heads for the Imnaha River. There is a signpost at this junction.

From the second Deadman Canyon Trail junction, the Sugarloaf Trail heads west southwest. At first it climbs towards Sugarloaf Mountain and then bears slightly to the left and begins a traverse around the south side of the mountain. It may be difficult to see in spots here. There is a trail marker sign 0.3 mile from the junction. The signpost is on the left side of the trail. Past the trail marker the trail becomes a two track, unused jeep road. Another trail comes in from the left (south) 0.2 mile, past the trail sign. There is another trail marker sign on the right side of the trail here. The trail goes through a saddle 0.3 mile past the second trail sign. Red Mountain comes into view straight ahead at the saddle.

After passing the saddle, the trail drops slightly then continues its traverse. The trail goes between two posts 1.1 miles past the saddle. A panoramic view of the upper Imnaha drainage opens up about 300 yards after going between the posts. The trail goes around the hill to the north for 200 yards. Then it makes a switchback and heads to the southwest. The switchback is difficult to see. The trail heads southwest for a short distance, then drops to the west. The trail drops for 0.25 mile to a saddle. There is a pond in this saddle. The saddle (El 7,380 ft.) is one of the better campsites along Sugarloaf Trail. The trail is difficult to see near the pond.

Pick up the trail on the west side of the pond. There is a broken down corral just past the pond on the left side of the trail. The trail comes to a burned area 0.3 mile past the saddle. It climbs 0.1 mile through the lightly burned area to another saddle (El 7,550 ft.). The trail goes around the north side of a low hill and comes to a spring 0.5 mile past the saddle. The small spring is right in the trail. After passing the spring, the trail drops steeply west for 0.3 mile to another saddle. The junction with Blue Creek Trail 1865 is 0.6 mile past the saddle on the left (south) side of the ridgeline. The area between the saddle and the trail junction may be nearly covered with phlox in early summer. The elevation at this junction is 7,320 feet. See Hike 87 East Pine Creek/Blue Creek and Hike 88 East Lakes Reservoir. This junction is 8.7 miles from Twin Lakes.

Past the junction the trail soon becomes difficult to see. It goes west, then southwest, and crosses a very small stream, which may be dry 150 yards from the junction. There is a post marking the trail 100 yards past the stream. Here the trail becomes easy to see again. There are also some rock cairns marking it along here. Two hundred fifty yards past the post the trail gradually turns to the west. In about 100 yards more it fades out again in an open area. The trail goes up the right (north) side of a little valley to the west, then climbs over a small rise and bears slightly to the left. Here the trail can be seen ahead as it heads up to a pass. There are also blazes on the scattered trees. The trail climbs to the pass (El 7,930 ft.), the high point of this trail.

Looking west from the pass, there is a good view of Red Mountain. To the northwest across the South Fork Imnaha River Canyon is Cusick Mountain. From the pass the trail heads down steeply, first to the west southwest, then to the west. It is difficult to see in spots but is never gone too long. It drops for 0.4 mile to the junction with Norway Basin Trail 1896. See Hike 86 Norway Basin. The Norway Basin Trail junction (El 7,630 ft.) is 9.9 miles from Twin Lakes.

Sugarloaf Trail generally follows the rim on the Imnaha River Canyon, and parallels the Eagle Cap Wilderness Boundary from Twin Lakes to Norway Basin Trail. After climbing the first mile from Twin Lakes, the trail stays above 7,000 feet elevation all the rest of the way. All of this trail goes through excellent elk summer range, and there is a good chance of seeing these large animals.

A one way trip can be made by combining Sugarloaf Trail with the south 3.6 miles of Norway Basin Trail and the south 1.2 miles of East Pine/Blue Creek Trail. See Hikes 86 and 87. Doing this involves a car shuttle to Cornucopia. See Hike 87 for directions to Cornucopia Trailhead.

90   *DEADMAN CANYON*

Trail 1869

General description: A 6.1 mile backpack, or long day hike from Deadman Trailhead near Fish Lake to the Imnaha River.
Difficulty: Moderate to strenuous.
Trail maintenance: Infrequent.
Best season: July through October.
Traffic: Moderate.
Elevation gain: 700 feet. Loss: 2,150 feet.
Maximum elevation: 7,460 feet.

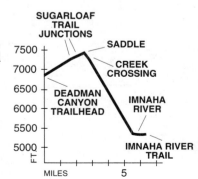

Maps: Imus Geographics Wallowa Mountains Eagle Cap Wilderness, or Deadman Point and Cornucopia USGS quads.

For more information: U.S. Forest Service at Wallowa Mountain Visitors Center, Enterprise, Oregon, or U.S. Forest Service at Halfway Ranger Station, Halfway, Oregon.

90 *Deadman Canyon*

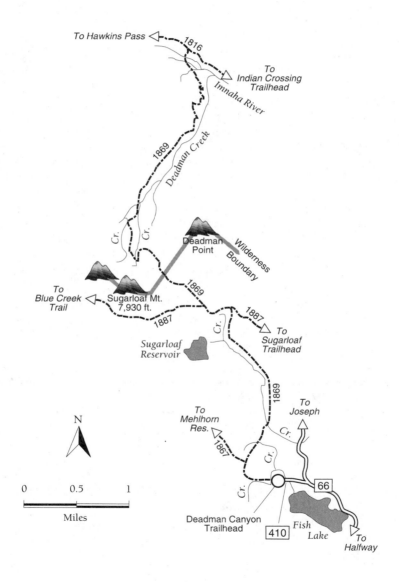

Finding the trail: Deadman Canyon Trail begins at Deadman Canyon Trailhead just north of Fish Lake. To reach the trailhead, first follow the directions to Twin Lakes, see Hike 91 Twin Lakes. From Twin Lakes, follow Forest Road 66 for 4 miles to the southwest to the junction with Forest Road 410. Turn right (west) on FR 410 and go 0.4 mile to Deadman Trailhead. The junction of Forest Road 66 and FR 410 is just north of Fish Lake. Fish Lake can also be reached from Halfway by taking East Pine Creek Road north from town. East Pine Creek Road becomes FR 66 and leads to Fish Lake and the junction with FR 410. The Imus Geographics map mentioned above is a big help for finding your way around the roads in this area.

0.0	Deadman Canyon Trailhead.
1.8	First trail junction with Sugarloaf Trail.
2.1	Second trail junction with Sugarloaf Trail.
2.6	Trail crosses saddle.
6.0	Trail fords Imnaha River.
6.1	Trail junction with Imnaha River Trail.

The trail: From Deadman Canyon Trailhead (El 6,760 ft.) Deadman Canyon Trail starts out as a road that is closed to motor vehicles. There is a sign at the trailhead pointing to the Imnaha River. The trail, or road, heads west to start. About 150 yards from the trailhead, the trail crosses a creek as it climbs gently through the timber. Another 300 yards and a creek flows down the trail for a short distance. The junction with the trail to Clear Lake Reservoir 1867 is reached 0.4 mile from the trailhead.

The trail to Clear Lake turns to the left (northwest). A short distance past the junction, the Deadman Canyon Trail bears to the north and leaves the closed road. The trail crosses a creek 0.3 mile after leaving the old roadbed and crosses another one 0.2 mile farther along. The trail comes to the junction with Sugarloaf Reservoir Trail 0.8 mile after the last creek crossing. The reservoir is 0.25 mile to the left (west) across the meadow. Deadman Trail goes straight ahead (north) 0.2 mile more to the junction with Sugarloaf Trail 1887. The junction (El 7,230 ft.) is 2.1 miles from the trailhead. This junction area is where this description disagrees with both the Imus Geographics and USGS maps. See Hike 89 Sugarloaf and the map accompanying this description.

At this junction Deadman Canyon Trail turns to the left and follows Sugarloaf Trail to the west southwest. There is a sign here pointing out Sugarloaf Trail. There is a path that goes straight ahead (north) here, but it dead ends. Turn left and follow the posts that mark Sugarloaf Trail.

After following Sugarloaf Trail for 500 yards and crossing a couple of small streams there is another junction with a sign post. The signs can be confusing here. The Deadman Canyon Trail turns to the right (northwest) and climbs gently, through mostly open meadows to the saddle between Deadman Point and Sugarloaf Mountain. This saddle (El 7,460 ft.) is 0.2 mile northwest of the junction. The trail crosses the Eagle Cap Wilderness Boundary in the saddle.

After crossing the saddle, the trail begins to drop through burned timber. The trail soon leaves the burn area. It crosses a small creek 0.2 mile below the saddle. A few yards farther along, the trail crosses Deadman Creek (El 7,280 ft.). The forks of the creeks run together just below the trail. There is a meadow to the left and possible campsite here.

After the creek crossing, the trail turns to the north and heads down Deadman Canyon. It crosses a couple more streams 0.75 mile after crossing Deadman Creek. Another 0.8 mile down there is an open area with a good view of the Imnaha Canyon below.

The trail begins a mile long series of nine switchbacks 1.9 miles after crossing Deadman Creek, as it drops steeply through the forest. Below the switchbacks the trail becomes less steep and soon heads left (west) on the flat ground, crossing a small stream. A short distance farther there is a campsite on the left side of the trail. The Imnaha River is 50 yards to the right at this point.

The trail heads west up river for 300 yards, crossing another small stream, to the point where it fords the Imnaha River. This crossing can be dangerous during times of high water. After crossing the river the trail heads northeast, then north, for 0.1 mile to the junction with the Imnaha River Trail 1816. The elevation at the junction is 5,310 feet. See Hike 100 Imnaha River. There are good campsites here near the river, and the fishing can be excellent. Check with the Oregon Department of Fish and Wildlife regulations before fishing, as there are some special regulations for the Imnaha River.

A one way trip can be done by combining Deadman Canyon Trail with Imnaha River trail and coming out at Indian Crossing Trailhead. This would necessitate a car shuttle to Indian Crossing Trailhead. See Hike 100 for directions to Indian Crossing Trailhead and a description of the Imnaha River Trail.

91 TWIN LAKES

Trail 1874

General description: A 3.1 mile day hike or backpack from Twin Lakes Trailhead and Campground to the Imnaha River. This area was burned in the Twin Lakes Forest Fire of September 1994. Because of this at present the trail is difficult to follow but it is supposed to be maintained in the future.

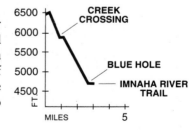

Difficulty: Moderate to strenuous.
Trail maintenance: Infrequent
Best season: Mid-June through early November.
Traffic: Light.
Elevation gain: 30 feet. Loss: 1,770 feet.
Maximum elevation: 6,490 feet.

Blue Hole. *Photo by Gary Fletcher.*

For more information: U.S. Forest Service at Wallowa Mountain Visitors Center, Enterprise, Oregon, or U.S. Forest Service at Halfway Ranger Station, Halfway, Oregon.

Finding the trail: Twin Lakes Trail begins at Twin Lakes Trailhead and Campground. To reach the trailhead, take Oregon Highway 86 from Halfway, east for 9 miles. Turn left (north) on Forest Road 39 and go 14 miles to Forest Road 66. Turn left (west) and follow FR 66, 12 miles to Twin Lakes Campground and Trailhead. FR 39 can also be reached from Joseph, Oregon. See Hike 100. Once on FR 39 continue south to the junction with FR 66.

0.0 Twin Lakes Trailhead.
2.9 Trail crosses Imnaha River at Blue Hole.
3.1 Trail junction with Imnaha River Trail.

The trail: The area around the Trailhead and along most of this trail was burned in the September 1994 Twin Lakes Forest Fire. The trail heads northwest from the trailhead (El 6,480 ft.). After a short distance it crosses the creek that connects the lakes. There is another creek crossing 0.2 mile farther along. Just past this second creek crossing is the Eagle Cap Wilderness Boundary. Soon after passing the wilderness boundary, the trail starts to descend through

91 *Twin Lakes*

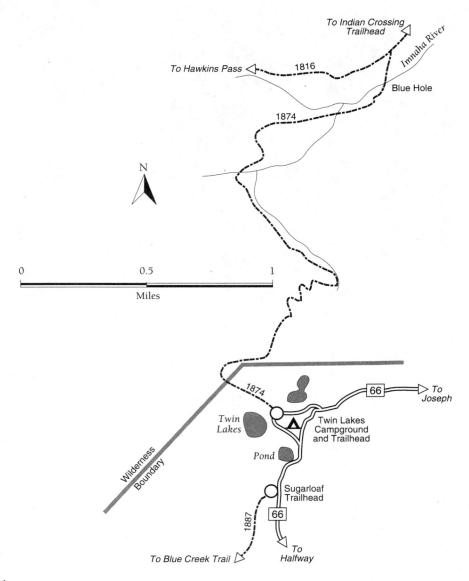

the now completely burned forest into the Imnaha River Canyon. The trail may be difficult to follow through this burned area.

The trail descends for 200 yards then follows a bench to the right (east) for 125 yards before bearing to the left (northeast) and dropping steeply again. The trail descends for 0.8 mile more, then crosses a creek (El 5,820 ft.). After crossing the creek, the trail bears left and heads northwest. This area can be confusing, as the creek, during times of high water, may fork into two channels, in which case the trail heads down between the channels.

The trail comes to an open bench area 0.1 mile after the creek crossing. There is a campsite on the bench, if you don't mind camping among the burnt snags. The elevation here is 5,760 feet. There is a rock outcropping on the right side of the trail on this bench. The top of the outcropping provides a good viewpoint overlooking the Imnaha Canyon.

The trail drops off the bench and descends fairly steeply for 0.4 mile to the northwest. Then it flattens out and heads west, finally reaching an area which was not completely burned in the forest fire. It doesn't flatten out for long, and soon drops to a creek crossing. After crossing the creek, the trail heads west southwest through a meadow. Here there are smooth glacier carved rock outcroppings on the right side of the trail. The trail winds its way down through these outcroppings and crosses another stream 0.25 mile past the last stream crossing.

After the stream crossing, the trail goes between and over some more outcroppings. Watch for cairns to follow the route. The trail gets back into the partly burnt woods 400 yards past the stream crossing. Here the trail drops steeply for a short distance, then heads east again. There is another creek crossing 0.4 mile after getting back in the woods. The trail crosses two more streams in the next 0.25 mile, then it comes along side of the Imnaha River which is in a gorge here. There is a viewpoint overlooking the gorge 100 feet to the left of the trail. The trail crosses the Imnaha River 0.2 mile after passing the viewpoint.

The crossing is at a place called Blue Hole (El 4720 ft.). This crossing can be dangerous during high water. It is usually a safe but wet waist deep crossing in August, September and October, but in June and July it may be much deeper and very swift. Be careful. There is a good but heavily used campsite just across the Imnaha River on the north side. The junction with Imnaha River Trail is 0.2 mile past the crossing. See Hike 100 Imnaha River.

The return trip may be made by the same trail, or a one way trip can be made by heading east for 2 miles on the Imnaha River Trail to Indian Crossing Trailhead. See Hike 100 for directions to Indian Crossing Trailhead. A car shuttle can be made by going north on FR 39, as mentioned in the finding the trail section above, to Upper Imnaha River Road 3960, then turning left, and following it 10 miles to Indian Crossing Trailhead. FR 39 is the Wallowa Mountain Loop Road, from Halfway to Joseph.

Trail 1820 and 1816

General description: A 12.6 mile backpack along the South Fork Imnaha River, from West Fork Wallowa River Trail, over Hawkins Pass, to the junction with North Fork Imnaha Trail. This trail, used in conjunction with West Fork Wallowa River Trail and the Imnaha River Trail, makes a great several day trip through the north-central and eastern parts of the Wallowa Mountains. Access to Cliff Creek, Blue Creek, Boner Flat, North Fork Imnaha River, Lick Creek, Deadman Canyon and Imnaha River Trails can be had from this trail.
Difficulty: Moderate.
Trail maintenance: Yearly or more often if necessary.
Best season: July through September.
Elevation gain: 1,190 feet (3,680 feet if coming from Wallowa Lake Trailhead). Loss: 2,930 feet.
Maximum elevation: 8,330 feet.
Maps: Imus Geographics Wallowa Mountains Eagle Cap Wilderness, or Eagle Cap, Krag Peak, Cornucopia and Deadman Point USGS quads.
For more information: U.S. Forest Service at Wallowa Mountain Visitors Center, Enterprise, Oregon.
Finding the trail: This trail begins as Hawkins Pass Trail 1820 at its junction with West Fork Wallowa River Trail 1806. Trail 1806, goes on up to Glacier Lake. Trail 1820, which is also West Fork Wallowa River Trail, comes up from Wallowa Lake Trailhead. See Hike 4 West Fork Wallowa River and Hike 13 Glacier Pass.

0.0   Trail junction with West Fork Wallowa River Trail.

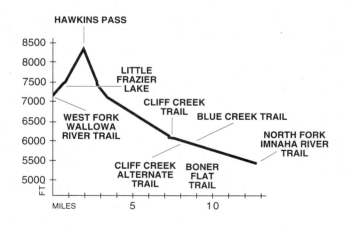

0.7	Little Frazier Lake.
2.1	Hawkins Pass.
7.2	Trail junction with Cliff Creek Trail.
8.0	Trail junction with Cliff Creek Alternate Trail.
8.6	Trail junction with Blue Creek Trail.
10.2	Trail junction with Boner Flat Trail.
12.6	Trail junction with North Fork Imnaha River Trail, Trail 1816 becomes Imnaha River Trail.

The trail: The Hawkins Pass Trail, which is also the South Fork Imnaha River Trail, turns left (southwest) off the West Fork Wallowa River Trail at the junction (El 7,140 ft.) just west of Frazier Lake, 9 miles from Wallowa Lake Trailhead. The trail crosses a stream 0.25 mile from the junction. This is the outlet stream of Glacier Lake, part of the headwaters of the Wallowa River. After crossing the stream, the trail climbs a ridge between the stream it just crossed and the outlet stream of Little Frazier Lake. The outlet stream from Frazier Lake is another part of the headwaters of the Wallowa River. After climbing the ridge for 300 yards, the trail crosses the Little Frazier Lake outlet stream. Another 0.3 mile and five switchbacks more is Little Frazier Lake (El 7,430 ft.).

The trail goes around the left (east) side of the lake. The waterfall across the lake is the outlet from Prospect Lake. The trail climbs above the south side of Little Frazier Lake for 0.5 mile, then makes a switchback to the left. It makes seven more switchbacks in the next 0.3 mile. Here there is a hand built rock wall about 75 yards to the right of the trail. This is part of the mining operations which took place in this area. There is also a small stream in and cross-

Author near Hawkins Pass. *Photo by Gary Fletcher*

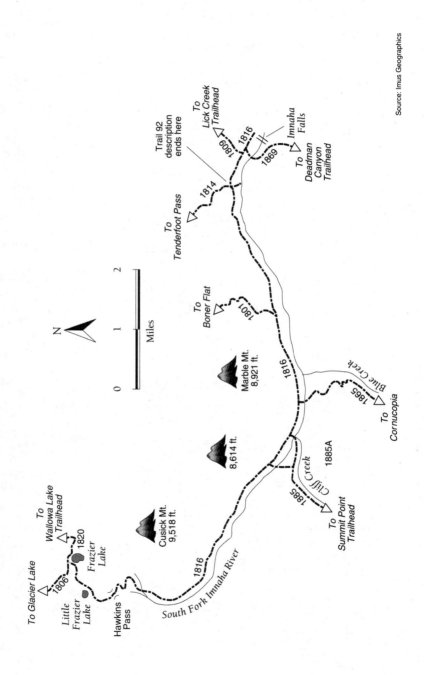

ing the trail. The trail makes six more switchbacks getting up the 0.4 mile more up to Hawkins Pass (El 8,330 ft.).

There has been a lot of mining activity at Hawkins Pass. There is evidence of this to the right, up the hill from the trail. This area is very interesting geologically. There are many types of rock strata, ranging in color from white to black. To the south and southeast at the head of the South Fork Imnaha Canyon there is a huge limestone wall. Eagle Cap Mountain can be seen to the northwest. This area is private land as of 1994, so please respect it. No permission is necessary to cross this private land on the trail.

After going through Hawkins Pass, where the trail number changes to 1816, the trail starts to descend into the glacial valley at the head of the South Fork Imnaha River. This is one of the most spectacular valleys in the Wallowa Mountains. Flowers carpet the area in summer. After going 150 yards, there is a switchback to the right. On the main trail there are five more switchbacks in the next 0.7 mile. In that 0.7 mile the trail drops 720 vertical feet. There is an older trail heading down here. It is shorter and cuts off some switchbacks, but it is also steeper. For your knees and for the environment it is better to use the main trail.

After the last switchback the trail heads down the valley. There is a spring to the left of the trail 300 yards past the last switchback. The trail goes past the first grove of trees since Hawkins Pass, 150 yards past the spring. It crosses the South fork Imnaha River about 0.4 mile after going past this first grove of trees. There is no bridge at this crossing (El 7,100 ft.). We are now 3.5 miles from the junction with West Fork Wallowa River Trail.

Beyond the river crossing the trail may be difficult to see for a short distance in a lush grassy area. Actually a lot of the "grass" is not grass, it is wild onions. This area may be quite wet. The trail goes along about 50 yards to the left (east) of the river. Three-tenths mile after the river crossing, there is a campsite to the right of the trail. In this area the trail alternates, going through groves of trees and flower covered meadows. Soon it gradually makes its turn to the east. It crosses a couple of streams and comes into a large open area 1.25 miles past the campsite.

To the left in this open area is a huge exposed limestone slope. This is the south side of 9,518 foot high Cusick Mountain. In the next 1.5 miles, the trail crosses three streams before coming to the junction with Cliff Creek Trail 1885 (El 6,100 ft.). Cliff Creek Trail turns off to the right (south). See Hike 82 Cliff Creek. This junction is 7.2 miles from the junction with West Fork Wallowa River Trail.

There is a small stream crossing 0.5 mile past the Cliff Creek Trail junction. One-third mile after the stream crossing is a campsite in the trees to the right of the trail. There is an unmarked trail junction 75 yards past the campsite. The unmarked trail is an alternate to Cliff Creek Trail, and it joins Cliff Creek Trail on its way south. Between this junction and Blue Creek Trail 1865 junction, 0.6 mile farther along, there are three small stream crossings which may be dry in late summer. Sego lilies are common here in the open areas. There are also some very large tamarack (western larch) trees in this area. After the Blue Creek Trail junction the trail continues for 1.9 miles to the unmarked junction with Boner Flat Trail 1801. There are several small stream crossings between the trail junctions.

Boner Flat Trail is very difficult to spot from the South Fork Imnaha River Trail. It heads up to the left (north) through an open grassy area, but there may be no sign of it on the ground. There is a sign marking it on a tree 50 yards off the Imnaha River Trail. But this sign is almost impossible to see from the South Fork Imnaha River Trail. See Hike 95 Boner Flat. The elevation at this junction is 5,680 feet.

After passing the Boner Flat Trail junction, the South Fork Imnaha River Trail heads down the river. It crosses several more small streams in the 2.1 miles from the Boner Flat Trail junction to the bridge over the North Fork Imnaha River. Just past the bridge is the junction with North Fork Imnaha Trail 1814 (El 5,400 ft.). See Hike 93 North Fork Imnaha River. This junction is 12.6 miles from the junction with West Fork Wallowa River Trail. There are some very large tamarack trees growing in this area. From here to Indian Crossing Trailhead Trail 1816 is the Imnaha River Trail. See Hike 100 Imnaha River.

The junction with Lick Creek Trail 1809 is 600 yards past the North Fork Imnaha River Trail junction. Lick Creek Trail turns off to the left. There is a sign at this junction. See Hike 96 Lick Creek. One hundred fifty yards past the Lick Creek Trail junction is the junction with Deadman Canyon Trial 1869. This trail turns off to the right. See Hike 90 Deadman Canyon. There is a good campsite here. The trail crosses a small stream 350 yards past Deadman Canyon Trail, and another small stream 275 yards farther. Three hundred fifty yards past the second stream a path drops off to the right. This path goes 100 yards to Imnaha Falls.

The area around Deadman Canyon Trail junction is a great place to camp and explore the many trails that come together in this area. This description overlaps with the description of the Imnaha River Trail in this area. The description of Trail 1816 from here to Indian Crossing Trailhead is written as though coming from the opposite direction, because of this section's popularity as a day hike from Indian Crossing Trailhead. A one way trip can be done from Wallowa Lake Trailhead to Indian Crossing by combining Hikes 4, 92, and 100. This involves a 53 mile car shuttle and 29.8 miles on the trail. Allow at least 2 days to make this one way trip, if the whole party is in excellent shape. A better schedule would be 3 days, with a camp at Frazier Lake the first night and one around the junction with Cliff Creek Trail the second night.

Trail 1814

General description: An 8.1 mile backpack down the North Fork Imnaha River, from Tenderfoot Pass to the Imnaha River Trail. This trail accesses Polaris Pass, Tenderfoot Wagon Road, Middle Fork Imnaha River, and Boner Flats Trails.

Difficulty: Moderate.

Trail maintenance: Yearly.

Best season: July through September.

Traffic: Light to moderate, with moderate horse traffic.

Elevation loss: 3,100 feet.

Maximum elevation: 8,500 feet.

Maps: Imus Geographics Wallowa Mountains Eagle Cap Wilderness, or Aneroid Mountain and Cornucopia USGS quads.

For more information: U.S. Forest Service at Wallowa Mountain Visitors Center, Enterprise, Oregon.

Finding the trail: The North Fork Imnaha River Trail is a continuation of the East Fork Wallowa River Trail 1804. See Hike 2 East Fork Wallowa River. The North Fork Imnaha River Trail begins at Tenderfoot Pass.

0.0	Tenderfoot Pass.
0.3	Trail junction with Polaris Pass Trail.
1.8	Trail junction with Tenderfoot Wagon Road Trail.
5.5	Trail junction with Middle Fork Imnaha River Trail.
8.1	Trail junction with Imnaha River Trail.

The trail: From Tenderfoot Pass (El 8,500 ft.) the trail drops to the south for 0.3 miles to the junction with Polaris Pass Trail 1831 (El 8,210 ft.). See Trail 3 Polaris Pass. The junction with Trail 1814A is 250 yards past the Polaris Pass Trail junction. Trail 1814A, which bears to the right, is an alternate trail for descending into the North Fork Imnaha River Canyon. The alternate trail is a bit shorter than the main trail; however, it misses the junction with Tenderfoot Wagon Road Trail and is somewhat steeper than the main trail.

After passing the junction with Trail 1814A, the trail heads on down at a moderate grade through mostly open country. There are lots of flowers in this area including asters, whitetops, and many others. There is also some sage on these open south facing slopes. The trail crosses two streams in the 1.3 miles from the junction with Trail 1814A to the junction with Tenderfoot Wagon

Road Trail 1819. See Hike 97 Tenderfoot Wagon Road. The altitude at the Wagon Road junction is 7,570 feet. The North Fork Imnaha River Trail turns to the right (southwest) and heads down the wagon road.

After going down the wagon road for 300 yards, the trail makes a switchback to the left in the bottom of a stream bed. The trail goes down the stream bed for a few feet. At certain times this stream bed is a regular flower garden. After leaving the stream bed, the trail goes 400 yards then makes a switchback to the right. After making the switchback, it crosses one more stream in the 400 yards to the junction with Trail 1814A (El 7,000 ft.). This is

93   North Fork Imnaha River

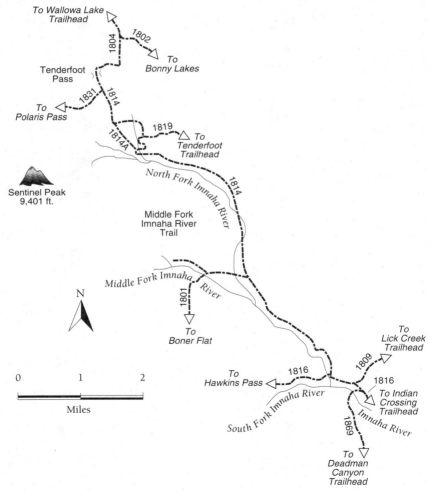

North Fork Imnaha River Canyon from near Tenderfoot Pass.
Photo by Gary Fletcher.

the lower end of the alternate trail mentioned earlier. Just past the junction, the trail makes a switchback to the left and heads down the bottom of the North Fork Imnaha River Canyon.

From here down to the junction with the Middle Fork Trail there are many good campsites. However, it is a good idea to camp back away form the river in this area because this river does flash flood occasionally.

After going down the canyon for 1.9 miles and crossing numerous small streams, the trail fords the cold waters of the North Fork Imnaha River. The elevation at the crossing is 6,400 feet. Most maps show the junction with Boner Flat and Middle Fork Imnaha River Trails to be just below this crossing. However, the Middle Fork Trail from here to the Middle Fork of the Imnaha River is difficult to find. It is better to go on down the North Fork Trail approximately 1.1 miles to the marked junction. See Hike 94 Middle Fork Imnaha River.

After going down along the right (west) side of the river for 400 yards, the trail crosses the North Fork Imnaha River again. The trail heads on down the left (east) side of the river for 0.9 mile to the junction with Middle Fork Imnaha River Trail (El 6,010 ft.). It crosses three small streams before reaching the junction. The junction is marked with a sign on a tamarack tree on the left (east) side of the trail. This junction is 5.5 miles from Tenderfoot Pass.

The trail crosses a stream 350 yards past the junction with Middle Fork Imnaha River Trail. There is a campsite on the right 0.25 mile past the stream crossing. One-half mile past the campsite the trail crosses another stream. After going 0.3 mile past this stream crossing, it begins to climb away from the river.

The trail climbs for 350 yards then drops for 300 more yards to a switchback to the right. After the switchback the trail continues to descend, crossing a couple of stream beds as it drops to the river level again.

Half a mile past the switchback the trail climbs again for a short distance and makes a switchback to the right. Another 75 yards and the trail begins to drop again. It drops at a moderate grade for 600 yards to the junction with the Imnaha River Trail 1816 (El 5,400 ft.). Some of the trail in the last 600 yards before reaching Trail 1816 may be badly eroded, nearly washed away. See Hike 92 South Fork Imnaha River and Hike 100 Imnaha River. This junction is 8.1 miles from Tenderfoot Pass. Many wonderful campsites are to be found along the Imnaha River, and fishing can be very good. Check for the special regulations on bull trout (dolly vardon) which inhabit these waters.

From the junction with Imnaha River Trail one can head on down the Imnaha River to the east 6.8 miles to Indian Crossing Trailhead. This requires a car shuttle. See Hike 100 Imnaha River for directions to Indian Crossing Trailhead. For the more ambitious hiker, a loop trip can be made by going up the South Fork Imnaha River Trail, over Hawkins Pass, and back down the West Fork Trail. Allow one and one-half days to get to Frazier Lake and another half day to get back to Wallowa Lake Trailhead.

94   MIDDLE FORK IMNAHA RIVER

General description: A 1.6 mile side trail from North Fork Imnaha River Trail to a campsite. Middle Fork Imnaha River Trail is not maintained anymore; however, it does connect with Boner Flat Trail, and gets enough use to be fairly easy to follow up to the junction.

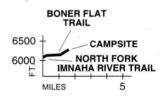

Difficulty: Easy, but the path fades out above Boner Flat Trail.

Best season: June through November.

Trail maintenance: Rare or none.

Traffic: Generally light, with most of its use by horse traffic during fall hunting seasons.

Elevation gain: 290 feet.

Maximum elevation: 6,300 feet.

Map: Aneroid Mountain USGS quad covers the area, but does not show this trail. Some of the older Forest Service and Eagle Cap Wilderness maps show this trail.

For more information: U.S. Forest Service at Wallowa Mountain Visitors Center, Enterprise, Oregon. Further information may be very limited.

Finding the trail: The Middle Fork Imnaha River Trail leaves the North Fork Imnaha River Trail 1814 approximately 2.7 miles up river from its junction with the Imnaha River Trail 1816. See Hike 93 North Fork Imnaha River. The elevation where the Middle Fork Trail leaves the North Fork Imnaha River Trail is 6,010 feet. The junction is marked with a sign pointing to Boner Flat.

0.0   Trail junction with North Fork Imnaha River Trail.
0.7   Trail junction with unmarked trail.
1.0   Trail junction with Boner Flat Trail.
1.7   Campsite and trail disappears.

The trail: The Middle Fork Imnaha River Trail turns west off the North Fork Imnaha River Trail. After heading west a few feet, it fords the cold rushing waters of the North Fork Imnaha River. There is a junction with an unmarked trail that turns to the right (north) 0.75 mile after crossing the river. This unmarked trail, is the trail which is shown on most newer maps. The unmarked trail contours around to the north and joins the North Fork Trail about 1 mile up river from the marked junction we turned on. The Middle Fork Trail heads west from the junction.

There is a metal trail sign on a tree on the left side of the trail 350 yards past the unmarked trail junction. The sign says "Middle Fork Imnaha River Trail." The Boner Flat Trail 1801 turns to the left, a short distance past the sign. See Hike 95 Boner Flat. The elevation at this junction is 6,180 feet.

Past the Boner Flat Trail junction the Middle Fork Imnaha River Trail becomes difficult to see as it heads up the right side of the river. The trail is generally within 20 yards of the river in this area. After five or six hundred yards the trail disappears completely in an open area. Across the open area is a well-

94 *Middle Fork Imnaha River*
95 *Boner Flat*

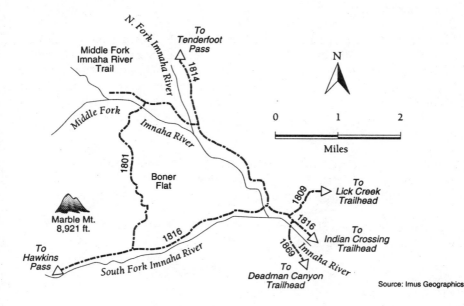

Source: Imus Geographics

used campsite. This campsite (El 6,300 ft.) is about 1.7 miles from the North Fork Imnaha River Trail.

The trail becomes just a route past the campsite. It is generally not visible on the ground and is not shown on newer maps. The Middle Fork Imnaha River forks 200 yards southwest of the campsite. This campsite makes a good base camp from which to explore the upper part of the Middle Fork Imnaha River drainage. There are fish to be caught in the Middle Fork.

Return by the same trail or make a loop trip over Boner Flat Trail and back down the South Fork Imnaha River Trail. See Hike 92 South Fork Imnaha River.

95   BONER FLAT

Trail 1801

General description: A 4 mile connecting trail from the Middle Fork Imnaha River Trail, up and over the ridge top meadows of Boner Flat, to the Imnaha River Trail.

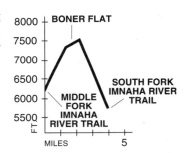

Difficulty: Strenuous.
Trail maintenance: Infrequent.
Best season: Mid-June through October.
Traffic: Light, with light horse traffic.
Elevation gain: 1,330 feet. Loss: 1,830 feet.
Maximum elevation: 7,510 feet.
Maps: Imus Geographics Wallowa Mountains Eagle Cap Wilderness, or Aneroid Mountain and Cornucopia USGS quads.
For more information: U.S. Forest Service at Wallowa Mountain Visitors Center, Enterprise, Oregon.
Finding the trail: Boner Flat Trail leaves the Middle Fork Imnaha Trail, 1 mile from its junction with North Fork Imnaha River Trail. See Hike 94 Middle Fork Imnaha River. The elevation at this unmarked junction is 6,180 feet. The Middle Fork Imnaha Trail is not shown on most newer maps, including USGS quads, so be sure to refer to the Middle Fork Imnaha River Trail section in this book before trying to take this trail, since most maps show Boner Flat junction differently than this description.

0.0   Trail junction with Middle Fork Imnaha River Trail.
2.2   Summit on south side of Boner Flat.
4.0   Trail junction with Imnaha River Trail.

The trail: The Boner Flat Trail turns left off the Middle Fork Imnaha River Trail. It crosses a meadow, then crosses the Middle Fork Imnaha River. After crossing the river, the trail heads south and up. It is a bit difficult to see in some of the open areas, so watch for blazes on the trees. The trail climbs steeply 0.4

mile to a small stream crossing (El 6,540 ft.). It crosses the same stream again 0.3 mile farther along. Between the stream crossings the trail goes almost straight up the hillside for a short distance. It is sometimes hard to see the trail in this area.

After crossing the stream the second time, the trail turns to the left. It flattens out a bit for a short distance then starts to climb again. The trail climbs for 0.25 mile, then makes a series of eight switchbacks in the next 0.4 mile. Above the switchbacks the grade moderates and the country opens up.

The trail now goes through more rolling country. This area of large sloping meadows spotted with wild flowers and groves of subalpine timber known as Boner Flat. It is about 0.9 mile from the top of the switchbacks across the meadow to the summit (El 7,510 ft.). Before reaching the summit, the trail is deeply eroded in places. In other places it is difficult to see. It heads generally south. Watch for blazes on the trees. Mule deer and elk are often seen on Boner Flat. Boner Flat is not a good place to be in a thunderstorm, as happened to me.

After passing the summit, the trail heads down to the southeast for a short distance. It then turns to the south southwest. The trail makes three switchbacks 0.25 mile below the summit. After passing the switchbacks, it winds down steeply for 0.25 mile more to another short series of switchbacks. After these switchbacks, the grade moderates again and heads southwest. A couple hundred yards past the switchbacks the trail crosses a small stream. It then goes down a small ridge for 300 yards and turns to the left (east) for 125 more yards before heading down another series of switchbacks. The trail makes five switchbacks then crosses the same stream again.

After crossing the stream, the trail enters an open area and becomes difficult to see. It goes down along the left (east) edge of the open area, passing a very large tamarack tree. There is a blaze on a small fir tree 40 yards to the right of the tamarack tree. Follow the blazes. There is another blaze on a small lodgepole pine on the right side of the opening 125 yards below the small fir. Thirty yards past the lodgepole is another blaze on a larger fir. This tree also has a sign on it which points back up the hill to Boner Flat. South and down 50 yards, is the junction with South Fork Imnaha River Trail 1816 (El 5,680 ft.). See Hike 92 South Fork Imnaha River. The junction is not marked and Boner Flat Trail is not visible on the ground at the junction. The junction with South Fork Imnaha River Trail is 4 miles from the junction with Middle Fork Imnaha River Trail.

Boner Flat Trail is very difficult to find when hiking along the Imnaha River Trail. I walked past it twice before I found it. The Forest Service maps are not too good in this area. If you are going to go up the Boner Flat Trail from the south, I suggest you get a USGS quad map, or better yet, take someone along that knows exactly where it leaves the Imnaha River Trail. The USGS map you need for this end of the trail is Cornucopia quad. The other end of the trail is covered by the Aneroid Mountain quad.

This trail can be done as part of a loop hike from a base camp on the Imnaha River near Imnaha Falls. This loop is hiked by going up the North Fork Imnaha River Trail to the Middle Fork Imnaha River Trail, then taking the

Middle Fork Imnaha River Trail to Boner Flat Trail, following Boner Flat Trail to South Fork Imnaha River Trail and taking South Fork Imnaha River Trail back to the campsite. This loop makes a long day hike of about 13 miles. There are lots of campsites along the Imnaha River Trail near it junction with North Fork Imnaha River Trail. Imnaha Falls is 0.9 mile down river (east) of the junction. See Hikes 90, 92, 93, 94, 96 and 100 for more information about the area around the junction.

96 LICK CREEK

Trail 1809

General description: A 5 mile day hike or backpack from Lick Creek Trailhead to the Imnaha River, near Imnaha Falls.
Difficulty: Moderate.
Trail maintenance: Infrequent.
Traffic: Light.
Elevation gain: 950 feet. Loss: 1,680 feet.
Maximum elevation: 7,020 feet.
Maps: Imus Geographics Wallowa Mountains Eagle Cap Wilderness, or Lick Creek and Deadman Point USGS quads.

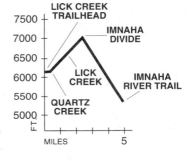

For more information: U.S. Forest Service at Wallowa Mountains Visitors Center, Enterprise, Oregon.
Finding the trail: Lick Creek Trail starts at Lick Creek Trailhead, 25 miles southeast of Joseph. To get to the trailhead take the Imnaha Highway east from Joseph. After going 8 miles, turn right on Wallowa Mountain Loop Road (Forest Road 39). Follow Wallowa Mountain Loop Road 15.75 miles, to Lick Creek Campground. At the entrance to the campground, turn right (south) off the Loop Road on Forest Road 3925, the campground is to the left, across FR 39 from FR 3925. Go 0.15 mile on FR 3925, then turn right of Forest Road 015. Follow FR 015 for 2.2 miles to the trailhead (El 6,080 ft.). The area around the trailhead was near the edge of the 1994 Twin Lakes Forest Fire. There were a few spot fires next to the road, but the major part of the burn was to the south.

0.0   Trail begins at Lick Creek Trailhead.
0.2   Trail crosses Quartz Creek.
0.5   Trail crosses roadbed.
1.8   Trail crosses Lick Creek.
1.9   Eagle Cap Wilderness Boundary.
2.5   Trail crosses Imnaha Divide.
5.0   Trail junction with Imnaha River Trail.

The trail: At first the trail is an old roadbed. It traverses around a hillside to the west for 0.25 mile to Quartz Creek. At the crossing (El 6,140 ft.) the trail leaves the roadbed. Just after crossing the creek it turns to the left. The roadbed goes on up along Quartz Creek to the Zollman and Wells Mine which is about 500 feet from the trail. There is a trail sign just past the crossing pointing out Lick Creek Trail 1809. The trail crosses another creek 300 yards farther along. Just after this crossing there is a burn area on the right side of the trail. The trail climbs up to and crosses an old roadbed (El 6,420 ft.) 0.25 mile after the creek crossing. The burned area is passed before reaching the roadbed. Watch for Brown's peonies along the trail in this area.

After crossing the roadbed, the areas which the spot fires burned get smaller and farther apart and are completely gone by the time the trail crosses another creek (El 6,710 ft.) 0.8 mile after crossing the roadbed. Just after this creek crossing the trail is built up with log sides, which makes crossing a wet area easier. The trail crosses a couple of streams in the next 0.5 mile. It then crosses Lick Creek (El 6,650 ft.). There is no bridge at this crossing. It is easier to cross Lick Creek a couple hundred feet upstream from the trail. A short distance after crossing Lick Creek, the trail enters Eagle Cap Wilderness. There is a sign marking the boundary (El 6,680 ft.).

After entering Eagle Cap Wilderness, the trail continues to climb gradually for another 0.6 mile to the top of Imnaha Divide. Imnaha Divide is the ridge between the Imnaha River and Sheep Creek drainages. The elevation where the trail crosses the divide is 7,020 feet. There are some good campsites on the top of the divide, but no water.

After crossing the divide, the trail starts to switchback its way down towards the Imnaha River. Just over 1.5 miles below the divide it crosses a creek.

96   Lick Creek

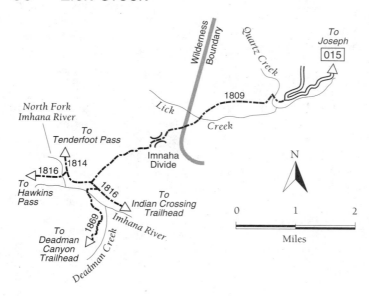

After the creek crossing there are some good viewpoints looking into the Upper Imnaha Canyon. The trail continues to descend crossing four more small streams in the next 0.75 mile. It then makes some switchbacks and comes to the junction with Imnaha River Trail 1816 (El 5,340 ft.). See Hike 92 South Fork Imnaha River and Hike 100 Imnaha River. The distance from Lick Creek Trailhead to the junction with the Imnaha River Trail is 5 miles. This junction is quite close to the junctions with Deadman Canyon Trail and North Fork Imnaha River Trail and not far upstream from Imnaha Falls. See Hike 90 Deadman Canyon and Hike 93 North Fork Imnaha River.

The area around the junction with Imnaha River Trail was also hit by some spot fires from the Twin Lakes Forest Fire, but most of the damage from the fire was to the east and south. There are many good campsite along the Imnaha River. Fishing can be very good, but be sure to check the current angling regulations for special rules. A one way trip can be made by combining Lick Creek Trail and Imnaha River Trail. This combination would involve a 20 mile car shuttle to Indian Crossing Trailhead. See Hike 100 for directions to Indian Crossing Trailhead.

97   TENDERFOOT WAGON ROAD

Trail 1819

General description: Tenderfoot Wagon Road Trail is an 11.2 mile backpack from Salt Creek Summit Sno Park and Trailhead to the North Fork Imnaha River Trail. From the trailhead to just past the Tenderfoot Trailhead connecting trail junction, our trail goes through the burn area of the 1989 Canal Forest Fire.

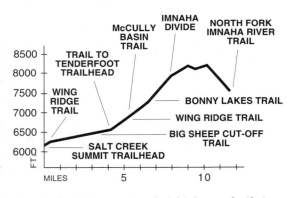

This route follows the historic Tenderfoot Wagon Road, which was built in the first decade of the twentieth century. The wagon road was built as an access route to the Tenderfoot Mine and Town site. It was soon discovered that the mine had been salted, and the only real mining that had been done was done from the pockets of the investors from the east.

Difficulty: Easy, except for a short stretch just before reaching Imnaha Divide, where it is fairly steep.

Trail maintenance: Infrequent.

Best season: For hiking, June through October up to the junction with Big Sheep Cut-off Trail, past the junction July through mid-October. For skiing, December to April up to Bonny Lakes Trail.

Traffic: Light from Salt Creek Pass to Tenderfoot Trailhead connecting trail, then moderate to Bonny Lakes Trail, light past there. Horse traffic is heavier during fall hunting seasons, and the part of the trail between Salt Creek Summit and the trail to the nordic ski shelters is used quite heavily by skiers in the winter. This trail is also occasionally used by mountain bikers from Salt Creek Summit Trailhead to Tenderfoot Trailhead.

Elevation gain: 2,000 feet. Loss: 530 feet.

Maximum elevation: 8,100 feet.

Maps: Imus Geographics Wallowa Mountains Eagle Cap Wilderness, or Lick Creek and Aneroid Mountain USGS quads. The part of the trail between Salt Creek Summit and Tenderfoot Trailhead connecting Trail is not shown on the USGS quad maps.

For more information: U.S. Forest Service at Wallowa Mountain Visitors Center, Enterprise, Oregon. For skiing and use of the ski shelters, contact Wing Ridge Ski Tours. The address and phone number are in the address section of this book.

Finding the trail: The trail begins at Salt Creek Summit Trailhead and Sno Park, for the first 0.3 mile Tenderfoot Wagon Road Trail and Wing Ridge Trail 1828 follow the same route. See Hike 99 Wing Ridge for driving directions to Salt Creek Summit Trailhead.

To reach Tenderfoot Trailhead, drive a couple of miles on Forest Road 39 past Salt Creek Summit, then turn right (southwest) on Forest Road 100. Follow FR 100 to its end, at the trailhead approximately 4 miles. From the trailhead, a short connecting trail crosses Big Sheep Creek and joins the Tenderfoot Wagon Road Trail.

Wagon Road. *Photo by Gary Fletcher.*

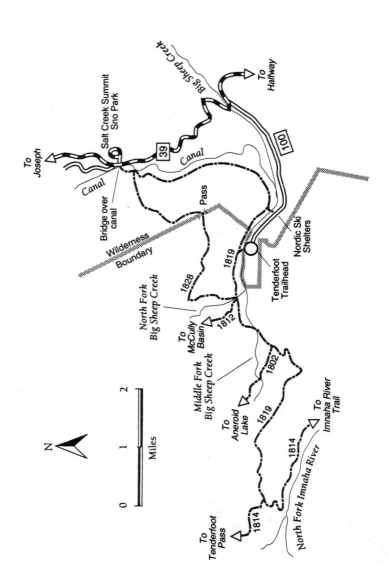

0.0   Salt Creek Summit Trailhead and Sno Park.
0.3   Trail junction with Wing Ridge Trail.
3.3   Trail junction with Big Sheep Cut-off Trail.
4.1   Trail junction with connecting trail to Tenderfoot Trailhead.
5.0   Trail junction with Wing Ridge Trail.
5.1   Trail junction with McCully Basin Trail.
6.2   Trail junction with Bonny Lakes Trail.
7.9   Trail crosses top of Imnaha Divide.
11.2   Trail junction with North Fork Imnaha Trail.

The trail: From Salt Creek Summit Trailhead (El 6,100 ft.) cross the canal bridge and follow Wing Ridge Trail 0.3 mile to its junction with Tenderfoot Wagon Road Trail. See Hike 99 Wing Ridge. The Wagon Road goes straight ahead (south) at the junction, and Wing Ridge Trail turns to the right. Both trails are marked with the blue diamonds that are used to mark cross country ski trails. Soon the trail crosses the bridge over Salt Creek. Just after crossing the bridge, the trail is elevated on two boardwalks to cross a wet area. The trail then climbs slightly around the point of a small ridge. From the ridge there is a good view of the Seven Devils Mountains to the east across Hells Canyon in Idaho. The trail crosses a couple more small creeks, one of them on another bridge, then begins to climb steadily but gently to 6,430 feet at about 3 miles from the trailhead. In early summer many elk use this area, and bear tracks may be seen on the trail. For a short distance near the high point the trail goes through green timber which was missed by the fire. At 3.3 miles the Big Sheep Cut-off Trail turns to the left (south), drops a couple hundred feet in switchbacks, crosses big Sheep Creek, on 2 wooden bridges, and goes to some nordic ski shelters. These shelters which are about 0.5 mile off Tenderfoot Wagon Road Trail are mostly dismantled in summer. The shelters are next to Big Sheep Creek Road which is the access road to Tenderfoot Trailhead. At the junction, Tenderfoot Wagon Road Trail heads straight ahead to the west north-west. The Big Sheep Cut-off Trail is marked with blue diamonds, but from here on the Wagon Road is not.

The junction (El 6,500 ft.) with the short connecting trail to Tenderfoot Trailhead is 0.8 mile past the trail to the nordic shelters trail junction. The trail to Tenderfoot Trailhead turns to the left (south). The unmarked Wing Ridge Trail 1828 junction is another 0.9 mile, and 0.1 mile farther, after crossing the North Fork of Big Sheep Creek, is the junction with McCully Basin Trail 1812 (El 6,750 ft.). See Hike 99 Wing Ridge and Hike 1 McCully Basin. Both Wing Ridge and McCully Basin Trails turn to the right (north). One and one-tenth miles after passing McCully Basin Trail junction is the junction with Bonny Lakes Trail 1802 (El 7,200 ft.). Bonny Lakes Trail bears to the right (west). See Hike 98 Bonny Lakes.

From the Bonny Lakes Trail junction the Wagon Road heads southwest. It quickly starts to climb out of the Middle Fork Big Sheep Valley. The trail goes by a melt pond 0.9 mile after leaving the junction. This pond may dry up in late summer. The trail heads up a stream bed 300 yards after passing the pond.

After going up the stream bed a few yards, it climbs out on the right side. The trail reaches the ridge line (El 7,900 ft.), of Imnaha Divide 0.6 mile after leaving the stream bed. This ridgeline divides the drainages of Big Sheep Creek and the North Fork Imnaha River. Evidence of the old wagon road is not always easy to see between Bonny Lakes Trail junction and the top of the ridge, but it becomes quite obvious from here on.

At the top of the ridge the trail turns right. It heads up the ridge line, climbing approximately 100 feet in 0.5 mile. After going up the ridge 0.5 mile, the trail begins a traverse on the left side of the ridge. This traverse climbs slightly to 8,080 feet, then descends back to 8,000 feet and climbs again to 8,100 feet. The traverse is 1.5 miles long, and goes along a fairly open south facing slope. The open area along the traverse makes for a good view of North Fork Imnaha River Canyon and the high peaks above its headwaters. There are some very large whitebark pines along this traverse.

Just past where the trail starts to head down at the end of the traverse there is an unmarked path that turns off to the right. This path is a way to connect to Tenderfoot Pass without dropping down into the North Fork Imnaha River Canyon. It is not a maintained trail and may be hard to follow. It should not be used by horses because of the damage they cause to this alpine terrain.

The Tenderfoot Wagon Road Trail continues to descend for 1.25 more miles to the junction with North Fork Imnaha Trail 1814 (El 7,570 ft.). The junction with North Fork Imnaha River Trail is 11.2 miles from Salt Creek Pass Trailhead. At this junction the Wagon Road becomes the North Fork Imnaha River Trail.

The old Tenderfoot Town site, the reason the wagon road was built, is a couple of switchbacks down the North Fork Imnaha River Trail next to the river. See Hike 93 North Fork Imnaha River. Several one way hikes are possible by connecting Wagon Road Trail with other trails. All of them except Wing Ridge require a car shuttle. See Hikes 1, 2, 92, 93, 98, and 99. One can also end their hike at Tenderfoot Trailhead.

Trail 1802

General description: A 5.5 mile backpack or day hike, from Tenderfoot Wagon Road Trail to East Fork Wallowa River Trail. A 7.8 mile hike if coming from Tenderfoot Trailhead.

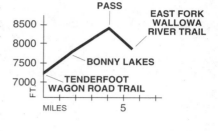

Difficulty: Moderate.
Trail maintenance: Infrequent.
Best season: July through mid-October for hiking, January through April for skiing.
Traffic: Moderate, heavier during fall hunting seasons, with moderate horse traffic. This trail has light cross-country ski traffic in winter. In winter, skiing is done from Salt Creek Summit Sno Park via Tenderfoot Wagon Road, or from Wallowa Lake Trailhead via East Fork Wallowa River Trail. In winter, there is avalanche danger along this trail.
Elevation gain: 1200 feet. Loss: 600 feet.
Maximum elevation: 8,420 feet.
Map: Aneroid Mountain USGS quad.
For more information: U.S. Forest Service at Wallowa Mountain Visitors Center, Enterprise, Oregon. For winter ski information or use of the nordic shelter contact Wing Ridge Ski Tours, see address in back of book.
Finding the trail: Bonny Lakes Trail leaves Tenderfoot Trail 1819, 2.25 miles west of Tenderfoot Trailhead. The elevation at the junction is 7,200 feet. See Hike 97 Tenderfoot Wagon Road.

0.0	Trail junction with Tenderfoot Wagon Road Trail.
2.0	Bonny Lakes.
4.0	Trail junction with path to Dollar Lake and trail crosses pass.
5.5	Trail junction with East Fork Wallowa River Trail.

The trail: Bonny Lakes Trail heads to the right (west) off Tenderfoot Wagon Road Trail. The trail crosses a creek 0.75 mile (El 7,310 ft.) after leaving the Wagon Road Trail. After going 0.3 mile more there is another creek crossing (El 7,440 ft.). Bonny Lakes (El 7,800 ft.) are 0.9 mile past the second creek crossing. The trail goes between the lakes, but only the one to the left can be seen from the trail. There are campsites at Bonny Lakes, but the mosquitoes may be bad in July and August.

After passing Bonny Lakes, the trail climbs through thinning timber for 2 miles to Dollar Pass. This pass (El 8,420 ft.) is on the ridge dividing Big Sheep Creek and the East Fork Wallowa River drainages. To the north of the pass the dark brown 9,702 foot summit of Aneroid Mountain reaches well above timberline. To the south is Dollar Lake (El 8,450 ft.) and Dollar Mountain. To reach the alpine tarn called Dollar Lake, follow the faint trail along the ridge top to the left (south).

Trail 1802 continues west over the pass and drops straight down a small valley. The trail is very faint in this area, but there are cairns to follow. It soon becomes easier to find again as it drops down to the junction with East Fork Wallowa River Trail 1814 (El 7,820 ft.), 5.5 miles from Tenderfoot Wagon Road Trail.

At the junction Tenderfoot Pass is to the left (south) 1.5 miles, and to the right (north) it is 1 mile to Aneroid Lake. See Hike 2 East Fork Wallowa River. From the junction a return trip requiring a car shuttle can be made to Wallowa a Lake Trailhead. Wallowa Lake Trailhead is 7 miles from the junction via Aneroid Lake.

98   Bonny Lakes

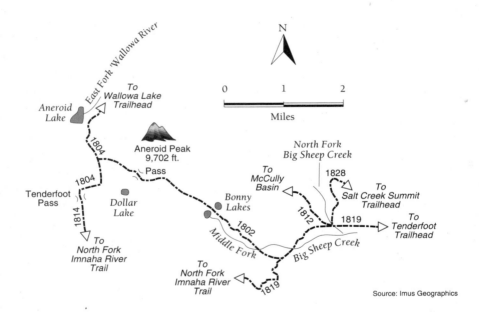

Trail 1828

General description: A 4.7 mile day hike from Salt Creek Summit Trailhead, over Wing Ridge, to Tenderfoot Wagon Road Trail. This trail can be used as a more scenic, also far more strenuous, alternate to Tenderfoot Wagon Road Trail.

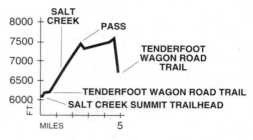

Difficulty: Moderate to strenuous.
Trail maintenance: Infrequent.
Traffic: Light during summer, and moderate during fall hunting seasons. The part of this trail near Salt Creek Summit Sno Park is used heavily during winter by cross-country skiers.
Elevation gain: 1,635 feet. Loss: 985 feet.
Maximum elevation: 7,585 feet.
Map: Lick Creek USGS quad.
For more information: U.S. Forest Service at Wallowa Mountain Visitors Center, Enterprise, Oregon. For winter skiing information contact Wing Ridge Ski Tours; see address section in the back of this book.
Finding the trail: To reach Salt Creek Summit Trailhead and Sno Park, take Imnaha Highway, Oregon Highway 350, also known as Little Sheep Creek Highway and Hells Canyon Scenic Byway, for 8 miles east, from Joseph. Turn right on Forest Road 39, Wallowa Mountain Loop Road, and follow it 10 miles south to Salt Creek Summit. The parking area is a short distance to the left (east) of FR 39 at the summit.

0.0	Salt Creek Summit Trailhead.
0.3	Trail junction with Tenderfoot Wagon Road Trail.
1.2	Trail crosses Salt Creek.
2.5	Pass over Wing Ridge.
4.7	Trail junction with Tenderfoot Wagon Road Trail.

The trail: The first 3 miles of this trail goes through an area burned by the 1988 Canal Forest Fire. From Salt Creek Summit (El 6,100 ft.) go west across FR 39 and the canal bridge. After crossing the bridge, bear left and climb past the cross-country ski trails, which are marked with blue diamonds, as is the Wing Ridge Trail at this point. At 0.3 mile the trail crosses the top of a small rise then drops slightly. A short distance farther is the junction with Tenderfoot Wagon Road Trail 1819. See Hike 97 Tenderfoot Wagon Road. Turn right (west) at the junction.

Past the junction the trail begins to climb steeply, passing two more cross-country ski trails. At 1.2 miles the trail enters an unburned area and crosses

Salt Creek (El 6,690 ft.). A short distance farther (El 6,850 ft.) the trail enters the burned area again, turns right and goes 200 vertical feet up a steep open ridge. Just below the top of the open area the trail turns left and the grade moderates. Soon it turns steeply uphill again, climbing to 7,220 feet. Watch for blazes on the trees, because the trail is faint on the ground. There is a stock driveway sign on a burnt tree at the top of this open area. The blazes and stock driveway signs may be difficult to spot in this burned area.

Soon the trail turns left and enters an area of small, partly-burned trees. It then continues up to the ridge top and enters a semi-open area (El 7,350 ft.). In the open area there is a good view of the Seven Devils Mountains to the east. The trail soon crosses the Eagle Cap Wilderness Boundary, then makes a switchback as it climbs the last few feet to the pass, over Wing Ridge (El 7,490 ft.). The pass is 2.5 miles from Salt Creek Summit Trailhead.

Beyond the pass the trail comes into an area that was only partially burned and becomes difficult to see. It crosses Wing Ridge then descends slightly for 0.1 mile to the west. At this point (El 7,340 ft.) the trail appears to turn steeply downhill to the left into some small timber. However, here one must contour, on the level to the right (west) for a short distance. Soon the trail shows up again. This is the easiest place to lose the route. If one descends below this point, it will be difficult to find the trail again. An altimeter can be a real help here.

A couple hundred feet more and the trail climbs slightly again to a gully crossing. Just before the gully, some logs have been sawed off clearing the trail, and marking it. The trail goes 5 feet straight up the gully then climbs out on the other side. Past the gully the trail climbs slightly around a small ridge (El 7,425 ft.) and then it flattens out for a period. Watch for the yellow rectangular "Stock Driveway" signs. They are difficult to spot, but they mark the trail in this area.

The trail crosses an open sage covered hillside, then enters scattered timber again. It then drops slightly into another gully with a small stream. Just before the gully is a yellow "Stock Driveway" sign (El 7,520 ft.). After crossing the stream, the trail leaves the partly burned area for good. It climbs slightly through a rocky area where it may be difficult to spot for a few yards. At 4.2 miles the trail rounds another small ridge (El 7,510 ft.).

The trail continues to contour along, crossing a couple more gullies to a small stream (El 7,585 ft.). This is the highest point on this trail. This stream is a little odd, as it is not in a gully, but rather on a flat slope. After crossing the stream, the trail turns left and goes downhill to the south.

It passes a campsite (El 7,530 ft.) and then continues downhill. The trail soon bears right and crosses a small gully. A short distance after crossing the gully, the trail goes straight down a poorly defined ridge. It makes a right switchback in an open area (El 7,350 ft.). It then drops straight down the ridge to the junction with Tenderfoot Wagon Road Trail 1819 (El 6,750 ft.). This junction is 4.7 miles from Salt Creek Summit Trailhead.

This trail requires considerable route finding. The return trip can be made by turning left (east) on Tenderfoot Wagon Road Trail and following it back to Salt Creek Summit Trailhead. See Hike 97 Tenderfoot Wagon Road. This makes a 9 mile loop trip. The Wagon Road is slightly longer than going back over Wing Ridge, but it is nearly flat and usually takes less time to cover.

100 IMNAHA RIVER

Trail 1816

General description: A 6.8 mile day hike or backpack from Indian Crossing Trailhead to the junction with North Fork Imnaha River Trail, along the Imnaha River.
Difficulty: Easy.
Trail maintenance: Yearly or more often if needed.
Best season: May through October.
Traffic: Heavy, with heavy horse traffic.

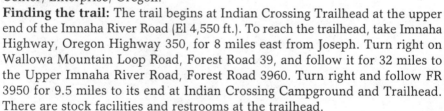

Elevation gain: 850 feet.
Maximum elevation: 5,400 feet.
Map: Deadman Point USGS quad.
For more information: U.S. Forest Service at Wallowa Mountain Visitors Center, Enterprise, Oregon.
Finding the trail: The trail begins at Indian Crossing Trailhead at the upper end of the Imnaha River Road (El 4,550 ft.). To reach the trailhead, take Imnaha Highway, Oregon Highway 350, for 8 miles east from Joseph. Turn right on Wallowa Mountain Loop Road, Forest Road 39, and follow it for 32 miles to the Upper Imnaha River Road, Forest Road 3960. Turn right and follow FR 3950 for 9.5 miles to its end at Indian Crossing Campground and Trailhead. There are stock facilities and restrooms at the trailhead.

0.0	Indian Crossing Campground and Trailhead.
0.7	Trail junction with trail to pack station.
1.5	Eagle Cap Wilderness Boundary.
2.0	Trail junction with Twin Lakes Trail.
5.7	Imnaha Falls.
6.1	Trail junction with Deadman Canyon Trail.
6.2	Trail junction with Lick Creek Trail.
6.8	Trail junction with North Fork Imnaha River Trail, Trail 1816 becomes South Fork Imnaha River Trail.

The trail: The trail heads up river (west) from the parking area. Just after leaving the parking lot there is a fenced area and some small buildings on the right side of the trail. At 0.7 mile is a trail junction (El 4.650 ft.). The trail to the right goes back to the pack station, so bear left and head on up the Imnaha

Pool below Imnaha Falls. *Photo by Jerry Lavender.*

River Trail. Just after passing the junction, the trail enters the burned area of the 1994 Twin Lakes Forest Fire. At first the burn was not too hot, and most of the larger trees, especially the big ponderosa pines, survived, but a little farther along the trail the fire became hotter and killed nearly everything. The beginnings of a new forest are evident, as there are many little pine seedlings poking their heads up through the ashes.

At 1.5 miles is the Eagle Cap Wilderness Boundary (El 4,710 ft.). Up to this point the trail appears to have been a road at one time. One-tenth mile farther the trail crosses Quartz Creek, and at 1.8 miles is another creek crossing. There is a short wooden bridge at 2 miles, and a few yards farther is the Twin Lakes Trail 1874 junction (El 4,740 ft.). The Imnaha River Trail continues on straight ahead. To the left a short distance, is Blue Hole. There are nice campsites next to the river at Blue Hole. See Hike 91 Twin Lakes.

After passing the Twin Lakes Trail junction the forest is more lightly burned. The trail climbs up a gully for 0.3 mile. At the top of the gully (El 4,970 ft.) the trail begins a traverse along a talus slope. To the left and below the trail, along the traverse the Imnaha River boils through a steep canyon. After crossing the 0.25 mile wide talus slope, the trail climbs three switchbacks to the top of a small rise, then drops slightly making two more switchbacks. It crosses three small streams in the 0.8 mile to the top of the next outcropping. From the top of the outcropping the patchwork pattern of the Twin Lakes Forest Fire can be seen to the south across the Imnaha River, and the high peaks of the upper Imnaha drainage come into view to the west. After passing the outcropping, the trail drops slightly, then climbs gently for 1.1 miles, crossing nine small streams to reach the top of another rocky outcropping (El 5,290 ft.) with a viewpoint overlooking the Imnaha River Canyon. There is a well-used campsite below the trail to the left 0.4 mile past this outcropping. One-third mile after passing the campsite is the unmarked junction with the path to Imnaha Falls. The falls can be seen through the trees to the left of the trail a short distance before reaching the path. The path goes 100 yards to Imnaha Falls. A beautiful little gorge and swimming hole are below the falls. There are strong currents in the pool, so be very careful if you decide to swim.

For the next 0.25 mile above Imnaha Falls the fire burned most of the trees on the left side of the trail between the trail and the river. The trail crosses a couple of small streams then leaves the burn area. The junction with Deadman Canyon Trail (El 5,310 ft.) is 0.5 mile past the path to the falls. Deadman Canyon Trail 1869 turns to the left (south) and crosses the Imnaha River. See Hike 90 Deadman Canyon. There is a campsite a few yards to the left of the Imnaha River Trail next to Deadman Canyon Trail. One hundred fifty yards past the junction with Deadman Canyon Trail is the junction with Lick Creek Trail 1809. Lick Creek Trail turns to the right (north). See Hike 96 Lick Creek. The junction with North Fork Imnaha River Trail 1814 is 600 yards past the junction with Lick Creek Trail. See Trail 93 North Fork Imnaha River.

North Fork Imnaha River Trail junction (El 5,400 ft.) is 6.8 miles from Indian Crossing Trailhead. The area between Imnaha Falls and the junction with North Fork Imnaha River Trail is an excellent area to camp and explore the surrounding territory. To continue on the South Fork Imnaha River Trail see Hike 92 South Fork Imnaha River. The description for the South Fork Imnaha River Trail, which overlaps this description from the falls to the junction with North Fork Imnaha River Trail, is written from the other direction. Several loops are possible by combining this trail with the other trails mentioned above.

100 *Imnaha River*

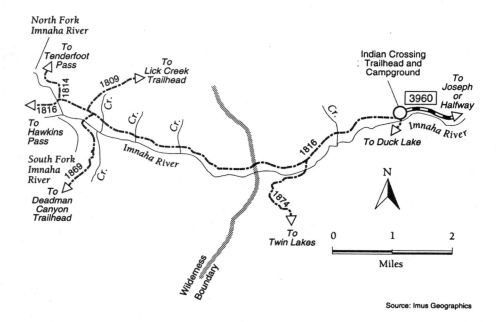

Source: Imus Geographics

CLIMB 1   *ANEROID MOUNTAIN*

General description: A moderate scramble up Aneroid Mountain from East Fork Wallowa River Trail.

Difficulty: Moderate.

Estimated time up: 3 to 5 hours from East Fork Wallowa River Trail.

Best season: July through September.

Traffic: Light.

Elevation gain: 2,572 feet from East Fork Wallowa Trail, 5,052 feet from Wallowa Lake Trailhead.

Maximum elevation: 9,702 feet.

Map: Aneroid Mountain USGS quad.

For more information: Wallowa Lake General Store in the Wallowa Lake resort area, or U.S. Forest Service at Wallowa Mountain Visitors Center, Enterprise, Oregon.

Finding the route: This route to the summit of Aneroid Mountain begins 4.4 miles south of Wallowa Lake Trailhead on the East Fork Wallowa River Trail 1804. See Hike 2 East Fork Wallowa River. The elevation where the route leaves the trail is 7,120 feet. Turn left (east) off the trail in a meadow, 0.25 mile south of the point where the divided inbound and outbound trails join back together.

The route: Go east off the trail on flat ground through the timber for a short distance. Then head up a ridge, which will be to your right. Climb directly up the ridge to timberline, at 8,650 feet elevation. This is where Hidden Peak climbers head straight up. See Climb 4 Hidden Peak. At timberline angle to the right and continue to climb slightly to the saddle on the ridge between Hidden Peak and Aneroid Mountain. The elevation at the saddle is approximately 8,850 feet. Go south on the ridge for 1 more mile. Then scramble the last few feet to the summit of Aneroid Mountain (El 9,702 ft.).

From the top of Aneroid Mountain, Aneroid Lake is below to the west. McCully Basin is to the east and Bonny Lakes is to the southeast. There is beautiful alpine country in all directions. Carry all the water you will need, as there may be none above the East Fork of the Wallowa River.

The descent can be made by the same route or by taking a 3 mile longer but easier route down the south ridge of Aneroid Mountain to Bonny Lakes Trail 1802. Bonny Lakes Trail is reached near Dollar Lake (El 8,020 ft.). See Hike 98 Bonny Lakes. Upon reaching Bonny Lakes Trail, turn right (west) and follow it to East Fork Wallowa River Trail. Turn right on East Fork Wallowa Trail and follow it for 7 miles, passing Aneroid Lake to Wallowa Lake Trailhead. See Hike 2 East Fork Wallowa River.

Climb 1 *Aneroid Mountain*
Climb 4 *Hidden Peak from East Fork Wallowa River*

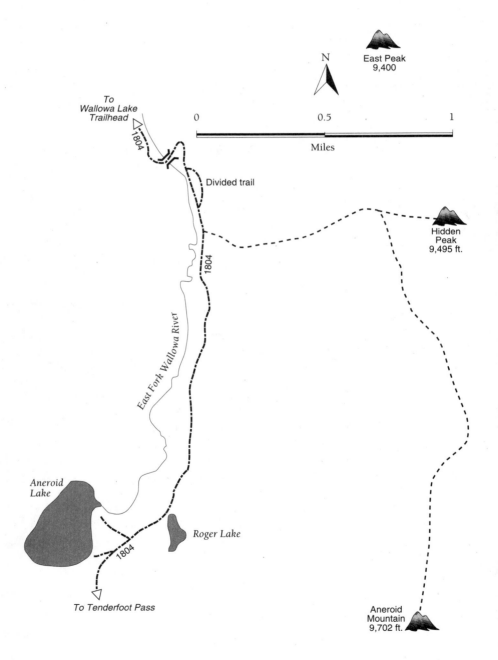

CLIMB 2   EAST PEAK FROM MOUNT HOWARD

General description: A 2 mile, mostly uphill, hike and scramble from the top of Mount Howard Gondola to the summit of East Peak.
Difficulty: Moderate.
Estimated time up: 1.5 to 3 hours.
Best season: July through mid-September.
Traffic: Heavy on the nature trails near the gondola, moderate past there.
Elevation gain: 1,400 feet. Loss: 150 feet.
Maximum elevation: 9,400 feet.
Maps: Joseph and Aneroid Mountain USGS quads.
For more information: Wallowa Lake General Store in the Wallowa Lake resort area, or U.S. Forest Service at Wallowa Mountain Visitors Center, Enterprise, Oregon.
Finding the route: The bottom terminal of the Mount Howard Gondola is located in the resort area at the head of Wallowa Lake. Take the gondola to the upper terminal, where this hike begins.
The route: From the south side of the top terminal of the gondola (El 8,150 ft.), follow the nature trail south, then southeast, 0.1 mile to the summit of Mount Howard (El 8,280 ft.). The view from here is wonderful, with the Wallowa Mountains to the south and west, and the Seven Devils Mountains in the distance to the east. From the top of Mount Howard, drop down (south) to the saddle dividing Royal Purple Creek which flows to the west and upper Prairie Creek which drains to the east. Nature trails can and should be followed to this point, if the ground is not covered with snow. Alpine vegetation is fragile and this is a high use area, so please use the trails. Two latrines are located in the saddle.

From the saddle follow the trail south, climbing an ascending traverse around the right (west) side of the first small peak on the ridge, to another saddle (El 8,400 ft.). After passing this saddle, the trail climbs 200 vertical feet, to the south, then goes around the left (east) side of the next peak on the ridge. Just past this peak the trail comes close to another saddle but does not quite reach it. This is the point where the East Peak and the Hidden Peak routes separate. See Climb 3 Hidden Peak.

From the point where the trail is closest to this saddle, climb west (straight up) to the ridge line (El 8,680 ft.), then turn left (south) and scramble up the ridge to the summit of 9,400 feet, East Peak.

The summit of East Peak can also be reached by following the trail on around to the left (east) of the peak, then climbing directly to the summit. This route is not difficult, but does not offer the spectacular views that the ridge route does.

From the summit the view is great. To the south Hidden Peak is close by, and 9,702 foot high Aneroid Mountain is about 2.5 miles away. To the northeast, you look across the Imnaha Canyon and Hells Canyon to the Seven Devils

Climb 2   *East Peak from Mount Howard*
Climb 3   *Hidden Peak from Mount Howard*

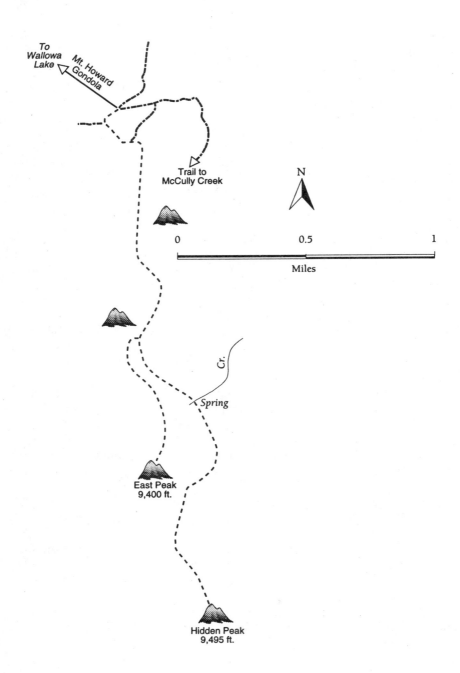

Mountains. Be sure to watch the time, so you can get back to the gondola before it closes. This climb may take several hours. Also watch the weather, a whiteout above timberline can be quite dangerous for the unprepared.

CLIMB 3 HIDDEN PEAK FROM MOUNT HOWARD

General description: A 2.5 mile hike and scramble from the top terminal of Mount Howard Gondola to Hidden Peak.
Difficulty: Easy to moderate.
Estimated time up: 2 to 3 hours from the top of the gondola.
Best season: July through mid-September.
Traffic: Heavy on the nature trails on Mount Howard, light to moderate after passing the first saddle.
Elevation gain: 1,495 feet. Loss: 150 feet.
Maximum elevation: 9,495 feet.
Maps: Joseph and Aneroid Mountain USGS quads.
For more information: Wallowa Lake General Store in the Wallowa Lake resort area, or U.S. Forest Service at Wallowa Mountain Visitors Center, Enterprise, Oregon.
Finding the route: From the top of Mount Howard Gondola follow the trail to the south past East Peak to the saddle (El 9,010 ft.) between East Peak and Hidden Peak . See Climb 2 East Peak.
The route: From the saddle climb southeast directly to the summit of Hidden Peak (El 9,495 ft.).

CLIMB 4 HIDDEN PEAK FROM EAST FORK WALLOWA RIVER

General description: A short scramble from timberline on Aneroid Mountain route to Hidden Peak.
Difficulty: Moderate.
Estimated time up: 45 minutes from Aneroid Mountain Route, 2 to 4 hours from East Fork Wallowa River Trail.
Best season: July through September.
Traffic: Light.
Elevation gain: 845 feet from Aneroid Mountain Route, 2,365 feet from East Fork Wallowa River Trail, 4,845 feet from Wallowa Lake Trailhead.
Map: Aneroid Mountain USGS quad.
For more information: Wallowa Lake General Store in the Wallowa Lake resort area, or U.S. Forest Service at Wallowa Mountain Visitors Center, Enterprise, Oregon. Further information may be limited.

Finding the route: From the Wallowa Lake Trailhead take the East Fork Wallowa River Trail 1804, 4.4 miles south, to the point where Aneroid Mountain Route leaves the trail. See Hike 2 East Fork Wallowa River. See Climb 1 Aneroid Mountain. Follow Aneroid Mountain Route east and up to the timberline. At this point, Hidden Peak and Aneroid Mountain Routes separate.

The route: To climb Hidden Peak, climb straight up to the summit, which is directly above to the east.

CLIMB 5 *BONNEVILLE MOUNTAIN EAST SIDE*

General description: Bonneville Mountain is the pyramid-shaped peak directly south of Wallowa Lake. It is the first major peak on the ridge dividing the East and West Forks of the Wallowa River. The east side route is a steep scramble with some moderate rock climbing from the East Fork Wallowa River Trail to the summit.

Difficulty: Strenuous.

Estimated time up: 3 to 5 hours from East Fork Wallowa Trail.

Best season: July through September.

Traffic: Very light.

Elevation gain: 2,940 feet from East Fork Wallowa River Trail, 4,210 feet from Wallowa Lake Trailhead.

Maximum elevation: 8,860 feet.

Map: Aneroid Mountain USGS quad. Most maps incorrectly show one of the sub-peaks north of the true summit as the summit of Bonneville Mountain.

Bonneville Mountain, east side.

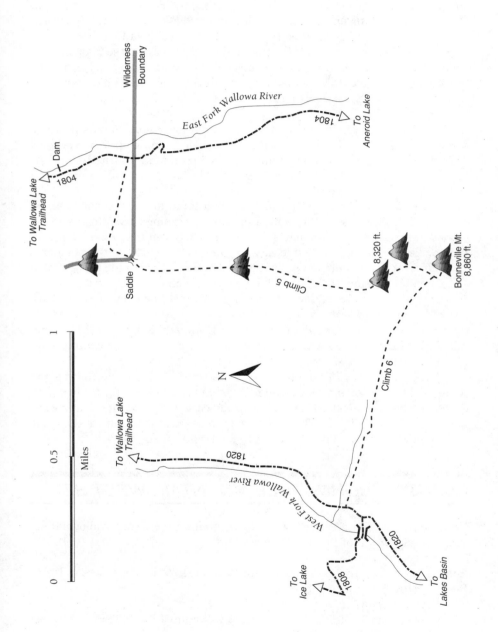

For more information: U.S. Forest Service at Wallowa Mountain Visitors Center, Enterprise, Oregon. Further information may be very limited.

Finding the route: The east side route on Bonneville Mountain leaves the East Fork Wallowa River Trail 1804, 2.3 miles above Wallowa Lake Trailhead. The spot to leave the trail is 0.3 mile above (south of) the Pacific Power and Light Company intake dam and 100 yards below (north of) the Eagle Cap Wilderness Boundary sign (El 5,920 ft.). See Hike 2 East Fork Wallowa River.

The route: The route turns off the trail to the right (west) in a semi-open area. Climb the low ridge between the obvious gullies. Continue to climb, on game trails when available, to a saddle on the north ridge of Bonneville Mountain. Just below the saddle, traverse left (south) to reach its lowest point (El 7,320 ft.).

From the saddle climb up the ridge to the south, to a false summit (El 7,970 ft.), which is actually the second peak on the ridge, coming up from Wallowa Lake. From here the light gray summit of 9,845 foot, Matterhorn Mountain is in view to the west. To the southwest is Eagle Cap Mountain, and Mount Howard is to the northeast.

From the false summit follow the ridge on south to the next sub-peak (El 8,320 ft.), then traverse to the right of the ridge dropping down slightly to the second gully. This gully originates in the notch between the twin summits of Bonneville Mountain. Turn left (east) and climb up the gully over the boulders and ledges. Stay generally to the right (south) of the bottom of the gully. Watch and listen for possible rock fall. Just below the notch at the top of the gully is a large boulder. At the boulder traverse right 75 feet to a smaller gully. Turn left and climb straight up the gully to the ridgeline. At the ridgeline scramble right a few feet to the summit of Bonneville Mountain (El 8,860 ft.). The summit block of Bonneville Mountain has a distinctly castle-like appearance with rock pillars.

Climbing Bonneville Mountain requires considerable route finding and some moderately steep rock climbing. A rope may be necessary for inexperienced climbers. No water is available on the east side route after leaving the East Fork Wallowa River. The easiest way to descend is to retrace the route back down to the East Fork Wallowa River Trail.

CLIMB 6   *BONNEVILLE MOUNTAIN WEST SIDE*

General description: A fairly long steep climb from West Fork Wallowa River Trail to the summit of Bonneville Mountain.

Difficulty: Strenuous.

Estimated time up: 3 to 6 hours from West Fork Wallowa River Trail.

Best season: July through September.

Traffic: Very light.

Elevation gain: 3,340 feet from West Fork Wallowa River Trail, 4,210 feet from Wallowa Lake Trailhead.

Bonneville Mountain, west side.

Maximum elevation: 8,860 feet.
Map: Aneroid Mountain USGS quad.
For more information: U.S. Forest Service at Wallowa Mountain Visitors Center, Enterprise, Oregon. Further information may be very limited.
Finding the route: To climb Bonneville Mountain from the west side, take the West Fork Wallowa River Trail. From Wallowa Lake Trailhead hike 2.5 miles south to an open area, just before coming to Ice Lake Trail junction. See Hike 4 West Fork Wallowa River.
The route: Turn off the West Fork Wallowa River Trail and climb the gentle open slope to the east (left) to a point where two gullies can be seen ahead. The two gullies run nearly parallel. Climb up the left gully all the way, nearly 3,000 vertical feet, to the large boulder just below the notch, which is described in the Bonneville Mountain East Side Route. Some rock fall is possible in the gully, so watch and listen for it. Above the large boulder follow the route described in the east side route. See Climb 5 Bonneville Mountain East Side. The easiest way to descend is via the east side route.

This route is more difficult than the east side route. It takes a fair amount of rock climbing to get up the gully, and in some places it is quite exposed. A climbing rope may be necessary for less experienced climbers. Water is not available after entering the gully.

CLIMB 7 *CHIEF JOSEPH MOUNTAIN VIA FIRST CHUTE*

General description: The First Chute Route is the easiest way to the summit of Chief Joseph Mountain, from the resort area at the head of Wallowa Lake.
Difficulty: Moderate to strenuous.
Estimated time up: 4 to 8 hours from Wallowa Lake Trailhead, 3 to 6 hours from the Chief Joseph Mountain Trail.
Best season: Late June through early October.
Traffic: Heavy on Chief Joseph Mountain Trail, light on the route.
Elevation gain: 3,235 feet from Chief Joseph Mountain Trail, 4,965 feet from Wallowa Lake Trailhead.
Maximum elevation: 9,617 feet.
Maps: Chief Joseph Mountain and Joseph USGS quad .
For more information: Wallowa Lake General Store in the Wallowa Lake resort area, or U.S. Forest Service at Wallowa Mountain Visitors Center, Enterprise, Oregon.
Finding the route: This route begins 4.4 miles up Chief Joseph Mountain Trail 1803, 4.7 miles from the Wallowa Lake Trailhead. See Hike 5 Chief Joseph Mountain.
The route: At the switch back (El 6,380 ft.) described in Hike 5 of this book, the First Chute Route to the summit of Chief Joseph Mountain leaves the trail. Go straight up the high valley, west for 400 yards. Look to the left at the face of Chief Joseph Mountain. The first open avalanche chute on the southeast end of the face marks our route.

To the left of the chute is timbered hillside, and to the right is a rock ridge with scattered trees. Make your way through the trees and bushes to the base of the chute. Climb up along the left side of the chute through the timber to the top of the main ridge at about 8,000 feet elevation. At the top of the main ridge Marina Ridge Route and B C Ridge Route join the First Chute Route. See Climb 8 Chief Joseph Mountain via B C Ridge and Climb 9 Chief Joseph Mountain via Marina Ridge. Follow the faint trail in a northwesterly direction along the main ridge, passing around the left side of a rock outcropping to the summit (El 9,615 ft.). The summit is about 1 mile and 1,600 vertical feet above the point where our route first reached the main ridge.

This is probably the easiest and quickest route to the summit from the Wallowa Lake resort area. Early in the season when there is snow, there may be avalanche danger in the chute. As with other routes on Chief Joseph Mountain, water will be difficult to find so carry what you will need. Watch for mountain goats near the summit. They are usually seen on the ridge just past, northwest of, the summit or in the cliffs below to the northeast. Return via the same route.

Climb 7 *Chief Joseph Mountain via First Chute*
Climb 8 *Chief Joseph via B C Ridge*
Climb 9 *Chief Joseph Mountain via Marina Ridge*

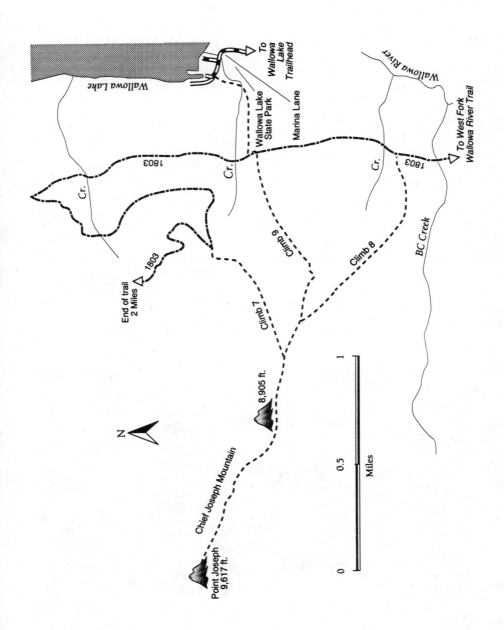

CLIMB 8 CHIEF JOSEPH MOUNTAIN VIA B C RIDGE

General description: A fairly steep, direct route from Chief Joseph Mountain Trail to the summit of Chief Joseph Mountain.

Difficulty: Strenuous.

Estimated time up: 3 to 7 hours from Chief Joseph Mountain Trail.

Best season: Mid-June through September.

Traffic: Very light.

Elevation gain: 4,450 feet from Chief Joseph Mountain Trail, 4,965 feet from Wallowa Lake Trailhead.

Maximum elevation: 9,615 feet.

Maps: Joseph and Chief Joseph Mountain USGS quads.

For more information: Wallowa Lake General Store in the Wallowa Lake resort area, or U.S. Forest Service at Wallowa Mountain Visitors Center, Enterprise, Oregon. Further information will probably be very limited.

Finding the route: From Wallowa Lake Trailhead take West Fork Wallowa River Trail 0.3 mile to the junction with Chief Joseph Mountain Trail. Turn right at the junction and follow Chief Joseph Mountain Trail to an unmarked point approximately 0.25 mile north of B C Creek. See Hike 5 Chief Joseph Mountain.

The route: From the unmarked point on Chief Joseph Mountain Trail, look to the left (up); above the rock slide is a prominent cliff. The route goes up just to the right of the cliff, then bears slightly left to reach the ridge above it. From here follow the ridgeline as closely as possible, getting off it only to go around rock outcroppings. Up to 7,500 feet elevation this route is quite steep and involves a lot of scrambling.

Above 7,500 feet, the ridge becomes less steep and the timber starts to thin out. Follow the broadening ridge to the point where it joins the main ridge of Chief Joseph Mountain at 8,170 feet elevation. This is the point where First Chute, B C Ridge, and Marina Ridge Routes join. See Climbs 7 and 9.

Turn left on the main ridge and follow a faint trail. The trail goes around the left side of the rock outcropping then comes back to the ridge. After regaining the ridge, follow it approximately 1 mile to the summit (El 9,615 ft.) Carry water, as there may be none above B C Creek. Watch for mountain goats near the summit. This route is much more difficult to follow and climb than is the First Chute Route. It should only be attempted by experienced mountaineers. Descend via First Chute Route as B C Ridge Route can be very difficult to follow when coming down.

CLIMB 9 *CHIEF JOSEPH MOUNTAIN VIA MARINA RIDGE*

General description: A direct route from the large parking lot at the south end of Wallowa Lake to the summit of Chief Joseph Mountain.
Difficulty: Strenuous.
Estimated time up: 4 to 8 hours from the parking lot.
Best season: Mid-June through September.
Traffic: Very light.
Elevation gain: 5,215 feet.
Maximum elevation: 9,615 feet.
Maps: Joseph and Chief Joseph Mountain USGS quads.
For more information: Wallowa Lake General Store in the Wallowa Lake resort area, or U.S. Forest Service at Wallowa Mountain Visitors Center, Enterprise, Oregon .
Finding the route: This route begins at the southwest corner of Wallowa Lake Marina's parking lot (El 4,400 ft.) in Wallowa Lake State Park. To reach Wallowa Lake State Park take Oregon Highway 82 and go 6 miles south from Joseph. Turn right at the intersection at the south end of Wallowa Lake next to Wallowa Lake General Store. Go 0.3 mile more, passing the campground, to the large parking lot next to the Wallowa Lake Marina. The trail leaves the parking lot at its southwest corner (El 4,400 ft.). See map on p. 283.
The route: Take the nature trail south from the parking lot. In a short distance the trail crosses a small creek on a wooden bridge. Just after crossing the creek, turn right off the trail and climb steeply on a path to the west southwest to where the route intersects Chief Joseph Mountain Trail (El 5,200 ft.). Turn left (south) on Chief Joseph Mountain Trail and go 100 yards or so, then turn right off Chief Joseph Mountain Trail. The turn-off spot can be difficult to find. It is just a few yards south of a small gully in a brushy spot with some burnt snags sticking up. This point can also be reached by taking the West Fork Wallowa River Trail and Chief Joseph Mountain Trail from Wallowa Lake Trailhead, but the exact spot is more difficult to find when coming this way.

After leaving Chief Joseph Mountain Trail, climb straight up 150 yards, then bear slightly to the left. Follow the ridgeline to the southwest, staying just to the right of a semi-open cliffy area. At 6,950 feet elevation this ridge intersects the main ridge of Chief Joseph Mountain. Turn right on the main ridge, go around the rock outcropping on the right side and through the notch, then drop down a few feet and traverse along the left side of the rock outcropping above the notch, to the bottom of a gully. Climb straight up the gully to the gentler slope above the outcropping. Turn left at the top of the gully and climb straight up the ridgeline.

At 7,500 feet elevation the timber begins to thin out, and by 8,000 feet, there are only a few scattered small trees left. At 8,170 feet Marina Ridge Route joins B C Ridge and First Chute Routes. See Climbs 7 and 8. From here follow the faint trail along the ridgeline to the northwest 1 mile to the summit of Chief Joseph Mountain (El 9,615 ft.).

This is a fairly difficult route, which involves considerable route finding and a little steep scrambling. Take water, as there is none to be found along the way. The descent is best made via the First Chute Route, which is much easier to follow going down. As is true with the B C Ridge Route, an altimeter can be very helpful with navigation.

CLIMB 10 *MATTERHORN MOUNTAIN FROM ICE LAKE*

General description: A moderately steep hike of about 2 miles, from Ice Lake to the Summit of Matterhorn Mountain.
Difficulty: Moderate.
Estimated time up: 1.5 to 4 hours.
Best season: July through September.
Traffic: Moderate to heavy.
Elevation gain: 1,996 feet from Ice Lake.
Maximum elevation: 9,845 feet.
Maps: Eagle Cap Mountain USGS quad.
For more information: Wallowa Lake General Store in Wallowa Lake resort area, or U.S. Forest Service at Wallowa Mountain Visitors Center, Enterprise, Oregon.
Finding the route: From Wallowa Lake Trailhead take West Fork Wallowa River Trail to the junction with Ice Lake Trail. Take the Ice Lake Trail to Ice Lake. See Hike 4 West Fork Wallowa River and Hike 6 Ice Lake.
The route: To climb the Matterhorn, follow the trail around the north side of Ice Lake to the northwest corner (El 7,849 ft.). Climb to the northwest on a poorly defined trail. Soon the trail turns to the west and is marked with cairns. Climb steadily up a small ridge until you are a couple of hundred feet below the summit. Turn left and do an ascending traverse to the summit of Matterhorn Mountain. There is a path all the way to the top. This path will not

be difficult to follow if you look some distance ahead for the faint path and cairns marking it. Route finding could be difficult during times of poor visibility. The return trip is best made by retracing the same route.

Matterhorn Mountain, at 9,845 feet elevation, is the highest peak in the Wallowa Mountains. Some newer maps dispute this and claim that Sacajawea Peak is a few feet higher, but this seems to change with each new survey. The entire summit area and the Matterhorn are white limestone, which is part of the Martin Bridge formation. This makes the Matterhorn a very distinct peak, especially when viewed from the west. The west face is a 3,500 foot wall of this white limestone. It is interesting to note that this limestone is the compressed skeletal remains of tiny marine animals, probably coral, which were deposited on the ocean floor, many millions of years ago. Just below the summit to the northeast is good evidence of recent glacial action in the form of a well defined cirque and moraines. Mountain goats are common in this area. Watch for them on the ridge to the north of the route and near the summit. Navigation above Ice Lake can be difficult during times of poor visibility, and thunderstorms are common most of the summer, so keep an eye on the changing weather.

Climb 10 *Matterhorn Mountain from Ice Lake*

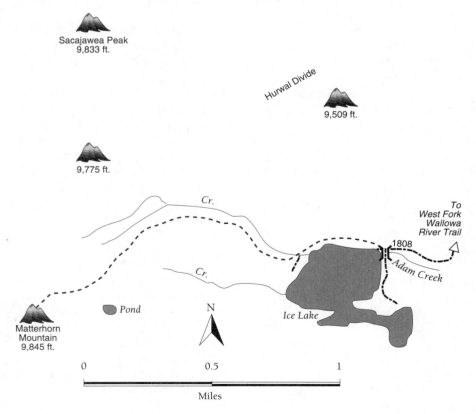

Sacajawea Peak
9,833 ft.

Hurwal Divide

9,509 ft.

9,775 ft.

Cr.

To
West Fork
Wallowa
River Trail

1808

Adam Creek

Cr.

Pond

N

Ice Lake

Matterhorn
Mountain
9,845 ft.

0   0.5   1

Miles

CLIMB 11 *SACAJAWEA PEAK VIA THORP CREEK BASIN*

General description: A fairly steep hike of approximately 5 miles, from Hurricane Creek Trail to the summit of Sacajawea Peak.

Difficulty: Moderately strenuous.

Estimated time up: 4 to 8 hours from Hurricane Creek Trail.

Best season: July through September.

Traffic: Light.

Elevation gain: 4,413 feet from Hurricane Creek Trail; 4,808 feet from Hurricane Creek Trailhead.

Maximum elevation: 9,833 feet.

Maps: Chief Joseph Mountain and Eagle Cap Mountain USGS quads. Chief Joseph Mountain quad shows Thorp Creek Trail. Most other maps do not.

For more information: U.S. Forest Service at Wallowa Mountain Visitors Center, Enterprise, Oregon.

Finding the route: Thorp Creek Trail, which is the route we are taking to the summit, leaves Hurricane Creek Trail 0.25 mile south of Deadman Creek, 1.8 miles from Hurricane Creek Trailhead. See Hike 14 Hurricane Creek. Thorp Creek Trail is not marked but it usually has had enough use to be fairly obvious.

The route: Thorp Creek Trail turns left off Hurricane Creek Trail and goes 0.25 mile southeast to where it crosses Hurricane Creek (El 5,420 ft.). A few yards upstream from the crossing, there are some logs that can be used to cross the creek dry footed.

After crossing Hurricane Creek the trail goes east for a short distance and enters an open grassy area. It then climbs gradually to the southeast through the open area. The trail soon enters the timber again and crosses Twin Creek (El 5,650 ft.). After crossing Twin Creek the trail climbs steeply with switch backs to the top of the ridge overlooking Thorp Creek (El 6,170 ft.). At this point the north face of Sacajawea is in full view to the south across Thorp Creek Canyon. The trail continues to climb generally following the ridge top to 7,450 feet, then traverses to the south southeast into the beautiful alpine upper Thorp Creek Valley where the trail ends 3.5 miles from Hurricane Creek Trail.

To continue on to the summit of Sacajawea Peak, follow the creek on up the valley. Then bear to the right (south), passing a large spring (El 7,800 ft.). Head on up the creek bed to the south to what appears from below to be a saddle. It is really a point where the creek bed flattens out (El 8,100 ft.). At this point turn right (west) and climb the prominent ridge to the west. To your right and below will be the north face of Sacajawea Peak, and to your left will be the basin at the head of Thorp Creek. When you reach the false summit, traverse left (south) to the summit of Sacajawea Peak (El 9,833 ft.).

The total distance from Hurricane Creek Trail to the summit of Sacajawea is about 5 miles with a 4,413 feet of elevation gain. The route is steep but not technically difficult. There are plenty of good campsites in upper Thorp Creek

Climb 11 *Sacajawea Peak via Thorp Creek Basin*

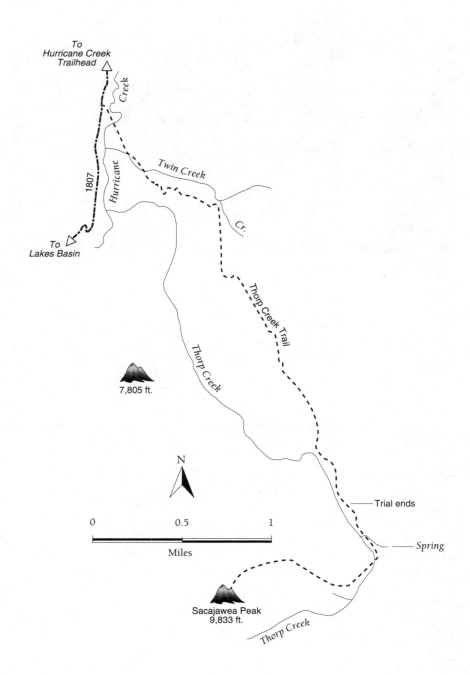

To
Hurricane Creek
Trailhead

Creek

Twin Creek

Hurricane

1807

Cr.

To
Lakes Basin

Thorp Creek Trail

Thorp Creek

7,805 ft.

N

0   0.5   1

Miles

Trial ends

Spring

Sacajawea Peak
9,833 ft.

Thorp Creek

Signing the summit register on Sacajawea peak.

Valley. Watch for mountain goats above timberline on Sacajawea Peak, especially in the huge basin on the west side. Return by the same route, or follow the ridge south for 2 miles to Matterhorn Mountain and descend via Ice Lake to Wallowa Lake Trailhead. Descending via Ice Lake requires a car shuttle to Wallowa Lake Trailhead. See Climb 10 Matterhorn Mountain, Hike 6 Ice Lake and Hike 4 West Fork Wallowa River.

CLIMB 12 *TWIN PEAKS VIA FALLS CREEK RIDGE*

General description: A steep 3 mile route, from Falls Creek Trail to the summit of Twin Peaks, with a short steep exposed scramble at the top.
Difficulty: Strenuous.
Estimated time up: 3 to 7 hours from Falls Creek Trail.
Best season: Mid-June through September.
Traffic: Light.
Elevation gain: 4,103 feet from Falls Creek Trail; 4,648 feet from Hurricane Creek Trailhead.
Maximum elevation: 9,673 feet.
Map: Chief Joseph Mountain USGS quad.
For more information: U.S. Forest Service at Wallowa Mountain Visitors Center, Enterprise, Oregon. Further information may be limited.
Finding the route: The route to Twin Peaks leaves the Falls Creek Trail 1807A, 0.75 mile from Hurricane Creek Trail 1807. See Hike 15 Falls Creek

Twin Peak

Climb 12

and Hike 14 Hurricane Creek. Falls Creek Trail makes a switchback at this point, and a rough path goes down to the North Fork of Falls Creek (El 5,570 ft.).

The route: Drop down to the left off Falls Creek Trail and cross the North Fork of Falls Creek just above the point where the North and South Forks of Falls Creek join.

After crossing the creek, follow a game trail south for a short distance, through a wooded area, then turn right and climb straight up a rock slide. Climb the band of moderate rock at the top of the rock slide (El 6,000 ft.). Above the rock band head up the prominent ridge, which divides the forks of Falls Creek. At 7,700 feet elevation is another steep rock band. Climb this rock band and continue up the ridge to 9,110 feet elevation. Here the ridge gets much steeper. Traverse to the left to a rib. Turn right on the rib and climb straight up to the south summit of Twin Peaks (El 9,646 ft.).

From the south summit traverse north, going around the smaller pinnacle, between the summits on the right (east) side to the base of the summit pinnacle. Go around the summit pinnacle on the right (east) to the north side. Then climb southwest up a ledge to a gully. Turn right and climb the gully to the summit of Twin Peaks (El 9,673 ft.).

Twin Peaks is one of the most prominent summits on Hurricane Divide, or in the Wallowa Mountains for that matter. It can be seen from most of the summits in the western part of the range. The summit pinnacle of Twin Peaks is composed of volcanic rock which sits uncomfortably on a softer layer of volcanic ash. The south peak slid away early in this century. Its remains are now a jumble of boulders at the foot of Frances Lake far below to the west. The present summit, which is North Twin Peak, will probably meet the same fate, eventually. The pinnacle overhangs on the the west, and its underlying strata does not look particularly stable.

The alpine area around Twin Peaks is a good place to observe both mountain goats and bighorn sheep which are fairly common in this area. The view from the summit is excellent, with Frances Lake below to the southwest and other high peaks in all directions.

The pinnacle of Twin Peaks is among the most difficult of the major Wallowa Mountain peaks to climb. A rope will be wanted by all but experienced and daring climbers. There may be no water available after crossing the North Fork of Falls Creek. An alternate descent can be made by following the ridge north of Twin Peaks for 0.3 mile then turning right (northeast) and dropping down the ridge just south of Legore Lake, the highest lake in the Wallowas. Then Falls Creek Trail can be followed back to Hurricane Creek Trail and Hurricane Creek Trailhead. This also makes a good ascent route. Campsites are available at Legore Lake. See Hike 15 Falls Creek.

Climb 12 *Twin Peaks via Falls Creek Ridge*

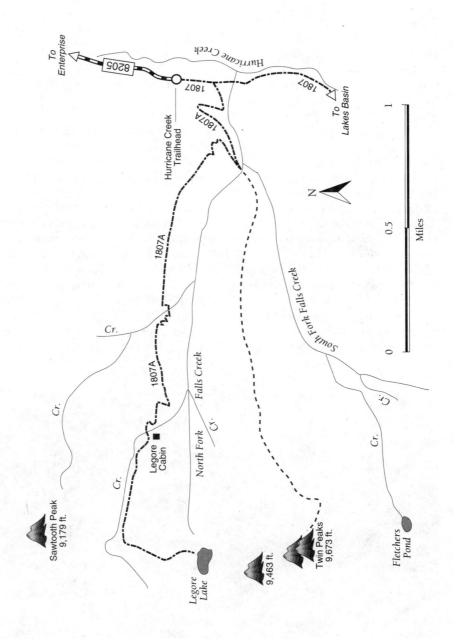

CLIMB 13 *RUBY PEAK FROM THE GAP*

General description: A scramble a little over 1 mile up the northwest ridge of Ruby Peak from Murray Saddle.

Difficulty: Moderate.

Estimated time up: 1.5 to 3 hours from the saddle.

Best season: Mid-June through September.

Traffic: Light.

Elevation gain: 1,594 feet from the saddle; 3,304 feet from the trailhead.

Maximum elevation: 8,884 feet.

Map: Chief Joseph Mountain USGS quad.

For more information: Wallowa Lake General Store in the Wallowa Lake resort area, or U.S. Forest Service at Wallowa Mountain Visitors Center, Enterprise, Oregon .

Finding the route: The route begins at Murray Saddle. (AKA The Gap). See Hike 28 Murray Saddle.

The route: Head left (southeast) at the saddle, cross the ditch, and climb on the right side of the ridge line following the faint bighorn sheep path. The route works its way up through rock outcroppings to the bottom of a large rock band. This band blocks the ridgeline route to all but technical rock climbers. Traverse to the right at the bottom of the rock band for 400 yards. Here a break in the band makes for a fairly easy scramble back to the ridgeline. After regaining the ridge, follow it to the southeast to the summit. Just before reaching the summit, the route is to the right of and slightly below the ridgeline. Watch for bighorn sheep on this route. There is no water after leaving the Gap. Easiest return route is via South Ridge. See Climb 15 Ruby Peak via South Ridge.

Climb 13 *Ruby Peak from the Gap*
Climb 14 *Ruby Peak via Silver Creek*
Climb 15 *Ruby Peak via South Ridge*

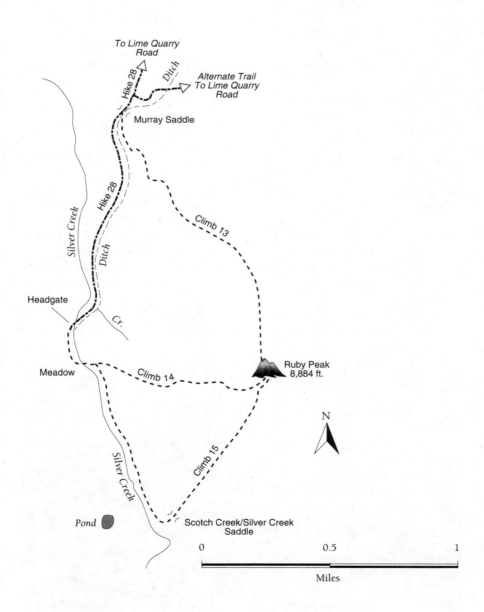

To Lime Quarry Road

Hike 28

Ditch

Alternate Trail To Lime Quarry Road

Murray Saddle

Silver Creek

Hike 28

Climb 13

Ditch

Headgate

Cr.

Meadow

Climb 14

Ruby Peak 8,884 ft.

N

Silver Creek

Climb 15

Pond

Scotch Creek/Silver Creek Saddle

0   0.5   1

Miles

CLIMB 14 *RUBY PEAK VIA SILVER CREEK*

General description: A steep but short 0.75 mile scramble from Silver Creek Ditch to the summit of Ruby Peak.

Difficulty: Moderate to strenuous.

Estimated time up: 1.5 to 3 hours from Silver Creek Ditch.

Best season: Mid-June through October.

Traffic: Light.

Elevation gain: 1,564 feet from Silver Creek Ditch; 3,304 feet from the trailhead.

Maximum elevation: 8,884 feet.

Map: Chief Joseph Mountain USGS quad.

For more information: U.S. Forest Service at Wallowa Mountain Visitors Center, Enterprise, Oregon. Further information may be limited.

Finding the route: The route begins at the upper (south) end of Silver Creek Ditch (El 7,320 ft.). See Hike 28 Murray Saddle.

The route: The route leaves Silver Creek Ditch at the headgate where the ditch gets its water out of Silver Creek, and goes up the the right side of Silver Creek. A quarter mile after leaving the ditch the route enters a meadow. There is a good campsite in the trees next to the meadow (El 7,400 ft.). At the meadow cross Silver Creek and head east up through the timber. The route climbs over a couple of benches to the open scree slope leading to the summit of Ruby Peak (El 8,884 ft.). It will be necessary to work around a few rock outcroppings, near the summit.

This route to the summit of Ruby Peak requires some navigational skills. There is a fairly steep scree slope, for the last 800 vertical feet which can be

a problem for the inexperienced off-trail hiker. An easier but slightly longer descent can be make by using the South Ridge Route. See Climb 15 Ruby Peak via South Ridge.

CLIMB 15 *RUBY PEAK VIA SOUTH RIDGE*

General description: A 2 mile off-trail, hike from the upper end of Silver Creek Ditch to the summit of Ruby Peak. This is the easiest route to the summit.

Difficulty: Easy to moderate.

Estimated time up: 1.5 to 3 hours from the upper end of the ditch.

Best season: Mid-June through October.

Traffic: Light.

Elevation gain: 1,564 feet from Silver Creek Ditch; 3,304 feet from the trailhead.

Maximum elevation: 8,884 feet.

Map: Chief Joseph Mountain USGS quad.

For more information: U.S. Forest Service at Wallowa Mountain Visitors Center, Enterprise, Oregon. Further information will probably be limited.

Finding the route: The route leaves the Silver Creek Ditch at its upper end, where the ditch takes its water out of Silver Creek. See Hike 28 Murray Saddle. See map on p. 295.

The route: From the end of the ditch follow Silver Creek up stream on a faint path on the right side of the creek. Go past the meadow 0.25 mile above the end of the ditch where Climb 14 leaves Silver Creek. See Climb 14 Ruby Peak via Silver Creek. Continue on up Silver Creek and pass through another meadow. Above the second meadow climb steeply, following the main fork of Silver Creek to the southeast to a large open timberline basin (El 8,200 ft.). A small side stream, sometimes dry, enters Silver Creek from the west as you climb above the meadow and before you reach the timberline basin. A short distance up this side stream is a pond with a few fairly good campsites near it. As soon as you enter the basin, turn left (east), and climb over a small rise, 0.1 mile to the saddle between Silver Creek drainage and Scotch Creek drainage.

At the saddle, turn left and follow a faint path along the right side of the ridge to the northeast to the summit ((El 8,884 ft.). It will be necessary to traverse along the right side of the ridgeline to avoid climbing over some rock outcroppings. This is the easiest route to follow when climbing or descending Ruby Peak.

The path this route follows from the Silver Creek, Scotch Creek saddle to the summit is a main route that bighorn sheep use when they travel from their winter range on lower Sheep Ridge to their higher summer range. The whole Wallowa Valley can be seen from the summit, as can the north end of Wallowa Lake. Return via the same route.

CLIMB 16 *CHINA CAP MOUNTAIN*

General description: A steep 0.5 mile hike from China Ridge Trail to the summit of China Cap Mountain.

Difficulty: Easy to moderate.

Estimated time up: 45 minutes from China Ridge Trail.

Best season: July through September.

Traffic: Light.

Elevation gain: 826 feet from China Ridge Trail.

Maximum elevation: 8,656 feet.

Map: China Cap USGS quad.

For more information: U.S. Forest Service at Wallowa Mountain Visitors Center, Enterprise, Oregon, or U.S. Forest Service at Halfway Ranger Station, Halfway, Oregon.

Finding the route: The route up the west ridge of China Cap Mountain leaves China Ridge Trail 1906 in a saddle 0.5 mile northwest of the peak. See Hike 66 China Ridge. Turn right (east) off the trail at the Eagle Cap Wilderness Boundary sign in the saddle (El 7,830 ft.).

The route: The route heads up the ridge to the east staying just to the right of the ridgeline, or by climbing the path just to the left of the ridge, for 200 yards, then crossing the ridgeline. After climbing a couple hundred yards, there is a path that traverses slightly to the right. Take this path for 200 yards, then climb to the left, back to the ridge. Turn right on the ridge and head up just

Climb 16 *China Cap Mountain*

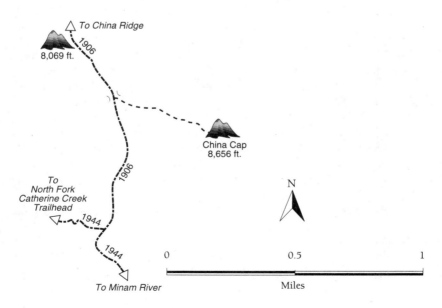

to the right of the ridgeline. There are high cliffs on the other (north) side of the ridge. Traverse on the right side just below the rock outcroppings. Turn left and climb up through the break in the outcropping on a grassy slope. Once on the ridgeline again, turn right and climb through a few small whitebark pines to the summit of China Cap Mountain (El 8,656 ft.).

This is a 30 to 45 minute climb from the saddle. From here the higher peaks of the north central Wallowa Mountains come into view to the east and northeast. There are many peaks in view, but Twin Peaks to the northeast and Aneroid Mountain to the east stand out and are easy to identify. Return by the same route.

CLIMB 17 *DIHEDRALS ROCK CLIMBING AREA*

General description: A poor 0.5 mile series of game paths from Chief Joseph Mountain Trail to Dihedrals rock climbing area.
Difficulty: Easy.
Estimated time up: 30 minutes.
Best season: July through November. Please do not climb the rocks when the eagles are nesting in the spring.
Traffic: Light.
Elevation gain: 200 feet from Chief Joseph Mountain Trail.
Maximum elevation: 5,200 feet.
Map: Joseph USGS quad.
For more information: Wallowa Lake General Store in Wallowa Lake resort area, or U.S. Forest Service at Wallowa Mountain Visitors Center, Enterprise, Oregon.
Finding the route: To get to the Dihedrals climbing area, drive to Wallowa Lake Trailhead 7 miles south of Joseph. The trailhead is at the end of Wallowa Lake Highway, Oregon Highway 82, one mile south of the Wallowa Lake resort area. At the trailhead, take the West Fork Wallowa River Trail. See Hike 4 West Fork Wallowa River and Hike 5 Chief Joseph Mountain. Follow the West Fork Wallowa River Trail to the junction with Chief Joseph Mountain Trail. Take the Chief Joseph Mountain Trail. The trail then drops slightly and crosses the West Fork Wallowa River on a bridge. After crossing the bridge, the trail climbs making five switchbacks. A short distance above the last switchback there is a faint path to the left. This path leads to the climbing area. The path turn off is approximately 600 yards from the bridge over the West Fork Wallowa River.
The route: The path, which is marked with cairns, heads southwest climbing slightly. Seventy-five yards up the path at the second cairn, the path turns right (west). It heads west for 30 yards to a blaze on a tree. Twenty yards past the blaze, the trail turns slightly to the left and climbs around a small rock outcropping. Thirty yards farther it bears to the right, climbing up and around another small outcropping. At the top of this outcropping it bears slightly to the left and

heads south for 300 yards. Here the trail drops 10 feet to the east. Then it heads on south for another 60 yards where it turns right (southwest) up a small gully. The trail heads up the gully for 15 yards to a large fir tree with a small blaze on it. Five yards past the tree, the trail turns left at the cairn and crosses the next small gully. There is a log crossing this gully. Turn left at the end of the log, go 5 yards, then climb right for 100 yards to a talus slope.

The path heads south into the talus slope. Eight yards into the talus slope the route to the back side of the Dihedrals turns to the right. It is a faint path, going straight uphill. The main path drops slightly and continues south along the base of the cliffs for another 50 yards. Here it drops steeply down a dirt slope for 20 feet. After dropping down the dirt slope, the path heads south again below the cliffs for 10 yards to an uprooted tree. It goes straight down the right (south) side of the tree for 10 yards. The path turns right again, along the base of the cliffs, then drops a few more feet to the east. The path then turns to the right again below the rock outcroppings. It continues to follow and climb around the base of the cliffs 15 yards to a large fir tree. Past the tree, climb steeply for 10 yards to the open area at the base of the Dihedrals.

This is one of the few areas in Northeastern Oregon where there is a large outcropping of fairly good rock for climbing. The main routes on the Dihedrals are two-pitch climbs. Because of their length, top roping may be difficult. Most of the routes have south or east exposure, so they are warm on sunny days. There are some bolts on the routes as well as an occasional pin. It is the climb-

Climb 17 *Dihedrals Rock Climbing Area*

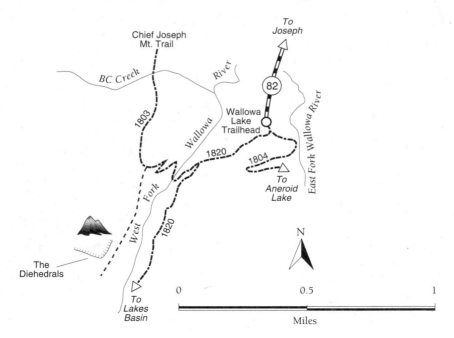

ers responsibility to make sure this hardware and its placement is safe. Only you can take care of your own safety when climbing. The Dihedral climbing area is in Eagle Cap Wilderness area, so wilderness regulations must be followed. Be careful when climbing.

APPENDIX

United States Forest Service
Wallowa Mountain Visitors Center
88401 Highway 82
Enterprise, OR 97828
(541) 426-5546

United States Forest Service
Halfway Ranger Station
Pine Ranger District
General Delivery
Halfway, OR 97834
(541) 742-7511

Wallowa Lake General Store
72784 Marina Lane
Joseph, OR 97846
(541) 432-9292

Spence Air Service
PO Box 217
Enterprise, OR 97828
(541) 426-3288

Wing Ridge Ski Tours
PO Box 714
Joseph, OR 97846
(541) 426-4322

GLOSSARY

Blaze — A mark on a tree formed by cutting away a small section of bark with a hatchet or ax. There may be one or two marks. Blazes can usually be seen some distance ahead.

Braided trail — A section of trail formed by two or more interconnecting paths. Not to be confused with cattle trails, which do not necessarily return to the main trail.

Cairn — A stack or pile of rocks that mark the trail or route.

Cirque — A glacier-carved bowl in a mountain, usually at the head of a valley, canyon, or gully.

Clearcut — An area that has been logged of all its timber.

Complete burn — An area where all the trees were killed by a forest fire.

Gully — A trench in the ground, smaller than a canyon. It may be steep and may or may not have a stream in it.

Jeep road — A road that is impassable for most two-wheel-drive vehicles. Roads may be blocked and closed to motor vehicles.

Notch — Naturally carved out sections of a ridge, much smaller than a saddle, with rock outcroppings on both sides.

Partial burn — An area where a forest fire killed some, but not all, of the trees.

Pika — A small mammal that lives in steep, rocky areas or talus slopes. Pikas are related to rabbits and do not hibernate.

Red digger — A species of ground squirrel.

Ridgeline — The top of a ridge, may slope steeply.

Outcropping — Bedrock protruding through the surface of the ground.

Saddle — The low point of a ridge, usually gently sloping. Much larger than a notch.

Scree — Loose rock on a slope. The size of the rocks in a scree slope are smaller than the rocks on a talus slope. May be tiring to climb.

Small stream — A stream 2 feet wide or less, smaller than a creek or stream. May dry up in late summer or fall.

Semi-switchback — A tight corner (120 degrees or less) in a trail.

Spur ridge — A smaller ridge protruding off the main ridge. May be quite steep.

Switchback — A tight corner (more than 120 degrees) in a trail where the trail turns back on itself as it traverses a hill. Allows hikers to negotiate steep slopes.

Talus slope — A slope covered with large rocks or boulders.

Tiny stream — A stream less than 1 foot wide. Usually dry in fall.

Traverse — The crossing of a slope, climbing or descending, but usually in a nearly straight line. This term is also used to describe a route or trail that follows a fairly flat ridgeline.

ABOUT THE AUTHOR

As a native Oregonian, Fred Barstad developed a keen interest in the remote high country of his state when he was young. As a teenager in the 1960s, Barstad roamed the Cascade Range in search of lakes to fish and peaks to climb. This search soon became an addiction for "bagging peaks." Barstad has climbed all the major Cascade peaks in Oregon, many of them several times, including sixty-three climbs to the summit of Mount Hood.

Barstad eventually developed a desire to climb mountains outside of Oregon, which took him to Mount Rainier in Washington, 20,320-foot high Mount McKinley in Alaska, Aconcagua in Argentina, and Popocatepetl and Citlaltepetl in Mexico.

Ever since he saw the Wallowa Mountains on a family vacation in 1961, Barstad has spent many years exploring, hunting, and fishing the canyons and peaks of this range. In 1987 he moved to Enterprise, Oregon, and began exploring the vast wild area of Eagle Cap Wilderness. He soon recognized a need for a guidebook of this spectacular area and eventually sold his business interest in the Wallowa Lake Marina to devote all of his attention to writing this book.

Barstad has hiked all the trails and routes featured in this book, nearly 1,500 miles worth. He hopes *Hiking Oregon's Eagle Cap Wilderness* will promote more interest to help preserve its pristine quality.